# LECTURES

AND OTHER

# THEOLOGICAL PAPERS

# LECTURES

AND OTHER

# THEOLOGICAL PAPERS

BY

J. B. MOZLEY, D.D.

LATE CANON OF CHRIST CHURCH, AND REGIUS PROFESSOR OF DIVINITY
IN THE UNIVERSITY OF OXFORD

WIPF & STOCK · Eugene, Oregon

Wipf and Stock Publishers
199 W 8th Ave, Suite 3
Eugene, OR 97401

Lectures and Other Theological Papers
By Mozley, J. B.
Softcover ISBN-13: 978-1-7252-9002-0
Hardcover ISBN-13: 978-1-7252-9001-3
eBook ISBN-13: 978-1-7252-9003-7
Publication date 10/29/2020
Previously published by E. P. Dutton and Co., 1883

This edition is a scanned facsimile of the original edition published in 1883.

## ADVERTISEMENT.

IN the following volume of DR. MOZLEY's literary remains, the greater number of original papers are taken from the Lectures delivered by him in the Latin Chapel, Christ Church, as Regius Professor of Divinity : to which office he was appointed in 1871. Of these a selection had to be made, as the Author, having no thought of publishing his Lectures, on some subjects availed himself freely of such passages from his earlier works as expressed his thought and opinion on the matter before him.

The paper on the Jewish and Heathen Conceptions of a Future State, a question on which he evidently felt great interest, was probably written about the year 1866.

The Reprints will be felt by the reader as deserving a permanent place among the Author's works, from the fulness and originality of their treatment and the lasting importance of their subjects. The Article on Dr. (now Cardinal) Newman's *Grammar of Assent*, which appeared in the *Quarterly Review* of July 1870, is given with Mr. Murray's kind permission.

# CONTENTS.

|  |  | PAGE |
|---|---|---|
| I. | EVIDENCES, . . . . . . . | 1 |
| II. | PHYSICAL SCIENCE AND THEOLOGY, . . . . | 17 |
| III. | JEWISH AND HEATHEN CONCEPTIONS OF A FUTURE STATE, . . . . . . . . | 26 |
| IV. | ON THE SUPPOSED OBSCURITY OF HOLY SCRIPTURE, . | 60 |
| V. | ST. PAUL'S TEACHING AN INTEGRAL PART OF HOLY SCRIPTURE, . . . . . . . | 74 |
| VI. | THE DOGMATIC OFFICE—ITS SCOPE AND METHOD, . | 86 |
| VII. | MYSTERIOUS TRUTHS, . . . . . . | 102 |
| VIII. | OF CHRIST ALONE WITHOUT SIN, . . . . | 116 |
| IX. | ORIGINAL SIN, . . . . . . . | 136 |
| X. | ORIGINAL SIN ASSERTED BY WORLDLY PHILOSOPHERS AND POETS, . . . . . . . | 148 |
| XI. | PERFECTIBILITY, . . . . . . . | 163 |
| XII. | MODERN DOCTRINE OF PERFECTIBILITY, . . . | 169 |
| XIII. | THE ATHANASIAN CREED, . . . . . | 183 |
| XIV. | THE HOLY EUCHARIST, . . . . . . | 200 |
| XV. | LETTER TO THE REV. PROFESSOR STANLEY ON THE ARTICLES, . . . . . . . . | 219 |
| XVI. | OBSERVATIONS ON THE COLONIAL CHURCH QUESTION, | 240 |
| XVII. | REVIEW OF DR. NEWMAN'S GRAMMAR OF ASSENT, . | 275 |
|  | NOTE ON EGYPTIAN DOCTRINE OF A FUTURE STATE, . | 301 |

# LECTURES AND OTHER THEOLOGICAL PAPERS.

## I.—EVIDENCE.[1]

THAT which a general course of Lectures on Theology like the present one naturally commences with, is the subject of Evidence. I shall not, however, enter into the consideration of the general fabric of the Christian Evidences, which is well known to you from the works of many able writers who have devoted themselves to that subject. I shall be doing perhaps something more useful if I call attention to some particular danger connected with the subject of evidence at this day, and endeavour to throw some light on the way in which it is to be met.

Apart from, and quite independently of, the particular arguments which unbelievers may use, it is to be observed that the mere existence of a large body of unbelief around us is itself a danger and a disturbance to us. It impresses the imagination. Such mere quantity of unbelief seems to be an argument in itself against revelation. We are perpetually reminded of it in the books of the day, in newspapers and reviews. It does not allow itself to be passed over; it obtrudes itself upon us at every turn; we cannot help observing it. All this affects the imagination. Unbelief is a great fact; it arrests us, and takes hold of our minds as such. It has a

[1] The first of an official course of lectures delivered in the Latin Chapel, Christ Church, Oxford.

threatening aspect. It is thus that, before going into the reasoning which it employs, a large mass of unbelief, as a simple fact, tends to produce a disturbing effect upon us,—to unsettle and to perplex us. As a mere fact it witnesses against religion. We may remark that anything that is constantly repeated tends to make itself credited, simply from the force of impression. So any standing assertion, quite apart from the grounds of it, influences us; there is a tendency in us to give way to the assertion itself, which gains its own admission in time from the mere circumstance that it demands it.

Such, then, being the disturbing nature of a great mass of unbelief, regarded simply as a fact, let us calmly consider whether this fact has any right in reason to make such an impression upon us. We shall find, I think, upon examination, that like many other great spectres which have frightened men, the terror of it goes upon a closer inspection; and that it ceases to possess any real pretension or right to unsettle and disturb our faith.

It must be remembered, then, that the conclusions which men arrive at are only valuable so far as they have possessed and apprehended the full data for forming them. We constantly reduce the value of men's conclusions on particular points on the ground either that they have not had opportunity of knowing the facts which bear upon them, or that they have not the special faculties and perceptions required for forming correct judgments upon them. The opinions men form on questions of poetry, philosophy, politics, trade, art, have thus constantly their weight challenged on this ground, *i.e.* that these men have not embraced certain preliminary special truths in their departments, which are necessary to be apprehended in order to the formation of correct conclusions further on. Vast masses of even strong judgment are very often set aside without any hesitation on this ground; they do not trouble at all those who arrive at different conclusions, provided only they see that those who have formed these judgments have not embraced certain principles necessary as preliminaries, and are wanting in the previous and introductory kind of truth.

To apply, then, these remarks to the subject before us: Christianity is founded upon certain great primary affections and wants of the human soul, which it meets, to which it corresponds, and of which it furnishes the proper objects and satisfactions. There is the feeling after a God; there is the instinct of prayer; there is conscience, and the sense of sin; there is the longing for and dim expectation of immortality. Christianity supplies the counterpart of those affections and wants of the soul, and it is as supplying this counterpart that it recommends itself in the first instance to us; it appeals to our belief upon the strength of its own characteristics at the same time that it comes before us as a subject of external evidence. The nature of Christianity, and its correspondence to our own nature, has a legitimate influence upon our minds, before any other consideration; it is one part of the whole Christian evidence, and a valid and necessary part, without which the other or the historical proof is reasonably and logically deficient.

For will any one consider the very nature of belief, and how it is constituted and composed? We never do, in fact, believe anything upon external evidence only. Somebody whom you meet in the streets tells you a piece of news; you believe it instantly, and as a matter of course; but what is it that makes you so believe it; his own assertion simply, without anything else? By no means; he might tell you some things, and you would not believe them, or at any rate you would remain a long time in suspense. There is something, then, besides the report of the witness, or the external evidence, which enters into the grounds of your belief, and that is the antecedent probability of the fact itself. If this is complete, and it is a fact of a common everyday sort, then you believe the report of it without the least hesitation. Thus the very commonest sort of credence shows upon what grounds belief is raised; that it is partly antecedent probability, and partly external testimony. Transfer the belief to a higher subject, and let the grounds of probability be not the mere experience of outward life, but certain inward instincts and affections, and the law of credence still holds. Your ground of belief is a sense of probability meeting and uniting with external evidence. These instincts and affections are what Christianity falls in with, and with which it coincides. This gives a reasonableness, a common-sense meaning to Christianity, that it does answer to our nature and gives the complement of it. And it is the reasonableness in the truths themselves of revelation, caused by this correspondence, which gives that foundation of belief which external evidence consummates. The two grounds, internal and external, make one whole. And with respect to Christianity, as with respect to other things, it is no mere report of facts which convinces us, it is also a congruity in the matter of the revelation itself. Whenever we believe a thing, in short, there must be something reasonable in it, reasonable to us. This is a primary condition. Nothing can engraft itself upon us which is alien to us. There must be a congeniality between ourselves and it before we can incorporate it by belief. We may not see the whole reason of it, but there must be some part at which the truth links itself on to our inward nature.

If, then, there are any considerable number of persons who do not feel and are not affected by those instincts and desires which form the preliminary argument for Christianity, and which are assumed in the effect of the external evidence upon us, the unbelief of these persons is accounted for. We know the reason why they do not believe, and it is a perfectly sound and valid reason. They are not, in fact, in possession of the full data relating to the question,—in possession, in the sense of inward apprehension of them. The same doctrines which completely fall in with the whole antecedent thought and feeling of some, and so to them are natural and reasonable, are to these persons extraneous and artificial, because there is no felt want and affection within them for the doctrines to lay hold of and join themselves on to. That law of belief then, which requires a probability in the thing itself to unite with the external evidence for it, is not complied with in their case —is not satisfied in the premisses of revelation as they apprehend them. There is no probability in the truths as they see them; they therefore disbelieve them.

Let us take the Comtists. Now, to the Comtists, every one of those inner wants and affections, which I mentioned just now as forming the introduction to Christian truth and making it reasonable and probable to us, is wanting. The Comtist says first, that to assert there is any sense of or feeling after a God in our nature is a total mistake; that it does not exist, and that the whole notion of our having it is an unfounded supposition put into our heads by theorists. Accordingly they erase this religious instinct altogether from the mind, and they stop at humanity. They deny of course, consistently with this, the instinct of prayer, and instead of praying they contemplate humanity. They do not acknowledge again a sense of sin or guilt in man as we understand it. Nor do they acknowledge an instinctive longing for, or expectation of, immortality in man. That instinctive feeling is completely obliterated in their system. The Comtists therefore are clearly without, as a felt thing, that whole foundation of mind upon which belief in Christianity arises. The conclusion of the Comtists therefore against Christianity is no perplexity to a Christian mind, because with them the premisses are wanting. The Comtists then avowedly and formally maintain as tenets those several denials of our instinctive feelings and instincts of which the Christian is convinced to begin with; but Comtism, after all, only lets out a secret of the substantial state of mind of a large number of those who do not call themselves Comtists; and only gives formal expression to negations which are practically entertained by a much more numerous portion of society than the Comtist sect. Comtism indeed is, in its blanks and erasures, the informal and unconscious philosophy of all who are absorbed in the sense of life, and to whom this world is the whole of existence.

But there is a portion of society also which, without calling itself Comtist, adopts these principles more or less formally and philosophically; which systematically does not concern itself with another world, or hold by any mysterious revelations of nature respecting God, conscience, sin, judgment. There are many in the first place who, without calling themselves Atheists, still do not feel any want of a God: He does not supply any need in their minds; they can do without Him; He is almost a superfluity in the world in their eyes; the world seems to go by laws of its own, and to be self-sufficient. To such, of course, prayer is no need of the mind. Again, the idea of morality which a great number entertain is not an idea involving any such deep affection as that of conscience and sense of sin. It is a public and social idea,— the idea of activity, public spirit, discharge of public duties, propriety of conduct, and the virtues which belong to a useful member of society. It goes a certain way in moral truth, but not to the depth of conscience with respect to obligation, or of sense of sin, supposing duty to have been violated or omitted.

The whole standard wants the element of sanctity. But this being the case, how can such a moral standard agree with or lead to Christianity? How can it lead, in the first place, toward a doctrine of an Atonement? If we feel a depth and a mystery in moral evil, then we are ready to accept a mystery in the remedy for that evil, and the restoration of man; but if we do not, such a remedy becomes immediately wholly out of place. It is eccentric and unmeaning, a simple anomaly, uncalled for and joining on to nothing in our nature. Again, there is no want of immortality felt by this class of minds. One might suppose beforehand, indeed, that human nature would long for an existence after death from the simple instinct of self-preservation; but as a matter of fact we find that a sense of present life which Nature has fixed in us (if we commit ourselves wholly to it) so completely shuts out the idea of death, as a realised and felt idea, that we do not feel any want of immortality. So long as we do not realise or feel that this life has an end, this life is endless to us; we have our immortality here, we do not want another immortality. There is no internal premiss then in such minds as these, to which the revelation of Eternal Life in the Gospel is a natural finish, and the revelation comes to them as an unconnected thing which their nature does not appropriate.

It is thus that the negations of Comtism, one after another, become the virtual premisses of a large number of minds; the sense of God, the sense of sin, the sense of eternity, are done away with as parts of human nature. The denials are not put expressly forward as tenets, nor are they formally held; but the whole groundwork of thought is in this direction. But if this is the case, the disbelief of such minds in Christianity need be no surprise to us. That is to say, we need not be surprised if such minds are not convinced by the external evidence for Christianity, when they do not possess those inward premises without which the external are necessarily defective; if they do not in fact accept a conclusion for which they have not the full argument. As was said just now, we never do in fact believe upon external evidence only; there is always an antecedent ground of some kind: with respect to common facts this is experience; in the case of religious doctrines, it is certain instincts and affections. This is a law of belief, and it argues no weakness in any given external evidence that it does not convince of itself; it is only that defect which constitutionally attaches to all external evidence as such. The existence, then, of a certain quantity of infidelity in society is accounted for; it need not trouble us as a riddle and an unexplained thing does; we can explain it, we can trace it to an intelligible source.

But when we call attention to this structure of evidence, we must be prepared to meet one common objection that is made. When any appeal is made to the inward affections in considering the grounds of Christian belief, it is commonly remarked that this is prejudging the question. You must argue the question of belief in Christianity, it is said, exactly as you would argue any other question, whether of history, or natural philosophy, or any other department. Questions of truth are not decided by the affections, but simply and entirely by evidence; and therefore it cannot make any difference, as far as the ascertainment of truth is concerned, whether persons have such and such affections, or are without them; the Christian evidences must be examined with perfect impartiality, like any other question of fact, and any bias—it is boldly asserted—which may arise from desire and affection must be altogether laid aside.

But where this objection is made to any appeal to the

affections of the soul in considering the evidences of religion, it must be remembered that there is a vast difference between some questions and others, with regard to the place which the affections hold in the argument relating to them. It would be absurd to say that the moral affections have any place in a question of natural history, or chemistry, or mechanics, or any department of science; because the moral affections have nothing to do with the faculties or perceptions which are concerned with that subject-matter; but in questions relating to religion, the moral affections have a great deal to do with the actual perception and discernment by which we see and measure the facts which influence our decision. Let us take, for instance, the question of a future life and the immortality of the soul. Now it is obvious that one of the chief arguments for a future state arises from human character—those high forms of it which we meet and with which we become acquainted, whether by personal knowledge, or by reading or hearing of them. But we cannot possibly enter deeply into character without affections; we cannot estimate or comprehend truly, we cannot embrace keenly, and with a living force, what is beautiful, profound, and touching in the mind and disposition of any person of extraordinary goodness, unless there are affections in us which enable us to seize hold of their moral traits, and inspire us with a vivid admiration and appreciation of them. Put before yourselves any one of the circle in which you have lived, or whom accident has brought before you, whose whole type has impressed itself upon you as uncommon, and who has stood out from the mass of average life as a being of a higher mould. Now it is evident that such a character as this is an argument for immortality; it is a reason to your mind for expecting it, because the very idea of such a being as this perishing is a shock to us. Was this spiritual creation made in order to come to nothing? In the case of such a character the whole look of life as a preparatory stage is particularly obvious. Life has matured its good tendencies, checked its wayward ones; it has become more perfect as it approached its departure from the world, more answering to the design which is stamped upon it; and the very final stage of all has taken its part in the development of it; there it attains its highest growth; the soul is more than ever a living soul; its feelings most alive and quick, the heart most tender, thought most deep. Is all this for nothing? Is the structure with such pains built in order that it may be overthrown, and the parts so elaborately and delicately put together in order that one rude moment may shatter the work in pieces? Is the Universe in which we live a system of treachery and mockery, of means for no end, frustrating every hope, and balking every purpose marked upon it? It is, if just when the character is formed the being is destroyed, and existence is over. That such a being should be extinguished, blotted utterly out of the tablet of the Universe—this is a thought which communicates a shock to our whole nature; and that it does communicate such a shock is the strongest of all arguments against such being the end of creation.

But can this premiss for a future life be apprehended without the affections? The moral affections are the very instruments by which we embrace it. This fact of human character is quite a different fact to us according as we see it with the affections or without. Without the affections we do not apprehend it, grasp it, or possess ourselves of it; we do rot take it in. And therefore to those who exhort us to divest ourselves of the influence of the affections when we come to judge of the evidence for Christianity and its doctrines, we reply that with respect to very considerable parts of the evidence of Christian doctrine, very important premisses for it, the affections are absolutely necessary even for the full force of the understanding. Affection is part of insight; it is wanted for gaining due acquaintance with the facts of the case. Feeling is necessary for comprehension; we cannot know a particular instance of goodness, we cannot embrace the true conception of goodness in general without it. Affection is itself intelligence; we cannot separate the feeling in our nature from the reason in it. When we come to examine the argument for a life eternal, we find that we cannot do it even bare justice without the help of the affections. One of the very first considerations upon the question of the destination of man to a state of eternal happiness is human character, the kind of goodness it is capable of, its worthiness of such a destination; and this is a matter which requires the affections as the condition of deciding it.

But let us take another point in the consideration of a future life, and in our relations of mind toward it; and we shall see a fresh reason why the affections are necessary for seeing properly the evidence of Christian truth. It is impossible that we can obtain a full insight into the evidence of the life eternal after death, unless there exists in our hearts the real and earnest wish for that future life. It may be said,—a strong wish prejudges the question, the wish is father to the thought. Certainly there is a strong tendency in it to act so; but on the other hand, to be without the wish for immortality is to be without the natural stimulus and motive to exert your reason on the subject, and to see what there is to be seen on the side of that doctrine. People are much mistaken if they think that no stimulus is required for the discerning of truth, for seeing the reasons and the evidences there are for any great conclusions connected with our prospects. Would Columbus, for instance, have seen all the evidences and probabilities which he did see of the existence of an unknown hemisphere; would he have elicited the different scattered facts which threw light upon it, and traced out the faint lines which converged in that direction, had he not been inspired with the intense longing for discovery? It was a great wish possessing itself of his whole mind which enabled him to see all the reasons there were for his conclusion. To have been without the wish would have been to be without the power of seeing them.

But again the wish for the life immortal is obligatory upon us; nor are we in a proper moral or reasonable attitude of mind upon this question unless we have it. If we ask a man to believe, he may say, I cannot; but he cannot say he cannot wish. If, then, there is any final issue of the whole of human existence which appears to be in the least possible, that is to say, our ascent into a glorious and endless state, we are at any rate bound, morally bound, to wish it to be true. We are under the rational obligation of wishing that to be the real issue which is obviously the best and highest. That the mere conception is offered to the mind, unless indeed it is impossible and involves a contradiction, constitutes an obligation to desire its truth. A man, therefore, is not in a reasonable attitude of mind, unless he has the strong wish that the idea of Eternal Life after death should be true in fact.

As, then, we saw before that affection was necessary for seeing the evidence for immortality, because we could not embrace the argument from human character for that conclusion without it; so now we see its necessity for that object, in the fact that without affection we cannot wish for immortality, and that without the wish we cannot see the full argument for immortality. Subjects of physical science do not require the affections, because the affections throw no light upon them, and are not wanted to understand them; but the truths of Christianity have a relation to our moral nature, and our moral nature both consists of affections and requires the affections to understand it.

When, then, the existence of a large mass of unbelief in society is felt, as it should be, as a painful and grave fact, let us at the same time remember that the real value and weight of such a fact must be tested by the proper conditions. Do these persons receive and acknowledge in the first place those preliminary truths which are assumed in the evidences of Christianity? Is there this sacred foundation of holy sentiment and affection in their characters? If there is not, they want the first conditions upon which Christian belief is formed; and therefore, their unbelief being accounted for by an actual want in their premises, the value of the fact as a witness against the Christian conclusion is annihilated. Without the felt need for prayer, without the sense of sin, without the wish for immortality, there is no antecedent ground of probability for Christianity; but there must always be some antecedent probability to create belief; we never in fact believe anything upon external evidence only.

I have called attention to one danger connected with the subject of evidence at this day, namely, the omission of the real place which the affections have in forming the ability to judge of the evidences of religion. I will ask attention now to another danger very much akin to this, namely, a narrow idea of what does or does not make an argument. There is a certain class of considerations which have a strong influence upon the most rational minds in aiding the formal evidences of religion, but if one of these is mentioned it will probably be met by the reply that it is not an argument. For instance, it is a consideration which makes a great impression upon us, that, as was just now mentioned, the issue of things which the Christian revelation teaches us, is the very highest issue imaginable or conceivable. Other religions, indeed, have taught various forms of a future life, but it has been either a state of vanity and emptiness, as the pagan future state was; or it has been restless and fluctuating existence, going through interminable changes and cycles, and connected with metempsychosis, and the passage of the soul through different animal and human lives, as the Egyptian and Oriental doctrines taught. A *glorious* eternal state is the revelation of Christianity alone. But when this is mentioned, that is, that the Christian issue of things is the very best imaginable; "This is not an argument," is the reply. That it is the *best imaginable* issue does not show that it is the *true* one. Thus, though a consideration may be one which we cannot help being impressed by,—and reasonably impressed,—though it is one which must have some weight, and a weight which, as far as it goes, is on the side of Christianity, it is still set aside altogether and allowed to contribute nothing to the Christian evidences, because it is not, as is said, an argument.

Now in answer to this, I think it may be fairly said that anything is an argument which, as far as it goes, tends rationally to bias the mind in a certain direction. We must have no narrow definition of an argument. The question is, Is there naturally any force in a given consideration—not an actually deciding force, but a force?—if so, it is an argument, as far as it goes. Thus, in the present instance, we cannot help ourselves being influenced by the consideration of the issue of the Christian scheme,—what it ends in,—that its end is the best possible one. It is so natural for us to think that this universe must be for good, that life, with all its capacities of development and discipline, must be for some great end, that when the highest and best conceivable end is announced in a revelation, its *being* the *best* end is a real argument to us that it is the *true* end. So when we are arguing the doctrine of a future state itself, and when we appeal to the natural wish and longing that we find within us for that state, as one of the *evidences* of its truth, we are met again with the reply, " This is no argument : that you wish for it does not prove that it is *true.*" It may be admitted that it is no proof : it would be absurd to say that it was, taken by itself. And yet it would be as unnatural to say that the innate hope we feel had no force whatever as an item of evidence on the subject. That a man *ought* to wish for this issue is clear, as I just said ; but now I say that the fact that man, when his nature is not suppressed, does wish for it, that he *has* a true longing and hope for it, is a real argument, as far as it goes, for it. The existence of such a wish must reasonably influence him. It is not a *mere* wish, such as we might have for some impossible thing. No, the wish that we actually find in our minds for a life to come is a wish accompanied with an idea of the possibility of it ; it is a practical hope. And that we have such a hope is an argument. Does Nature insert an instinct without a use? It may be said, indeed, the hope is not in vain if it cheers people at the time, and that *that* is a use for it. But is this the *kind* of use which we see in real nature ; that it is useful by deceit and by illusion ; by giving people ideas to which there is no responding reality merely that they may have the comfort of the ideas ? That is not the type of Nature's action. If she implants a presage or prognostication, it is that it may tell us of something. Her use and truth coincide.

The hope in our nature then for a future life is a reason, in a degree, for expecting that life ; it is a kind of forecasting of the future fact. And this accounts for the more believing temper which is often the effect of illness and approach of death. When people are well and strong, and enclosed in the sense of life, they entertain no real wish for another life, and have none of this forecasting. Amid the fulness of physical power and strength all these presentiments and presages are brushed aside as superfluous unmeaning shadows; but when this life is deserting them, and they really want another, then these presages and instincts come into force; then they have a meaning. Unbelievers have changed often upon the approach of death, and infidels say it is slavish fear, their understanding giving way. But is it their understanding giving way, or not rather their understanding awakening? They see tokens then within them to which their eyes were shut before, deep perceptions to what in the midday glare of life they were not alive.

And this may remind us again of another argument for religion which many disallow, namely, its utility. We appeal to the extraordinary utility of the Christian revelation, what motives it has supplied to virtue and benevolence, what stimulus its hopes and anticipations have given to our moral nature. But the answer is the same as before. Christianity may be *useful*, but it is not therefore *true*. And yet though usefulness is not formal proof, it is mockery to say that there is not something in it bearing upon evidence. We feel that we cannot wholly ignore utility in our estimate of the evidence of the truth of a revelation. For if a revelation truly comes from God, it must carry usefulness also as well as truth; usefulness must be one of its characteristics; and therefore where we see extraordinary and wonderful usefulness, we must take it as a note of truth. And indeed the progress of thought on the whole has been a decided testimony to utility as an argument. The philosophies of the old world and the ancient schools of legislation maintained the maxim of the utility of falsehood, and the great expediency of established religions, though they were not true; but the growth of thought has run counter to this. Lucretius condemned religion distinctly as being pernicious and injurious to society, as if he saw that to admit its utility would have been to go a long way in admitting its truth. And it is curious to observe that in the present day the position of "false yet useful" has been given up, and that modern Atheism expressly charges religion with the evils and disasters of society, and the grievances and miseries of humanity.

There is no mathematical criterion then of an argument. Everything is an argument which naturally influences us in one way rather than another; to think one thing true rather than another. In the preliminary region of evidence especially, we meet with considerations which have such a natural influence upon us in guiding our judgment, that it would be folly to dispense with them. And yet if we listen to some persons' objections, we shall have to believe there is nothing in these considerations, because, as it is said, they are not arguments. They do not indeed pretend to a technically conclusive force; and yet to shut them out from the judicial scope on account of their informal character as arguments, would be to imitate those narrow and pedagoguish tactics of law which fence in, with scrupulous jealousy, what are called the rules of evidence, till step by step they exclude as irregular the main and most important inlets of truth and channels of proof.

I have confined myself in this Lecture to the preliminary ground of Christian Evidence, and have called attention to some important considerations belonging to that introductory section of evidence. I have called attention first to the place which the affections hold in the Christian evidence; and secondly, to a wider and truer definition of an argument, which takes it out of a technical test, and makes it any consideration which reasonably influences us. And under this head I have alluded to the antecedent argument for Christianity contained in the fact that it offers to us the highest possible issue of human life and this whole scheme of things; to the antecedent argument of instinctive hopes; to the antecedent argument of utility. The substance of the Christian evidences of course lies in positive testimony, and in the proof of those historical facts upon which Christianity is based. But, referring you for the positive structure of Christian evidences to those well-known treatises which have issued at different times from our Church, I have preferred on this occasion directing your thoughts to those points connected with the introduction to Christian evidences; because, while antecedent ground is apt to escape our notice, it is ground of which it is very important to retain a proper hold and a just estimate. It is very material to establish our right to all the argument with which that ground supplies us,—not to allow ourselves to be deprived of it upon technical reasons; never to let a consideration of real weight, which has a genuine and natural influence upon us, be snatched out of our grasp upon the plea that it is not an argument. Everything is an argument which has a natural influence upon us in inducing us to think one way rather than another. If any persons have a criterion of an argument in their head, which lets all kinds of influential considerations slip, —casting them aside, and preventing their being turned to any use—because they do not come within this technical test; it is high time, not that we should give up these considerations, but that *they* should alter their criterion of an argument. Let us keep a firm hold upon the antecedent arguments for Christianity, upon all those reasons which induce us to welcome Christianity, and which prepare us for the reception of it when it is placed before us by positive evidence. These form a genuine and necessary part of the whole evidential structure, which is maimed and halt without it. We must have probabilities to aid external evidence in religion, just as in ordinary cases of reported facts; it is no fault of external evidence that it should be so, it is a constitutional limitation which attaches to it, and to which antecedent probabilities are the constitutional supplement. And as likelihood from experience is this supplement in ordinary evidence, so likelihood from moral considerations is in religious evidence.

## II.—*PHYSICAL SCIENCE AND THEOLOGY*.[1]

THERE is a current assertion relating to the existence of a Moral and Personal Deity, that the argument from *nature* for this truth is weak, and that the professed proof of it is taken from theological metaphysics. I will offer one or two considerations on this point. It may be admitted then that the existence of the human soul clears up many questions respecting the Deity which were not fully decided when we had only external nature before us. For example, as regards the question of design—we undoubtedly see a plastic power at work in nature before we take the human soul into consideration; but is this power intelligent or designing? We are involved in some perplexity. Mere material law is *methodical* in its operations, as in the case of crystals. Where do we get that plain evidence of an *end beyond the apparatus itself*, an object which is ulterior to the physical framework with which it is connected, which is the test of true design in nature? The answer is in all sentient life in its degree; but certainly the highest evidence of such an ulterior end, which throws all other evidence almost into the shade, is the human soul. That stands in such bold relief to the bodily structure belonging to it, as the *end of that structure;* the final cause is declared with such overpowering light, the purpose shines forth with such indubitable clearness and conspicuousness that the conclusion is irresistible : that power which constructed this body in order to the existence of myself—an intelligent being—must be itself intelligent.

Again, has the Deity will? On this question, too, we are much in the dark till we come to the human soul, which speaks and says :—" I have will, therefore that power which constructed this bodily apparatus for my existence has will too."

[1] Read by the Author at the Church Congress held in Dublin 1868.

Again, is the Deity moral? Here we are entirely in the dark before we come to the human soul, which says: "I am moral, therefore the power that made me is moral." In a word, He who thus obviously and elaborately provides for a moral and personal existence must Himself be a moral and personal Deity.

It must, therefore, be admitted that man, or the human soul, is the revelation of God in nature. Prior to this spiritual fact in nature, the mechanical system of nature reveals a First Cause of some kind, but it does not speak to the character of that Cause whether he is intelligent, moral, and has a will. We are groping in the dark amid the beginnings and *primordia* of things before nature interprets itself, and decides as to the character of its First Cause. But when we arrive at man or the human soul, the authorship of nature comes out like a disclosed secret, a light breaks forth which fills all space, which illuminates the whole fabric of the physical universe, and which reveals the moral source and end of nature. Of man it may be said, that not only as investigating man, but that as man, he is the interpreter of nature.

But is this proof of a moral Deity, as distinguished from law or plastic power, a metaphysical argument? Undoubtedly it is, if for convenience' sake we choose to call one part of our nature metaphysical; but let us, as we have a right to do, claim the term physical for *all* nature, and has not the human soul a place in physics? Is the instinct of any brute, any insect, to rank as part of nature, and is the instinct of man—namely, his soul—not to rank as such? In physical treatises the instincts of animals are invariably treated as just as much a part of physics as their bodies: the two are on a par as physical facts. And the soul is the instinct of man. We know indeed that the soul will one day exist out of this physical universe; but so long as it is *in* it, it is as plainly a part of it as the instinct of an ant or bee. The theistic argument, then, from the human soul is derived from something which is an element of this physical world; an instinct, a life, a power, an insight, an energy, going on in it, provided for by it, imbedded in the very centre of this whole physical apparatus. The great user of nature, the head and summit of nature, the rational soul which inhabits nature and reigns in nature, belongs *to* nature as much as the mechanical laws of nature. It is a part of physics taken as a whole. That marvellous spiritual insertion in this physical world is yet one of the contents of that world. We look down from the height of our own reason upon a vast shadowy scene below of blind and groping instinct;—instinct which may be called subterranean, its processes are so dark, so hidden from itself, so unconscious;—a maze of motions in all shapes and figures, following tame and homely or wild and eccentric lines, but all going on in rigid grooves, between invisible walls which bound the vision; all the movements of a deaf, dumb, and blind spirit which does not perceive, which does not think, which does not direct itself. All brute life has this sad impress stamped even on its liveliest play and action, that it does not know what it is doing. From this animal instinct in all its stages, the leap is so sudden and immense to the human instinct, with its inward light of self-consciousness, and all its other glorious perceptions and faculties, that we forget that that mental force which is so *supreme* in nature is still *in* nature, and that it does not cease to be *part* of nature, because it is the highest part. This enormous and prodigious instinct, which is so different from the other instincts as to look miraculous, is still within the system—though a spiritual insertion in it, still in it;—the property of an inhabitant of nature, a tenant of a physical frame—an animal—man. The First Cause of this whole physical apparatus has connected this apparatus with the human soul: and it is all one system, the physical kosmos which encloses, and the spiritual life which is enclosed.

When, therefore, it is asserted that the argument from nature for a moral and personal Deity is weak, it may be replied that this assertion is only made true by robbing the argument from nature of its principal contents. The human soul does not come under the head of metaphysics only, but it is a part of physics, or nature taken as a whole. But if, upon the plea of its being a metaphysical element in the question, it is *excluded* from a place in the argument from nature; if the spiritual is extracted from nature, before we are allowed to argue *from* nature, the natural argument for a God may well become weak. We reduce it then simply to an argument from methodical matter, from mechanical adjustments; and thus narrowed and reduced, no wonder if the argument from nature proves only a mechanical Deity.

I am aware, indeed, that this is only a question as to what head a particular argument comes under; and that the human soul is the same premiss under whatever head it may be placed; but I do not think the question is therefore unimportant. For the practical influence an argument has upon the mind, a great deal depends upon division. An arbitrary division excludes some great premiss from an area and enclosure in which it would have striking weight, banishes it from the field before our eyes, ostracises it, removes it to some distant quarter in which it is thrown entirely upon its own isolated strength instead of having all the aid of a familiar and recognised surrounding. So if we make the great theistic argument *nature*, the theistic evidence of the human soul is plainly disadvantaged if it is not allowed to come under the head of nature. As a metaphysical premiss only, it is deprived of a certain matter-of-fact aspect and bearing which it possesses as a physical. "Important in its place, but no part of the argument," is the reply to a proof which does not come under a main heading; "*we* are arguing from nature, *you* are introducing metaphysics." A premiss that is shut out of a great trunk argument fares like an incidental visitor, to whom we say: "Presently,—I will attend to you by and by." As soon as ever a man has handed over some point to metaphysics, he thinks he has entirely got rid of it, that he need not give himself any further trouble about it, that it is removed to a region of shadows. But remove mind or soul from its *technical* head of metaphysics, and place it under its *real* head of nature, and then we have at once two great facts of nature before us. All soul says of itself "I will," and "I ought;" and these two facts re-act by a necessary law of thought upon the character of the Divine Being. It is quite true that both of these are mysteries. It is true no one knows what "ought" means; no one has deciphered, no mortal key ever will decipher that unfathomable enigma. No one knows what "will" is, its source or basis; that, too, is an inaccessible secret. But it would be the greatest mistake in philosophy to say that mysteries cannot be facts. With the innate *impressions* of "will" and "ought" all nature vibrates; all history is founded on them; they are inherent in us, rooted in us, no human being can shake them off. When a man has deliberately and with choice before him done a wrong act, can that man really make himself think that he could not have done the right one? He cannot. It is an impossibility of nature. Can he cast off the sense of right and wrong? That too is an impossibility of nature. These impressions of "will" and "ought" are as plain, as obvious, as conspicuous facts of nature,—of physics in the large sense,—as electricity or the circulation of the blood. And with these two facts within us, we cannot, by a necessary law of thought, rest in a God who does not respond to them. If there is *no* God, there is no *moral* God; but if there *is* a God of some kind (as science admits), and the only question is what kind, that question is settled by these facts.

Now to bring these remarks to bear upon one particular point.

1. Scientific men sometimes appeal to an inward certainty which they feel, as to the impossibility of any interruption of the order of nature. They do not profess to give the reason of this idea; they only say they are possessed by it; that it is an intuition, a forcible impression, which grows by conversance with nature and insight into her laws. Now, with respect to such an impression as this, I would remark that it is well known as a truth of human nature, and one of wide application, and attaching to all kinds of subject—that nothing does produce a stronger sense of certainty in men's minds than forcible impressions for which they can give no reason. It is curious that the instant you begin to reason, in a certain sense you begin to doubt. The *element* of doubt is introduced. If you allege a reason for a thing, the question of proportion immediately arises—is it reason *enough*? is the premiss strong enough to support the conclusion? But if you have no premiss, and no reason, the whole element of doubt which arises from this source is avoided. There are such multitudes of examples of this species of certainty arising simply from

forcible impression, that they may be said to compose a chapter in the history of the human mind; nor is there any fact which experience teaches more strongly than that, for the absolute sense of certainty, there is nothing like being without a reason. Not, however, that I would exclude all forcible impressions, which are unable to give a complete account of themselves from philosophy; or say that because men have them absurdly, men may not sometimes have them wisely; but I would only remind those who possess such impressions, that the imagination simulates reason with wonderful success, and has an extraordinary power in making the view it suggests look like the only possible reality, and any other appear like fiction. It is the special effect of forcible impressions produced by the imagination, that it seems unnatural and artificial to resist them;—that imagination looks like reason, and reason like imagination. Human nature is operated on by mighty currents, which carry it in different directions; nor can science or philosophy, any more than action, be conducted without such impulses. Which current shall we trust ourselves to? What is imagination, and what is reason within us? The appeal must be made to our whole nature—for nature as a whole corrects the impetus of particular movements.

2. I would remark with great respect, and knowing that the liability is shared by other departments of knowledge as well, that physical science is capable—if I may dare to say such a thing—of breeding crotchets. A curious attitude of opposition to common sense is, I say, noticeable as an occasional feature of the scientific mind, rising up at sudden turns. It is a phenomenon to be attended to. We speak of poetry, romance, religious enthusiasm, generating strange fancies; but nothing can exceed the odd and unaccountable convictions which science sometimes takes up. Can there, for instance, be found a more curious quarrel with common sense, than that antipathy which some scientific schools, especially the French school, entertain to the idea of design in nature, so thrust upon us by nature? The vindication of physical causes can hardly be considered as more than a decent disguise for this grotesque prejudice of science; because it is so obvious that physical

causes can produce a chaos just as much as they can produce a harmony or system; that they are common to arrangement and disorder, and therefore cannot in themselves account for arrangement. Again, take the strange antipathy of one great inductive school to the idea of intuitive or necessary truth; everything with them is induction—even truths of mathematics, even truths of arithmetic. That two and three make five has been "invariably observed:" in no single instance have we seen them produce any other number. It is what is called a "completed induction," that is, as far as our opportunities of observation go; but not necessary; and if I understand Mr. Mill aright, he thinks it conceivable that in one of the heavenly bodies the result might be different. These curious scientifically generated points of view, these eccentric products of the scientific mind, show that science has, as a mental pursuit, its faulty habits, and that it can breed its own class of prejudices—aspects of things, caught in the first instance by the mind in peculiar junctures and angles of thought, and then permanently stamped upon the intellect.

3. I would remark respecting this forcible impression as to the impossibility of an interruption of the order of nature, that scientific men are in this instance doing what they generally disclaim doing—theologising: for unquestionably this is a theological conclusion; it affects the nature and the power of the Deity. Their general posture is that of claiming the right to investigate facts without being interfered with by theology; and there is justice in this claim; but here they leave the position of physical investigation, and diverge from the discovery of facts, to drawing a theological conclusion from them.

4. But, lastly, scientific men are not only theologising in this instance, but theologising altogether prematurely; they are judging about the Deity before they have a revelation of Him. The mechanical laws of nature do not of themselves reveal Him; man alone is the revelation of God. Let it be granted then, that a person might argue from the material and mechanical laws of nature, taken by themselves, to the inviolability of the laws of nature. Allow him to say, looking simply to these laws, "I do not catch here any glimpse of a

power which can interrupt nature : I see motion, orderly motion, but that motion does not hint at anything which can stop it : I must regard, therefore, this as an alien, arbitrary idea, and gratuitous fiction of the mind." But has he in these laws the whole of nature before him? No; he omits the human soul, which has a distinct, a strong and vigorous argument of its own on this subject. All soul, being conscious of will itself, declares for a Deity with will, upon which an interrupting power necessarily follows ; and soul, as has been said, is a fact in nature, its consciousnesses are facts in nature. This, which is disdainfully called the "old theological argument for miracles," is theological only in its conclusion ; its premises are, in the true sense, physical.

It must be observed that scientific men are by the order of their task and pursuit placed at a disadvantage with respect to a theological conclusion from nature—for this reason. A mechanical First Cause does not interrupt nature, because it has no will; man, as I have said, reveals a will in nature, a moral power. It is therefore not from the mechanical beginnings and elements of nature, but from the user and the end of nature—Man ; it is from the spiritual life in nature that we obtain the idea of a First Cause that can interrupt nature. But this being the case, scientific men have, by the very order of their pursuit, to do with the beginnings of nature and not with the end, with the mechanical and not with the spiritual power in nature. They see the grand edifice, as it were, upside down, they look away from *themselves, from* man, *from* soul, *from* mind, *to* matter, *to* mechanism, *to* material law. They look in a direction which is dictated by the very investigating purpose of their occupation itself, but which has still the inherent defect of setting nature in a wrong position before them. They look at nature, indeed, *with* the mind, *with* the rational soul, but working with it as an instrument, not contemplating it as an object : as the eye sees other things, but not itself, the soul overlooks itself in its survey of the universe. This is an attitude essential for the purpose of investigation, but an artificial and inverted one for the view of nature. It is the higher part of nature which interprets the lower. Nature ascends from matter to its head and vertex,—Man; and we ought to look at it in the direction of its ascent, from its base to its summit, like a building, not reversely, away from its vertex to its mechanical base. This is the upside-down position of nature in the process of physical analysis; which process therefore, however the fault may admit of being corrected, in itself puts man at a disadvantage with respect to the idea of nature as a whole. It is like the case of some peculiar occupation which may be necessary for the community, but which disadvantages those employed in it in some particular organ or function. Perpetual conversance with beginnings operates in this way. An incorrect attitude which is assumed for a special purpose, and thrown aside afterwards, does no harm, but it is injurious if it becomes the habitual position of the mind. He who looks *always* to the mechanics of nature will *never* see a God there; he looks far off, and does not see what is close to him—the evidence of a God which is within him.

## III.—*JEWISH AND HEATHEN CONCEPTIONS OF A FUTURE STATE.*

It has been remarked by those who have wished to derogate from the value and rank of the Jewish dispensation, that the Jews were worse off than the Pagans in one important point, namely, that they were without a doctrine of a future state, whereas Paganism taught that doctrine. This is a question, then, not only of speculative interest, but of great moment, considering the estimate of a Divine dispensation is affected by it. But in order to decide it, we must first have before us with some accuracy what the Pagan doctrine was, and what the Jewish absence of doctrine was; for we must know both of these conditions of thought in order to compare them together; and judge whether the positive conception of the Pagan was, being compared with the absence of definite conception in Judaism, a ground of superiority to him. Again we cannot estimate the Jewish attitude towards a Future State without a reference to the Christian conception of a Future State, for which the condition of the Jew was a preparation. Our subject therefore ranges itself under the following heads :—

    I. The Pagan conception of a Future State.
    II. The Christian conception.
    III. The Jewish preparatory absence of conception.
    IV. Comparison of Judaism and Paganism on this point.

    I. *The Pagan conception of a Future State.*

The doctrine of a Future State, or the Immortality of the Soul, and the Gospel doctrine of Eternal Life, are two distinct doctrines. The former is the general doctrine of a continuance of the soul's existence, and is necessary for the doctrine of Eternal Life; because the soul must continue to exist first of all, in order that it may exist in that way which is expressed by the doctrine of Eternal Life. But the former is only the substratum, or, as we may call it, the rough material out of which the doctrine of Eternal Life is formed. That rough material was worked up into many different forms, before the ultimate and true or normal form of it was produced in the Gospel. When persons speak then of the Pagan and the Christian doctrines of a Future State as if Paganism had been beforehand with the Gospel on this subject, and had made the same discovery which the Gospel made before the Gospel made it, they speak incorrectly. The two, the Pagan and Christian, are not the same doctrines.

The general doctrine of a Future State or the immortality of the soul was worked up in three principal forms in Paganism, which we may call respectively the Future State of the Poets, the doctrine of the Mysteries, and the doctrine of Philosophy. The division will suffice for practical purposes, although the heads of it run partially into each other, and both the Mysteries, and, in time, Poetry, were coloured by Philosophy.

1. The Future State of ancient legend and poetry was a state of shadowy, unreal, and ghost-like existence; that is to say, it was *not* existence, *not* true life at all. The inhabitants of the other world were *shades*, that is, they were men deprived of half their nature, and their existence was altogether without solidity; airy, dreamy, and deceptive, even in their own eyes. They remembered what they had been, and how far they fell short of that; they remembered how truly alive they had been upon earth, and what a solid reality their existence was then, only to compare it with their present ambiguous condition, which was half way between life and death; not life, for it wanted all the corporeal powers and sensations which were essential to being properly alive; not death, for they still, in a sense, *were;* they were still themselves, and conscious of themselves. The son in the old fables goes down to the infernal regions, sees the shade of his father, and forgetting for a moment the nature of departed spirits is going to embrace

him, but only clasps the air, and is bitterly reminded of the truth that the form which is so dear to him is but a vision that meets the eye, and wants the solidity of life.

The two great Epic poets of antiquity both describe the state of the dead. Criticism has justly awarded to Homer's representation the praise of life-like simplicity and vigour—that it is the representation of a real world of ghosts with an almost matter-of-fact truth imparted to it—such truth of conception, that is, as would naturally arise in a strong imagination regarding the scene as a real one. The shades have such ways and habits as gregarious ghosts might be supposed to have; the agitation and impetuous flutter of airy shadowy beings; the rushings to and fro in crowds, the thick gatherings, and the easy dispersions. They collect with excited curiosity about the stranger who has arrived, and, incommoding him by closing in upon him with their cloudy shapes, have to be kept off at the sword's point:

αἱ δ' ἀγέροντο
ψυχαὶ ὑπὲξ Ἐρέβευς νεκύων κατατεθνηώτων. . . .
αὐτὸς δὲ ξίφος ὀξὺ ἐρυσσάμενος παρὰ μηροῦ
ἥμην, οὐδ' εἴων νεκύων ἀμενηνὰ κάρηνα
αἵματος ἆσσον ἴμεν.[1]

Achilles expresses exactly the disgust which a hero and a powerful man, with enormous muscular strength and activities, fiery temperament and boundless courage, might be supposed to feel at finding himself converted into a thin mist. Homer thus communicates a genuine character and naturalness to the other world as the habitation of a population of ghosts; he vivifies in its own way a subterranean world; while, on the other hand, the touches of life and nature which occur in Virgil's description belong to this upper world really, and not to the subterranean one; they are derived from the spectacles of human sorrow around us, from the sad page of earthly destiny, and the struggles of unhappy man in this mortal state.

[1] *Odyssey*, Book xi. 36, 37, 48-50.
 Forth from the infernal gloom the phantoms trooping poured,
 Shadows that once were men. I drew my biting sword,
 That hung anear my thigh, and sitting there forbade
 If any feeble ghost to lap the blood essayed.

The poet utters piercing notes, and living nature speaks in the allusions to the griefs, sufferings, and wrongs of human life; but the subterranean world which he professes to describe lies before him as a scene upon canvas rather than an actual scene, displaying the softest and most delicate colouring, and the most sublime lights and shadows, but asleep.

The poetical account, then, represented existence after death as an unsubstantial shadow, and for that reason fell completely short of the true doctrine of a Future State. To constitute a true existence, such existence must convey to its possessor the sense of its reality and solidity. A man made of shadow is not a real man. Solidity is guaranteed to the Christian's future life by the doctrine of the resurrection of the body. The resurrection of the body is indeed an insoluble mystery; the evidence of it rests upon the evidences of revelation; but, assumed to be true, the effect of this doctrine upon the nature of a future state is plain, namely, that it provides for the solidity of our existence in that state. It secures the truth and completeness of the life in question; that it will have everything analogous to those properties of this earthly life which gives to this earthly life its reality; qualities which truly correspond to the palpableness and tangibleness of our present corporeal nature; that there will not be the slightest sense of defectiveness in it on that score; and that however spiritual it will not be an atom less solid than this present life. This doctrine provides in short that the life hereafter will be no hallucination, no deception, no half life, perplexing the possessor by its ambiguity, and paining him with the sense of a void unsupplied, and a natural appetite for life unsatisfied; but that we shall be and shall feel ourselves to be as thoroughly alive then as we are now.

It has been remarked indeed by an acute writer that the shadowy character which the ancients attributed to existence after death was a mode of betraying their own want of true belief in that existence.[1] When we reflect, we think of a person

---

[1] Whately's *Revelation of a Future State* (Sect. 4). He is more discriminating than Warburton, who is misled by the imagery of a future life in the Pagan legends, and does not see the want of true belief contained in this very imagery, and the peculiar characteristics of it.

either as existing or not existing; we know that there is no medium between the two, because, as Aristotle says, "substance does not admit of degrees," and we know that doubt about a person's existence can only arise from our ignorance which of two alternatives, his existence or his non-existence, is true. But though this state of the case is very clear to us when we reflect, the loose imagination of mankind is apt to confuse doubt and the object of doubt together, and to attribute to the object of doubt that ambiguity and uncertainty which only exists in our own minds respecting it; and this confusion it expresses by a compromise which gives to the object itself a midway and half-existence between being and not being. Thus inaccurate minds regard contingency as a quality inherent in the contingent events themselves, instead of only, as it is, an uncertainty in their own minds respecting those events, which in themselves must either be or not be. And on the same principle the heathen attributed a half existence to the departed; by which they really expressed their own uncertainty whether they really did exist or not. Reflecting men indeed put that doubt before them in its true light, as an uncertainty residing in their own minds; but the majority made it an ambiguity and defectiveness in the future condition itself.

2. If we go from the field of legend and popular fancy to a more regular treatment of the doctrine, we come across corruptions which wholly degrade the doctrine. With respect to the inculcation of a future state in the ancient mysteries, two points must be observed.

In the first place it must be remarked that it was wholly unnatural, and betrayed a want of real conviction of the truth of the doctrine, that the doctrine of a future state should be taught at all in the form of a mystery or secret. Why teach such a doctrine in such a way? The true evidence of a future state was strictly public evidence, and lay in the instincts of every heart. Why then adulterate by quackery a truth of nature, and supplant the light of day by the fictitious charm of a dark secret, if it were not that men believed this false evidence more than they did the true? Let a mystagogue take them into the dark, conjure up an awful scene, and then tell them as a secret that there is life beyond the grave, and they think they believe; but they do not believe the presage of their own conscience which is the voice of God speaking to them. Now this belief is not genuine belief, it is a counterfeit; it is bred out of the dark, and it vanishes with the day. True belief rests upon a public ground, upon the evidence which is contained in our common human nature, human conscience, and human reason. That faith which springs from stage mystery is no faith to last in ordinary life. A secret indeed, and to be kept as such, not to be promulgated, but to remain the privilege of the initiated! what true belief would submit to such terms as these? It is the first impulse of the human heart, when it really believes a truth of such universal interest, to communicate it. All mankind are eager to know something about what is to become of them when they die. It is the pressing want of the human heart. If I really believe, then, that there is a future life, shall I keep this a secret? No, I will tell it to the whole world. It is a proof that I only half believe it myself, if I keep it shut up in my own thoughts. It is of the essence of true belief to be communicative; as soon as man felt really convinced of a future life, he preached it.

But in the next place the doctrine of a future state, as taught in the mysteries, contracted that monstrous corruption, which preyed like a cancer upon all the belief in the soul's immortality which existed in the ancient world, draining whatever there was of natural truth in it—the doctrine of Metempsychosis; that the souls migrated at death into another body, passing through a succession of earthly lives; so that a man went on being born into this world again as other men. The doctrine of Metempsychosis is an organic corruption of the conception of a future life, because it interferes with that which lies at the very root of such a conception—personal identity. I am the same person throughout the whole of my life here: Eternal Life is being the same person throughout eternity. But the doctrine of Metempsychosis utterly confounds, at the very outset, this elementary notion. A man becomes several men in succession. A man goes through in one life the consciousness of being Pythagoras; he goes through another life with the consciousness of being Pericles; through a third life with the consciousness of being Julius Cæsar; he goes through a fourth life with the consciousness of being Vespasian.

These successive divided periods of consciousness, in each of which the man thinks himself to be the individual of that period alone, are but the outer coat and film of one pervading personality. Under the proviso of this one check upon his own multiplication—that if he cannot be many men alive at the same moment of time—he may become any number of persons succeeding each other in unconscious unbroken succession while the world lasts.[1] But in this career of one person who is an innumerable crowd of persons, personal identity is confounded wholly, and so a future life at the root vitiated. Shall I who live now be the same person that will live in a future life, or will that person be different from myself? I cannot understand upon this doctrine how he will be the same person with myself; but if he will be different persons, I have no interest in the question of eternity at all.

The doctrine of Metempsychosis has appeared to some a natural doctrine; and they have accounted for its popularity in the ancient world on the score of its naturalness. The notion did not launch the thought into another world, but kept life within the region of sense and this world; which to some is more natural. But it is a natural doctrine in a very superficial sense only. What becomes of a man when he dies? It was an obvious and very easy conjecture to suppose that he came up to the surface of life again in another body; into a world one endless succession of births and deaths, where the sun of life is always setting in one form and rising in another. A spectator then makes the off-hand guess that Nature does not waste her old materials in supplying the perpetual demand upon her, but uses the treasury of past life to fill up the void of the future. But though the doctrine offers a coarse puerile solution to the enigma of human life, it is totally repugnant to the inner instinct of man; dis-

[1] See *Essays, Historical and Theological*, vol. ii., "Indian Conversion."

organising his whole conception of himself, and cutting off his communication with futurity. Brought to this inner touchstone, it is a totally unnatural doctrine, one from which Nature revolts; no grosser corruption has ever issued out of the chambers of speculation.

The idea, indeed, is singularly adapted to the Brahmanical basis of total scepticism—that point of view from which the whole of present existence, from the peel to the core, from the coat of matter to the very centre of consciousness, is regarded as a mere surface and film which rolls away in the presence of the Infinite Mind. But it is melancholy to see Plato reversing, remodelling, and constructing a scientific basis for the gross and corrupt absurdity of Metempsychosis, establishing it upon the principle of mutual generation of contraries, upon which ensued an endless alternation of death issuing in life and life in death; neither ending in itself, but always in its opposite. The great vortex of the universe was thus always casting up its waves to the surface, and re-absorbing them by turns into the depths below; discharging the vast resources of life, and re-collecting them; sending forth being into the upper world and into corporeal frames, and gathering it back again into the abyss of death, to send it forth again when wanted. The mighty frame of the universe was thus sustained by an equilibrium which kept up an inexhaustible fund of production ever equal to the demand, saved the old stock of life for fresh supply, and instantly replenished the stream from the ancient reservoir. Otherwise, if the old material failed and passed away altogether, and was never available for use again, production must stop, and everything come to an end.

3. We come now from the popular legendary doctrine, and from the mysteries, to the philosophical doctrine of a future state. The ancient philosophers use sublime language about the soul; they assert the immortality of the soul; they speak of it as in its own nature indestructible. A person who comes across this language says the ancient philosophers believed in a future state. But when we examine what the sense was in which they held the doctrine, what they meant by the soul living after death, we find that the idea was a

totally different one from our own, we find that they meant by a future state something which we should regard as a *denial* of it; namely, that the soul upon death was reabsorbed into the Universal Soul, and with all its individuality decomposed and resolved into the great Unity and Whole. The resolution into τὸ ἕν professed to preserve the essence or substance of the soul, safe for ever from extinction, but without distinct sensations, or consciousness, or any peculiar and separate existence of its own; stripped of all these, it was reduced to its *common* life and elementary nature, and lived, not as this or that soul, but as *soul*. The soul was thus absorbed into the Deity at death, because it was a *part* of the Deity. This latter idea was at the root of the philosophic doctrine of resolution into τὸ ἕν. The soul was, according to ancient philosophy, a portion of God—not made or produced by Him, but an absolute fraction of Him; the idea was explained by the illustration of a vessel in the sea holding water that has got into it out of the sea; which water floats for a time within its receptacle distinct from the ocean around it; but upon a fracture of the vessel mingles with the ocean again. The soul is part of God, or the Universal Soul, just as the water in the vessel is part of the sea; it is contained for a time within the receptacle of a human personality, and then mingles with the Divine essence again.

Arrian, the interpreter of Epictetus, uses almost a bolder image. I am, he says, as a man a part of the τὸ πᾶν, as an hour is part of the day.[1] That is to say, the whole, or τὸ πᾶν, being God in this philosophy, a man is part of *God*, just as an hour is part of the day. The soul, says Plutarch, is not so much the work and production of God, as a part of Him, nor is it made by Him, but from Him and out of Him.[2] Plato laid the foundation of this language in his Νοῦς ἀεὶ θεος. Seneca says, "Why should you not believe something to be divine in him who is *part of the Godhead*—Dei pars? That whole in which we are contained is One, and *that One is God*,

---

[1] Εἰμὶ ἄνθρωπος, μέρος τῶν πάντων, ὡς ὥρα ἡμέρας.

[2] Ἡ δὲ ψυχὴ—οὐκ ἔργον ἐστι τοῦ θεοῦ μόνον ἀλλὰ καὶ μέρος—οὐδ' 'ΥΠ' αὐτοῦ, ἀλλ' 'ΑΠ' αὐτοῦ, καὶ 'ΕΞ αὐτοῦ γέγονεν.

and we are His companions and members."[1] Epictetus says, "The souls of men have the nearest relation to God, as being parts or fragments of Him discerped and torn from His substance."[2] The soul being part of God, then, and separated and broken off from Him at birth, is reunited to God, that is, to τὸ ἕν or τὸ πᾶν, at death; as re-absorbed into the Universal Soul from which it was divided. "You have hitherto existed as a *part*," says Marcus Antoninus; "you will therefore be absorbed and lost in the substance that produced you. . . . Every body will be soon lost and buried in the Universal Substance. Every soul will be soon absorbed and sunk in the Universal Nature."[3]

Such a doctrine of the immortality of the soul did not deceive the Fathers, who attacked especially the blasphemy of the foundation on which it rested, that the soul was part of God. They saw the difference between the true and the false sublime, and denounced that exaltation of the human soul to the rank of a divine substance, which ended in its reduction into nothing. Jerome protests against those "qui hominem *exaequant Deo*, et de ejus dicunt esse *substantia*."[4] Tertullian does the same; Augustine tells those "who could not for shame say that the body was God, and yet said that the soul was," that they inserted mutability into the Divine nature. What, he says, do you assert wanton, unjust, impious parts of God? do you mean to say, "Dei partem vapulare, cum puer vapulat?"[5] Some Fathers indeed went so far in this opposition to the divinity of the soul, that they maintained its materiality, and Dodwell, upon the strength of their language, actually maintained the corporeal nature of the soul as a doctrine of the Fathers.

If we turn to the origin of this assertion of ancient philosophy, that the soul was part of God, the ancients seem to have considered that they were compelled to adopt this position by two arguments of irresistible cogency from two different quarters. One was from the nature of God, that the

[1] Ep. 92.
[2] Epict. *Diss.* ii. 8, 12.
[3] Εἰς Ἑαυτὸν, Lib. ii. cap. 12.
[4] *Ctesiphon adver. Pelag.*
[5] *De Civ. Dei*, viii. 5.

universal soul contained all individual souls as portions of itself. The other was from the nature of the soul. The ancient mind was imprisoned within the vice of that old axiom that *whatever is generated must decay.* This being adopted as a self-evident truth, it followed upon it that the soul must be *ungenerated,* that is, must have an eternal pre-existence if it is to have an eternal after-existence. "It is a thing very well known," says Cudworth, "that according to the sense of philosophers, these two things were always included together, in that one opinion of the soul's immortality, namely, its pre-existence, as well as its post-existence. Neither was there ever any of the ancients before Christianity that held the soul's future permanency after death, who did not likewise assert its pre-existence; they clearly perceiving that if it was once granted that the soul was generated, it could never be proved but that it might not also be corrupted, and therefore the assertors of the soul's immortality commonly began here, first to prove its pre-existence."[1] In what mode then did the soul exist in this eternity, *a parte ante?* "If eternal," says Warburton, giving the ancient argument, "it must be either independent of God or part of His substance. Independent it could not be, for there can be but one independent being of the same kind of substance. The ancients indeed thought it no absurdity to say that God and Matter were both self-existent, but they allowed no third; therefore they must needs conclude that it was part of God."[2] The soul could not have lived from all eternity a separate individual life of its own; that would be to make every soul a distinct God; it must therefore have existed *in* the universal soul. It was then at birth discerped from the universal Substance, and at death it will be resolved into it again. Such was the conclusion of the ancients, based upon one, as it seemed, self-evident axiom, "whatever was generated must decay :" therefore whatever was not to decay must be ungenerated. *We* know what such axioms are worth, but *they* were under the yoke of these semblances of truth; they could see no alternative, therefore, between making the soul mortal and making it divine, and thought themselves

---

[1] *Intellectual System,* p. 38.  [2] *Divine Legation,* Book III. Sect. iv.

obliged in self-defence, as claimants of immortality, to endow the soul with original, self-existing, indestructible being; that is, with the attributes of God. The whole well-known demonstration of the soul's immortality which Cicero adopts from Plato derives its eternal existence from the premiss of self-existence. But the usurpation recoiled upon itself in the sequel; that which was discerped from the Divine substance was resolved into it at death, and the soul paid for its false and illegitimate dignity by ultimate impersonality.

"Pythagoras and Plato," says Plutarch, "held the soul to be immortal, for that, launching forth into the Soul of the universe, it returns to its Parent and Original."[1] We must distinguish between Plato the divine and Plato the philosopher. The exponent of old Pagan theology, who remodelled and dressed up afresh the old legendary material, took one ground; the philosopher took another. But the philosophy of Plato outlasted his theology, and his metaphysical basis for a future state produced its natural results in the doctrine of re-absorption, upon which Plato himself verges, and which became the declared doctrine of the Platonists. Socrates seems alone, of all the ancient philosophers, to have rested the proof of a future state upon a moral ground solely; and as a consequence, although his belief of a future state was of the nature of a conjecture rather than a conviction, still his idea of that state was that of personal existence without speculative alloy.

Such was the ancient doctrine of a future state. As a popular doctrine, derived from legend, it represented the future life as an ambiguous and a half-existence, oppressing the departed with the sense of an utter deficiency in their state of being,—being indeed more dead than alive,—wandering as they did to and fro as unsubstantial shadows and ghosts in the subterranean realms. As a doctrine taught more formally in the institutions of Paganism, it contracted the gross corruption of Metempsychosis. As a doctrine of philosophy, it deprived the future life of all personality, and represented it as a mere absorption of the particular soul in the universal soul. We have evidently, in the incoherent and debased mass

[1] *De Plac. Phil.*, Lib. IV. cap. vii.

of sentiment and opinion with respect to the future state, the wild and disordered guesses of the human mind, endeavouring to construct a true doctrine of a future state before it had the foundation on which to build one,—the foundation of an enlightened conscience; a *moral* foundation. In all this accumulation of imagery and speculation, is a future life ever once presented to us as a life that is worth living for? Not once. It was not presented in that aspect in the legendary doctrine, for who could look forward with joy to being an unsubstantial shadow? It was not in the gloomy migrations of Metempsychosis, for who could entertain gladly, or even properly entertain at all, the irrational conception of being changed into a different unknown person, or into a brute? It was not in the philosophical doctrine of futurity: for who could look forward with pleasure to the loss of his personal existence? The Pagan turned his eye from the dreary prospect, and said, "Let us eat and drink, for to-morrow we die," to-morrow we die to this life, and is there any other life to care for? What evidence is there of that point of view, in which we regard a future life, existing in classical ages? The crowd played with the imagery of another world, but it had no place as a truth in their hearts; nobody lived for it. How could anybody live for a future such as this?

From this wild medley of delusion and speculation which composed the Pagan doctrine of a future life, we shall have to turn before long to the negative and neutral creed of the ancient Jew. But before we can estimate properly the condition of belief on this subject, we must place before us that doctrine for which the condition of the Jew was a preparation, viz., the Christian conception of a future life. It is only when the end is before us that the means towards it can be understood; the germ of the true doctrine can only be judged of in relation to the true doctrine itself.

II. *The Christian conception of a Future State.*

1. The Gospel made the announcement of the Life Everlasting; no second mortal life which rises in birth and sets in death, but an eternal and unclosing day which has no night. Once does man die, but it is against the law of the Universe that

he should die again; that the mystery of an end should be repeated; that an event which is single in his existence should recur. After that one death he lives for ever; and his life is a state of glory, not merely a continuation, but an ascent of existence. Nor is this endless life of glory announced as a vision or an ecstasy. By virtue of the article of the resurrection of the body, all that is analogous to the substance, the visibility, delineation of form, the distinction of local presence, the sense of solidity, which attaches to this earthly life, belongs also to the life everlasting. This was a doctrine divided the whole width of the poles from the Pagan doctrine of a future state. It was another truth, a different truth. The Pagans held a future state, held the immortality of the soul, we are told, as if, that said, the subject were all over. But the subject, in fact, is only just begun. Is it enough that the soul after death exists? Is that all; as if so long as it existed it did not signify how it existed, what its life was? This is only the threshold of the true doctrine. The soul may be allowed to exist, and that existence may be represented, as it is represented in Paganism, as shadowy, or as impersonal, or as a perpetual restless change and succession of lives, going on through one condition of being after another by alternating gateways of life and death; the vagrant inhabitant of different bodies, carried backwards and forwards by the interminable flux and reflux of the great tide of existence, and the action and reaction of contraries, life producing death, and death life, for ever and ever. It is the questions which arise after the admission of future existence that are the critical questions. It is a poor thing to say that the soul exists after death, unless you add the mode of existence.

The mode is the real point. But all these questions as to the mode were decided wrongly in Paganism; and therefore the doctrine of a future life, in our sense of the phrase, had to be reconstructed from the very base after the erection of the Pagan fabric; the very first step must be to cast off the whole of Pagan tradition, in which there was nothing that could be used, all which was so much obstructive matter in the way. It was a preliminary absolutely essential for a true doctrine to arise, that the ground should first be cleared and a clean sweep made of this mass of rubbish. To build upon these rotten premises was useless; a new and fresh foundation was wanted; and this was just what the Jewish dispensation, with its *tabula rasa*, its vacancy, its want of all definite conception of futurity, supplied.

2. This personal endless life in another world, which is the announcement of the Gospel, is a most incredible idea at first to human nature. To the simple imagination it is a wilder, a more audacious flight, it more utterly leaves this world and all its forms, its ideas, its types, and impressions behind it than any of the three Pagan conceptions of immortality. All those, with their monstrous and unnatural character, combine an evident timidity; they cling to earth and shrink from the soaring truth of a spiritual eternal world; legend dared not conceive of the future life as more than a shadow cast off from the true life which it placed here; Metempsychosis evaded the conception of another and spiritual sphere of life by providing a cycle of *earthly* lives, and keeping the soul within the changing coil of mortal flesh; and in philosophy another life evaporated altogether. None of these conceptions then got out of the enclosure of this world. The Gospel conception did. It is then the most astonishing conception of all; the most overpowering to the imagination. If we reflect how low a creature man naturally is in his own eyes, how contentedly he measures himself by the span of this life, and thinks himself as a matter of course a creature of to-day; nay, who embraces his fate as a conclusion of common sense, and philosophises upon it; we must see how at once he must regard the idea that he is to live for ever. That period after period should pass, ages and countless millions of ages, and still find him the same person that he is now, upon the verge of no dissolution, approaching no close, looking to as much existence as he has enjoyed, and indefinitely as much more—how can he believe it? How incredible the total unlikeness to all present experience, the release from all sense of transiency, the withdrawal of the weight and presence of mortality upon the heart, the absence of all anticipation of an

end! That the man should thus survive in a new and glorious world the total and dreadful ruin which death is, the blow which shatters the mortal structure, and blots out the whole visible man;—this might be the fitting vision of a fanatic seeing, in second sight, on the other side the dark boundary of life, his own form illuminated by a mystical light; but to mere sober worldly common sense such an eternity would appear an impossibility, a fancy and a dream, a thing to which no belief could attach. Regarded as a real prospect before us, an actual life, which we may at some time, under the Divine government of the universe, be admitted to, it even now tries the faith of the Christian. As soon as he realises it he is wonderstruck. And the mass can hardly be said to believe it. One glimpse caught of the mere chance of this eternity as a fact is superior to the most positive verbal conviction of many —that stupor of certainty which is unbelief in disguise.

The conception of a personal endless life has indeed this double character, and combines these two, at first sight, opposites. It is the only genuine, the only natural conception of a future, and at the same time it is the most stupendous, most surprising, and overwhelming one. It is the only natural conception, for what is the natural idea of immortal life, what we mean by it in our own minds, but oneself living and continuing to live, the same person as one is now, endlessly and for ever. If existence ceases to be personal it ceases to be our existence—what we mean by it. But this conception of immortality is also the most stupendous and surprising. Thus, not to embrace this conception of immortality is to confess to our own annihilation, and yet to embrace it is to believe what seems incredible. Hence the bold front of modern unbelief on this subject. This infidel outbreak which is the visitation of our day, is, after all, only human nature, escaped from discipline, speaking plainly out on this matter. The doctrine of eternal life is, unless he is trained for the reception of it, simply incredible to man. He cannot think himself as a being for whom an endless personal being is designed. It is an absurdity to him, this personal eternity; a mockery offered to a poor transient being, who lives his day and then vanishes.

III. *Jewish preparatory absence of conception.*

1. To build up, then, the Christian doctrine of everlasting life, so incredible to human nature, a new foundation was necessary; and that foundation was a *moral* one. And it was this moral foundation which was laid in the Jewish law. It is as a moral being that man feels his value; that he feels himself not a creature made for this life only, but for another; that he feels even everlasting life, sublime and transcendent thought as it is, not unsuitable or unfit for him. The law was a schoolmaster that gave man a knowledge of himself, that awakened his conscience, enlightened his perceptions, and revealed him to himself; acquainted him with the moral purpose of his creation, and with his own moral nature and capabilities. The law was thus a preparation, an education, and a discipline for the revelation of this truth, and introduced man to the designs of God for him.

It is true that heathen law and philosophy inculcated moral duty and obligation, and so far as heathen law and philosophy did this, so far they supplied a preparation and a training for the Christian doctrine of Immortality. But there were two great defects in heathen moral teaching which prevented solid progress in it, and issued in a stunted growth; these two defects, which had a deep mutual connection, were first, the absence of a junction between morality and religion; and secondly, the absence of the doctrine of repentance, or, what is the same thing, the sense of sin. I read through Cicero's *Offices*, and see much admirable teaching in it, but it is defective on both these points. He teaches morality without any relation to God, and as a consequence of this, without the sense of sin and the duty of repentance in the case of moral transgression. But morality cannot be a deep thing in man's nature apart from these two. It is as conforming him to the will of God, and raising him to communion with God, and in connection with our relations to God, that the sense of duty becomes a penetrating and overpowering feeling. It only rests upon the surface of man's nature and does not take hold of it otherwise. So again what deep hold can moral ideas be said to have over man, if when he acts immorally and wrongly he has not the sense of guilt, and does not see that repentance is necessary for him? This defect has its root in the former one: as an offence against God immorality becomes sin, and needs the Divine pardon, but if there is no God in the case, then there is no sin, and no need of repentance.

Now morality was taught in the Jewish law in its full connection with religion. Man was taught it as that which was to make him acceptable to his Maker, and as a divine rule, the violation of which exposed him to the wrath of God, and therefore imposed on him repentance. The moral law thus gained a marvellous and mysterious depth in man's eyes which it wanted in paganism, even when paganism taught good morals. Among the ancients, although we have scattered traces in their traditions of a divine curse which pursued the wicked, and although Plato partially joined morals and religion, still on the whole morality tended towards being a political and secular thing. In Judaism it was a profound essential. It was armed with all the powers of the invisible world, it was proclaimed with thunder and lightning by the voice of God from Mount Sinai. Man became by the infraction of it a guilty creature. That this infraction produced so terrible a result only showed the sublimity of the law which was broken; and only disclosed the high nature of man as being made to fulfil that law. Now this was a foundation for the doctrine of eternal life because it was a revelation of man to himself, that he was such a being as eternal life was suitable to. It was also a revelation of God to him as a God who cared for man, was intent on improving and purifying him, made him the object of His counsels, magnified him, and regarded him with unspeakable love. The Bible ever inculcates man's value in God's sight. As the object of God's love, and admitted to communion with God, and great in His sight, he could even think the prize of everlasting life accessible to him. And thus the Jewish law, as a discipline which brought man to know God and to know himself, was a preparation for the doctrine of eternal life.

The gospel doctrine of justification was, as an exaltation of man to the level of the life everlasting, to the condition of perfect fitness for it, the completion of the Jewish law on this point. The law was only an awakening of his moral nature, and issued in exposing its weakness and inability: under the gospel the defect was supplied by the justification of man, by which he was clothed with the righteousness of Christ, and made an heir of immortality.

2. But while the foundation of the doctrine of eternal life was being laid in the Jewish law, the truth itself did not rise to the surface. What was the actual state of belief then in the pious Jew on this subject? Let us put before ourselves a religious Jew. It will be said, "Must he not think of what is to become of him when he leaves this world? It is the question of highest personal interest to him. He knows that life is short. He must therefore put the question to himself, and if he does, how can he decide it but in one way? Can he, with his faith in God, really think that the soul perishes with the body? And if he does not think that it perishes, he must decide that it lives after death." These are questions which arise when we think of the pious individual Jew. The natural instincts of a pious heart appear at first sight to be inconsistent with a neutral state of belief on this subject. It would seem that natural curiosity itself must raise the question, and that if the question is raised it must be decided, and can only be decided in one way. On the other hand, if this is our conclusion, we are immediately involved in the greatest difficulties. No doctrine of a future state is revealed in the Jewish law; or definitely taught in any of the religious writings of the Jews, till a late date. And yet, had it existed, must it not have come to the surface? Must it not, indeed, have become the belief of the people?—for the religious part of the community formed the sentiment and set the standard; and the rest followed it if even only verbally.

These questions must be met by observing as accurately as we can what was the actual state of mind of the Jew. On the one side, then, his belief evidently stood upon the very edge of the doctrine of a Future State. First the existence of a God contained in itself the existence of an invisible world. God is not part of this world. He exists out of this world. His sole existence is therefore an existence outside of visible nature. His existence is therefore in itself an invisible world. The Jew, in the very act of believing in God, believed in an unseen immaterial world, in which was Will, Design, Foresight, Love, Anger, Action; because all these belong to God. He believed in an inhabited invisible world because God was in it; an infinite Being to whom any number of beings was as nothing. Again, there being intelligent existence out of this world, as the object of God's care he had an implicit pledge that God would continue *his* existence out of this world, and not destroy him. Would love blot its object out of being? Had all been extracted then out of these two premisses which was contained in them, the Jew would forthwith have awakened to the conclusion of his own immortality; but inasmuch as no extracting process was applied to them, these premisses just stopped short of the conclusion; and the doctrine which trembled upon the very edge of disclosure remained latent and unexpressed. Our Lord extracted and brought to light the latent force of these premisses in the saying that "God is not the God of the dead, but of the living, for all live unto Him."[1]

In this latent doctrine, then, there was something of a sense of security, a general consciousness of standing well upon the question of existence, standing, as it were, upon *terra firma*. In fixing her eye upon an Eternal Being, the soul unconsciously engrafted herself upon Him, and in that junction with the Invisible One was carried safe. The Jew would obviously have lost much in the way of a general feeling of security for himself, had he been without this hold upon an Eternal Being. Indeed, in our own case, besides the distinct image of a future life, there enters largely into our religious support the trust in a present God, and the pledge contained in His character that He will do the best for us. We cannot easily distinguish how much we owe to the superstructure of the doctrine, how much to the base.

But while the belief of the Jews trembled upon the edge of the doctrine of a future life, it did not rise to the explicit doctrine. If the question is asked—How could he go on so

[1] Matt. xxxii. 32; Luke xx. 38.

long, not drawing the conclusion from the premises before him, holding the doctrine in the foundation only? the reply must be a reference of the inquirer to the known habits of the human mind. We know that the human mind is capable of holding truth for a long time in an elementary stage in science and in religion; and that premises in many cases remain unproductive for ages. One step is wanted to bring the latent truth to light, but that step does not occur to the human mind. It is, indeed, an enigma which follows us everywhere in the history of man, whether we take the world's progress, or the progress of individual minds—why people do not think of things sooner than they do. As soon as the idea has been caught, it then seems unaccountable how it has been so long missed; and after the discovery we wonder at the blindness which did not see it before, and passed over what is now so plain. And yet, for all this surprise, we cannot say that there may not be new truths close to our eyes now which we do not catch because the moment of opportune quickness has not yet come to the sight; up to which moment they are invisible. But though the *reason* of man moves slowly, how, it may be asked, could the Jew resist the strong impulses of curiosity and imagination? A future life, it will be observed, is no remote and recondite conclusion of reason, which it takes time and attention and effort to extract from dark premises; but it is an idea to which the human mind has leaped forwardly and impetuously, and in the treatment of which it has rather needed a check, having not only eagerly adopted the belief in a future state, but having allowed fancy to invent the details of it, and illustrate it with most luxuriant imagery.

I reply to this question, that curiosity and imagination could never have discovered the true doctrine of a future state had the Jews given way ever so much to their impulses. The doctrine of a personal endless life was too great a truth to be prematurely seized by such a grasp; only a moral preparation could lead to it, and the ancient Jew did not discover it because his moral condition was not ripe for it. But if it is asked why the Jewish mind did not yield to the natural impulse of curiosity and imagination to penetrate further into this mystery; and how it was that the Jew maintained such a suspense on this subject, stopping contentedly upon the very threshold of it,—we answer that, if the reason of the Jew did not hurry him in this matter, his curiosity and imagination fell under the check of duty. The Jewish dispensation was a dispensation of waiting and suspense,—that was its fundamental character; it professed to be incomplete and intermediate, wanting a head and consummation in the Messiah who was to be. The whole religion was in its very nature expectant, acknowledging to itself its own want of finality—that it was but an instalment of the whole Divine scheme, looking forward to its own future completion in the fulfilment of the great promise upon which its eye was fixed. It was the line of humility and obedience in the pious Jew, and in keeping with the curb and check inherent in his dispensation,—in the absence of a revelation of a future state, not to invent one for himself. It was his trial to restrain curiosity and fancy, and submit quietly to a midway position. It was a trial to the imagination analogous to that which Butler lays upon the intellect in a particular case. The impulse of the sceptical mind is to total disbelief as the decision of, and relief from, doubt. The impulse of the imagination is to the very contrary, not to illegitimate demolition but to illegitimate construction; but the motive is the same, namely, that of obtaining decision and relief. The false repose of the arbitrary settlement of a question, and having done with it without regard to the evidence, is the same in either case; and the discipline of resisting either impulse, namely, the restraining of impatience, is the same.

I may observe, too, that the Jewish dispensation, besides being a Divine dispensation, and *as* being a Divine dispensation, was also a school of thought; and a school of thought, when it becomes established, has great permanent power over men's minds, whether as an impulse or a check; whichever be its aim. The ancient lawgivers appear to have established, by the side of the direct institutions they raised, certain types of character and moulds of thought, which they were able to impress permanently upon the states they founded or remodelled. Lycurgus imprinted his own type upon Sparta; and both Mahomet and Confucius founded schools, and repressive and coercive schools of thought,—a fatalist and a utilitarian; both of which succeeded in repressing the spirit of inquiry in the communities which accepted them. For the Confucian maxim that man could not find out truth, and must therefore attend to what is practical, interdicted the first entrance upon the field of intellectual thought. If we want an instance of the moderating and sobering power of a school of religious thought, we have it close at hand in that school of which the great exponent is Butler. No one who observes can fail to see how deeply this school has struck its root among us, the wide area of its influence, and the great strength with which it moulds a large mass of thought in the English Church, how early it instils into successive generations of minds a certain attitude upon certain questions, a temper of content under difficulties, a disposition to rest satisfied with positions which stop short, and do not profess to be solutions, and the acceptance of the duty of bearing with speculative suspense.

Such an instance may assist us to understand the influence of the Jewish dispensation as a school of thought, how it could sustain the midway and expectant attitude of the pious Jew, his contented suspension of hope, stopping short as he did of the definite conclusion of a future life, of which he held the premises, because he had not authority to go further. It is the natural wish of man to carry thought to a conclusion. Stopping short is irritating to him, just like breaking off from something one has to do when it is half finished; one likes to end one's work when one is about it; leaving off at a fragment is annoying. But the Mosaic system was a school of thought which early used its disciples to withstand this impulse, and habituated them to abstain from conjecture. The nature of man is pliable; and by reason of this pliability, which within certain limits is advantageous for him, and conduces to his instruction and improvement, he is capable of receiving strong moulding and direction from ruling minds and from founders of schools of thought. He is susceptible of being permanently impressed; of being habitually prepossessed for or against any forms or directions of thought; his mind is capable of being put under regulations and prohibitions which dictate to him his attitude, whether of inquiry or suspense, and sustain him, if need be, in particular positions, upon the edges of great questions where he stops short with a trained content, in which he does not chafe or struggle against his situation, but keeps at a safe distance from temptations of curiosity or fancy. The Jewish lawgiver told the Jew that he was not to think of certain subjects; that he was not to look into certain questions; that he was to avert his mental eye and not try to see;—the very opposite attitude of mind to that which the Pagan adopted, to whom the impulse of curiosity was law, who rushed with eager and impetuous speculation into the darkness beyond the grave, and allowed his volatile fancy to revel in the fictitious details of a world of which he knew nothing.

Such a trial of curiosity may perhaps be illustrated by a trial of temper. When anger exists in tendency, solicited by certain objects and events, but is not raised into an emotion, there is this intermediate condition of passion. A religious person, for example, sees what Scripture calls the triumph of the wicked or the success of unprincipled men in this world; but though the scandal is permanently in sight, there is no indignant motion in the mind of the spectator, because this natural effect of the sight is habitually kept at bay; the feelings appropriate to the facts are recognised but held in reserve. Thus curiosity upon the subject of existence after death may, without being suppressed altogether, be guarded off by an habitual attitude of the mind.

This explanation applies to the backwardness of the Jew in drawing a definite conclusion from the scattered disclosures of the invisible world under the old dispensation. Enoch was taken away from the world supernaturally; Samuel was called up from the realms of the dead; Elijah was carried upon a chariot to heaven. Angelic visitations were the visits of the inhabitants of another world, though not belonging to the race of man. But though scattered openings were given into an invisible world, it was a further step to bring this fragmentary knowledge to a point and bind it into the form of a doctrine. It was a further step to see in these special cases a law. The particular instances remained such in the mind of the Jew; they were not made into a whole, and interpreted upon a principle. He did not see, in the persons of Enoch, Samuel, and Elijah,[1] mankind. Passing gleams of a future world were the natural precursors of the mature truth; but at the time they were fragments of which the full meaning was not realised, or the whole to which they belonged, discerned. Truth breaks forth in sudden inspirations before it settles into a doctrine; and thus Job bursts forth with that prophetic utterance—"I know that my Redeemer liveth, and that he shall stand at the latter day upon the earth; and though after my skin worms destroy this body, yet in my flesh shall I see God." Here was the gleam of a future life; but it would be premature to argue from the gleam the existence of the full doctrine. Warburton's interpretation of this passage as an expectation of temporal deliverance is inconsistent with the general argument of Job, who regards this world as a scene of injustice. An interpretation of it as the assertion of a *doctrine* of a future life would be also inconsistent with the argument, which implies that Job does not possess the key to the enigma of that injustice. But the interpretation of the passage as an inspired gleam of the truth does not contradict the argument, and gives a more natural sense to the words.

In describing the Jewish belief on the subject of a Future Life as a state of suspense, we have at the same time to recognise a good deal of language on the subject of death in the Old Testament, which appears at first to go beyond a state of suspense, and to exhibit death as the termination of existence. "Shall thy wonders be known in the dark?" it is said in the 88th Psalm; "and thy righteousness in the land of forgetfulness? wilt thou show wonders to the dead? Shall the dead arise and praise thee?" "The grave cannot praise thee," says Hezekiah, "death cannot celebrate thee; they that go down into the pit cannot hope for thy truth." But

[1] Warburton admits a dawn of the truth in the ascent of Elijah, and a gradual advance of the Jewish mind in that direction from that time.

though this description of the state of death is in startling contrast with that of the Gospel, in which the grave figures as the gateway of heaven and the entrance into life and glory, we see, when we examine it accurately, that it stops short of the fact of what does really take place in the mystery of death. These are simple descriptions of the phenomenon of death, and do not profess to enter into the inner reality. To the eye death is the phenomenon which they describe; it is a withdrawal from the light of day, the effacement of all the sensible tokens of existence. The dead cannot praise God because they cannot speak; they cannot be shown His wonders because they cannot see; they are in the land of forgetfulness because they give no outward sign of recollection; they are shut up in the pit because they are buried in the earth; they have no hope, because the grave is the apparent end of everything. This is a faithful picture of death as a visible change; but this language does not say more or enter into the question of what really happens to the soul at death; it is not a description of the real truth but of the outward phenomenon. The language in Ecclesiastes appears at first to place man on a level with the beasts at death; but the whole mode of speaking evidently assumes the sphere of visible nature as the scene in which the writer places himself, and to which he intends his observation to apply. "All go unto one place, all are of the dust, and all turn to dust again"—this is only the statement of a visible fact. "Who knoweth the spirit of man that goeth upward, and the spirit of the beast that goeth downward to the earth?"—that is to say, there is an immense difference between the spirit of a man and the spirit of a beast, the one is much superior to the other; the human soul having an alliance with God and heaven, while the animal nature creeps on the ground; but though we see this difference we cannot follow it beyond the boundary of this world, where both man and beast vanish from our cognisance, and are reduced by death to an outward equality. We must too, take the melancholy description of death in the Old Testament combined with more hopeful language which seems to pass beyond the line of neutrality. The saying, "The spirit shall return unto God

who gave it," confines itself indeed to the resumption of the
gift of life by the giver, stopping short of the question, whether
this resumption is for continuation in another state; but still,
as appertaining specially to man, this mode of speaking
declares the dignity and excellency, and favours the permanence of, the human soul. The language of the Old Testament
which points to the happy end of the righteous—" Let me die
the death of the righteous," "the end of that man is peace,"
does not of necessity contemplate consequences beyond this
life; because the man who has the support of his conscience at
that awful moment, even without the distinct prospect of what
is to follow, cannot but enjoy a sense of security and feel that
in some way or other all will be well with him; but such
language still borders upon the idea of a future life.

It is not, I say, the idea of annihilation which is expressed
in this language of the Old Testament, but the visible exterior
of death. If we want a specimen of language which does
express the idea of annhilation, we must go to Lucretius.
The language of Lucretius on the subject of death indeed, so
far as the mind of the poet is vigorously inspired, as we see
it to be, with the clear apprehension of the end of this life—
of a moment when that will be to us a past life, not belonging
to us—possesses a latent religion, and may be called spiritual
language. His words fix with an iron sharpness and strength
upon us the miserable thought that there is an end of this
world to us—that truth which Scripture appeals to as the
foundation of a religious life. The common mind does not
really apprehend what is so contradictory to experience as the
total cessation of its connection with this world; it cannot
embrace the true idea of an *end;* but dreams of another life
which is only the reflection in the glass of the life it knows.
Lucretius breaks in pieces this idol, and we see, as we have
said, a spirituality in the mind of a poet who is thus fiercely
at war with a dream of mortal flesh, and cuts with the unspar-
ing edge of reason through the mistake and the delusion. He
takes indeed the particular case in which this mistake is a
source of fear to man, who wrongly identifies himself beforehand with that miserable spectacle of death which will only

have begun when he will cease to be affected by it; but this sham eternity is much oftener a source of false comfort to man. Yet though Lucretius, so far as he fastens upon his reader's mind an end of this life, uses spiritual language, he goes beyond this idea, and devotes his poetical rage to representing the clear philosophical conception of total annihilation. And we therefore see from him what language that is which does express this latter idea, and we see how different it is from that of the Old Testament description of the phenomenon of death.

IV. *Comparison of Judaism and Paganism with respect to the belief of a Future State.*

With the Pagan doctrine and the Jewish absence of doctrine before us, we may now compare the two together as religious conditions. How stands the case with respect to the comparison of Judaism and Paganism on this point? It must be observed then, in the first place, that a great fallacy is involved in the usual mode in which this comparison is made. The case is stated as if the comparison lay between a religion in which the true doctrine of a future life was not taught, and a religion in which that doctrine was taught; but this is not the state of the case. The two beliefs between which the comparison lies are, on the one side, a gross misconception of the future life, which is the Pagan; and an absence of definite conception, which is the Jewish. We have not here to answer the question why the true doctrine of a future life was not revealed to the Jews; that is a question which has to be answered in its proper place, and it is incidentally answered in the course of this discussion; it is in fact part of the general question, Why was revelation progressive? Nor again have we to answer another question akin to it. It may be asked why should there have been an interval of complete vacancy? Granting that the Pagan doctrine of a future life must be thrown aside, and that the time was not yet ripe for the true doctrine;—why should not the element of truth which was in the Pagan creed have been separated from its corruption and been inserted in the Jewish Law? There was still room, it may be said, for some declaration of a Future State, instead of the omission of it. But we are not concerned here with the question why such and such a piece of knowledge was withheld in the old dispensation. We are concerned with no omission or defect in Judaism on its own account which belongs to the other general ground of progress of revelation; we are only concerned with such an omission as compared with a Pagan assertion; whether the silence of the law were an inferiority and a loss as compared with an erroneous and debased doctrine, in the religion of the Heathen.

This question may be met, in the first instance, in some such way as this. We know the religious belief of Abraham, of Jacob, of Joseph, of Moses, of Samuel, of David, of Hezekiah, and other saints of the Old Testament. Would it have been any improvement to their belief in our eyes, if instead of that state of mind with respect to futurity in which we perceive them to be, they declared their belief in the doctrine of Metempsychosis, or their belief in the legend of the infernal regions; or their belief in the doctrine of absorption and an impersonal existence of the soul in a future state? Would it add to the dignity, to the spirituality of their religious condition in our eyes, that they should have the conception, and definite conception, of a future life, but a conception of one or other of these kinds? It is evident that it would not; on the contrary, that it would greatly lower our estimate of the religious condition of these holy men. There is no scandal in a simple stopping short of the truth in those who held the solid groundwork of that truth. But to suppose, for example, David, the holy Psalmist, to have believed in the cycle of Metempsychosis, to have imagined that the human soul at death passes into other bodies of men or brutes, would be a conception so degrading to the spiritual character of David, that we cannot state it without revolting from it.

Now, if this is so, the comparison between Paganism and Judaism on this subject is decided, and decided in favour of Judaism. The alternative is not between some true conception of a future state and the want of a conception of it; but between a false conception and the want of one. We must not, in this comparison, take some abstract doctrine of the immortality of the soul to compare with the defect of one in Judaism; we are comparing two actual systems, and we must compare them as they stand. We must take the doctrine of the immortality of the soul as it was actually worked up, in the actual shapes in which it was held in Paganism. We may, indeed, and sometimes do, substitute for the actual doctrine of Paganism a philosophical abstraction of our own, and then sharply objurgate the omission of this in Judaism; but if we do so we commence the comparison by wholly mistaking one of the sides of it. It is the actual doctrine of Paganism and the actual doctrine of Judaism which must be brought together in this judgment and compared. The actual doctrine of Paganism existed in those three shapes I have mentioned, the life of shadows, the Metempsychosis, and the absorption into the infinite. Did any one of these shapes give the Pagan the superiority over the Jew? Common reason answers, No.

Again, we have an additional aid and support to the Jew in sustaining his position of suspense, and resisting the temptations of curiosity and fancy, in the opposition in which he was placed to Paganism. He could not have indulged in speculation and imagery without falling into the corrupt conception of a future state into which the Pagans had fallen; but the Pagan corruptions of the doctrine were before him, to deter him from such an attempt, and to warn him of his danger. In the Pagan doctrine the pious Jew saw not the elevation but the degradation of man; and as he abhorred the idolatry of the heathen so he would shrink from his idea of futurity. The Pagan belief then might be thrust before his eyes, but it would be before him not to captivate but to disgust him. It is at first sight difficult to understand how the Israelites could have had throughout their whole abode in Egypt that very marked and elaborate doctrine of a future life before them which stood out so prominently in the religion and constitutions of that country; and yet that the fact should have been wholly ignored, and that in a law, the institution of which followed almost immediately their exit out of that country, so long their abode, not a single mention of a future state should be made; but this is the answer. To the pious Israelite the Egyptian doctrine on this point and Egyptian idolatry and animal worship stood on exactly the same footing. Could he believe in the transmigration of the human soul at death into the bodies of brutes? His purer creed as to God and man would at once throw aside such an idea as monstrous. But this was a prominent part of the Egyptian doctrine of a future state, and could not be separated from it. All went together. It no more occurred to the pious Israelite to parley with the Egyptian doctrine of a future state, than to enter into terms with his very theology. He no more respected the Egyptian fancy when it played with futurity, than when it played with the Divine Nature.[1]

But again, did the Pagans really believe after all in the future state they talked about? or what was the sort of belief they had in it? A great drawback must be made on *this* head, in comparing the Pagan and the Jewish states of mind, as well as on the score of the debased conception of the state itself. The crowd caught up the imagery which poetry supplied. But it is not generally considered, as much as it ought to be, how small an element in the real belief of a future state is the mere image of it. People see a luxurious growth of imagery on this subject in Paganism, and leap to the conclusion of a belief; but let us examine a mere image in the mind— what is it? What does it amount to? If a man looks forward to a future state he must have an image of himself as existing or not existing. He takes of the two the image of himself as existing. It requires no high state of mind to do this; anybody can do it, the merest savage can and does so image himself. But there is no belief implied in what is a mere guess, a mere choice of that alternative of the two which is most liked; unless there are also some *reasons*, some principles in the conscience on which the mind goes. Yet this image taken up is expanded, is dressed out, is decked with the details of fancy and of story, and becomes a popular doctrine of a future state. After all, however, water cannot rise above its level; the belief is at the root a guess, and however it may be orna-

[1] See page 301.

mentally developed does not rise to more. The whole Pagan imagery was in reality an enormous advance upon their belief. The superstructure was wholly disproportionate to the basis. It was a luxurious growth of shell with hardly any kernel inside. It is a striking contrast when we turn from the scenic details, circumstantial disclosures, of another world in Paganism, the personal adventures connected with it, the reports brought back by visitors to the region of mystery, to the blank of the Jewish law. But vivid imagery, though it shows a warm and lively fancy, is very little index of faith. A pictorial creation, when once begun, advances so fast and gets so far ahead of conviction, that it ceases to be any guarantee for the latter. Man can imagine endlessly. Vivacity will give the smallest minutiæ of any scene; but it is mere picture-making. Do you believe in the scene which your own fancy has conjured up? I may imagine a certain kind of life going on in the planet Jupiter, animal forms, modes of nutrition totally different from those of this earth. Or I may imagine states and societies of men there, with a most elaborate geography. But I do not believe in the creation of my own fancy. There was a foundation of belief in a future world among the heathen, but to suppose that vivid and minute painting was any proof of the depth and solidity of the belief would be to mistake the habits of the human mind. There was entertainment, excitement, a gratification of the appetite for the marvellous in such descriptions; but to true belief they stood in the relation of a monster mask, which was out of all proportion to the head within it. It is not, then, the imagery of the Pagan—which is quite another thing—but the *belief* of the Pagan which we must consider in a comparison of Pagan and Jew upon this subject; we must take the small residuum of belief left after the deduction of pictorial matter, and put it side by side with the solid germ of the true doctrine of a future life in Judaism.

How stands the case then in the comparison of Paganism and Judaism upon the point of the doctrine of a Future State? On the one side, it is true that we have the express adoption of the doctrine, but it is grossly misconceived, while, moreover, the general *belief* in it is so weak and unsettled as to be hardly more than a name. On the other side, there is the omission of it, but a foundation is being laid for the true doctrine. Which of these two conditions or situations then is the better? I do not mean when the true doctrine came to light which was the better of the two—that is taken for granted. But in the interim, and while the truth was in its latent and germinal stage, which was best: to have the superstructure of the spurious doctrine, or the foundation of the true one? There can be no fair doubt on this point. The foundation of the true doctrine which was being laid in the communion of man with God, and the enlightenment of man's conscience by the Law, was in *itself* and at the *time* a most signal elevation to man, the most direct improvement of him. What if there was no clear idea of a future state? There was the actual present belief in God, and in a God who governed by rewards and punishments. To the authority of the divine law the direct belief in a future state is not essential, but, first, the conscience is bound by it prior to further sanctions; secondly, although the sanctions of rewards and punishment are practically necessary to the support of human obedience, such sanctions need not have express reference to a future life. The Divine Law was in fact able to move man in the old dispensation, and commanded in a pre-eminent degree, as compared with the Pagan moral law, the springs of action in his heart. The Law was a present effective influence. On the other hand, the practical influence of a doctrine of a future life, as they held it, upon the heathen was wholly inconsiderable. There is no evidence that the sort of motive was in any operation among them, or was known in classical times as a practical principle of life—the aim at the reward of future happiness. There is no proof that the living for another world was a recognised practical rule of life. There is no sign of their understanding such a scope and direction of life as this. Still less is there any sign that such an aim created any mass or body of holy men, or church. Whereas, under Judaism, we see a perpetual, standing body of pious men, whose idea of life was obedience to the Divine Law; we see a Church. We need not then argue the case from premisses; the proof lies in the facts. The Jewish belief bore fruits. The mere article of a future life is not in itself the test of superiority of one creed over another, for besides that it may be grossly misconceived, the bare image of a futurity is nothing, and merely shows a different condition of the popular fancy— unless it influences life. That is the criterion. But the Pagan belief with this article did not answer this test, while the Jewish belief without it did.

## IV.—ON THE SUPPOSED OBSCURITY OF HOLY SCRIPTURE.[1]

THERE appears to have been a tendency lately to exaggerate the obscurity of Scripture. I do not mean of particular texts or departments, such as the typical language of Scripture, or the prophetical section of Scripture, but of Scripture in matters of faith. This has been alleged sometimes in the interests of church authority, to create a more stringent view of its necessity, sometimes in the interests of doctrinal scepticism. Let us take first the *extreme* school of tradition. What it lays down is, that the language of Scripture is an indefinite ambiguous language, which is consistent with various interpretations; that, for instance, a Socinian could fix his own interpretation upon it, and that it would be difficult to show that the language itself did not admit of that interpretation, and that the reason why the Socinian interpretation is not the right one, is not that Scripture may not be so interpreted, but that it is not the interpretation of Tradition. Tradition determines the ambiguity and neutrality of Scripture to one point, and out of all the interpretations of which the language admits, assigns to it the true one. This is a position which goes beyond the Anglican doctrine of Tradition.

When these persons attribute this obscurity to Scripture, the reason seems to be that they confound *omission* with obscurity. Scripture, for instance, on the subject of the peculiar nature and virtue of the sacrament of the Eucharist; on the relation in which infants stand to the grace of the sacrament of Baptism; on the point of the extent of the administration of the Rite, whether it should be administered to infants or not, there is an absence of exact statement; Scripture lays down no doctrine of church-government, and no formal doctrine of any particular order of men as the channel of grace to the Church.

[1] Delivered in the Latin Chapel.

These are all points, however, upon which great dissension has arisen, and great separations taken place. It may be almost said that our Church *separated* from the Church of Rome at the Reformation upon the question of Transubstantiation, so much had the movement of the Lollards which roused the national mind hinged upon that doctrine, and so prominent was its place in the whole crisis of the Reformation. Upon the Baptismal question again, and the question of church-government, not only great disputes, but separations also have arisen.

When persons observe then the different disputes and schisms which have arisen upon these points they say generally and indefinitely, How obscure is Scripture, which gives room for so much difference! But omission is one thing, and obscurity is another. Before we pronounce the Bible to be an obscure book, we must be sure that there is no distinction to be drawn between its omission, its silence, or its reserve on some points, and its substantial clearness and openness on others; and we must be sure too that those two styles of treatment in Scripture do not respectively attach to fundamental matter of belief on the one hand, and to non-fundamental on the other. A book must not be called obscure because it leaves out some points which it does not care to decide; it is an obscure book only if it is ambiguous, reserved, and wanting in expression upon the great truths which it requires us to believe, and leaves them matter of guess.

Whether these omissions in Scripture then do or do not prove the obscurity of the Scripture, is not a question of the language of Scripture so much as of the quality and comparative importance of the truths omitted. The general opinion in our Church is that the truths which are adequately expressed in Scripture are the *fundamental* truths of the Gospel; and that that matter of belief which is passed by in silence, or is not decisively stated, is non-fundamental matter of belief. Those of our divines who maintained a certain definition of the grace of the Eucharist, or who maintained the necessity of Bishops for the Church, drew a distinction. It was essential for the Christian status of a person that he should be in a church thus organised, and that he should receive true sacraments; but it was not essential that he should *believe* in the necessity of this church organisation, or in the true nature of the sacraments.

Mr. Keble urges the distinction in his postscript to his sermon on Tradition.[1] Speaking of these two facts or truths, just mentioned, relating to the Eucharist and Episcopacy, he says, "The *doctrines or propositions* concerning them could not be necessary; it would be wrong to insert them as Articles of the Creed.... St. Ignatius writes, 'Let that Eucharist be accounted valid which is under the Bishop, or some one commissioned by him.' Wherein he lays down the rule which we know was universally received in the Primitive Church, that consecration by apostolical authority is essential to the participation of the Eucharist, and so far generally necessary for salvation." 'But,' adds Mr. Keble, this "could not be turned into a proposition and put into the Creed, because that would make, not only the rule itself, as observed by the Church, but, the knowledge of it also by the individual, necessary to salvation: and it may be thankfully admitted that knowledge of the true nature of the sacraments is nowhere required in Holy Scripture, as a condition of our receiving the grace they impart."[2] In the same way with respect to pædobaptism, which is another omitted point in Scripture, our great authority Wall says, "If it be *not* a fundamental point there is not ... any sufficient reason for men separating or renouncing one another" upon it. And "I think that such a question about the age or time of one's receiving baptism does not look a fundamental, nor is so reputed in the general sense of Christians."[3]

Such omissions in Scripture then do not go any way to prove that Scripture is an obscure book; that is, that it does not express with adequate clearness that which is essential, that which it is necessary for its purpose that it should express. Does not the admission which meets us on the very threshold of the great Roman controversies go to acquit Scripture on this

---

[1] *Primitive Tradition recognised in Holy Scripture*, preached September 27, 1836. The postscript was to the third edition, 1837.
[2] *Postscript*, pp. 13, 14.
[3] W. Wall, *History of Infant Baptism*, vol. ii. p. 422 (Part II. ch. xi.), 4th edition, 1819.

point of obscurity? The Roman Church professes to draw its peculiar claims and dogmas not from Scripture, but from tradition as an original independent source. But if this is so, Scripture cannot be answerable for that material which is committed to another authority altogether to communicate. If you have to be clear on any subject you must in the first instance have to speak about it.

I have tried to explain what appears to me to be a source of confusion on this subject; and one from which a prejudice has arisen with regard to the language of Scripture—a pre-occupation of persons' minds with the notion that Scripture is, in the matter of doctrine generally, a neutral and ambiguous document which tradition alone can interpret. I cannot but think that if Scripture had been allowed to speak for itself without any intercepting medium of this kind, it would have amply vindicated its own language. Take it up, seriously of course, and reverently, but still regarding it as a book which, like any other book, is to declare its own meaning by its own words, and I do not think that upon the great truths of the Christian Creed there can be any fair doubt as to what it says.

With respect to the doctrine, for instance, of our Lord's Divinity, it is difficult to understand how any one can read St. John's Gospel, and not see that that truth is contained in it; that is, read in the way in which we should read any other book. The same may be said of the doctrine of the Atonement; we do not want any more than that Scripture should be read according to those grammatical rules by which other books are read. Imagine yourself taking the sacred books of some pagan religion, for example the Hindoo, and finding some sublime personage occurring in them, to whom such language expressive of his being an Incarnation of the Deity was applied, as is applied to our Lord in numbers of passages in the New Testament, and you would not hesitate to say that such a personage *was* in this mythological book put forward as an Incarnation of the Deity.

Suppose any new Hindoo sacred book were discovered in one of the Temples which contained deifying language as clear regarding some person figuring in it, as that of Scripture concerning our Lord : one of our Oriental scholars who was reading a paper on it before the Asiatic Society would not scruple to say that that person was exhibited in that Oriental document as a Divine Incarnation. And so with respect to the doctrine of the Trinity, if in any Mexican or ancient Persian manuscript we found three great Divine Agents figuring, to whom personal characteristics and acts were attributed as openly as they are attributed to the three Sacred Persons in Scripture, we should have no doubt that a Trinity was exhibited in that manuscript.

It is true that the word Trinity does not occur in the New Testament, and this objection has been sometimes urged (by advocates of the extreme school of tradition) as proving that tradition alone communicates the doctrine of the Trinity. But such an objection, in order to be of any value, must show what Three Persons *can* be *but* a Trinity ; and if Scripture also proclaims from first to last the Unity of God, the natural and unavoidable interpretation of Scripture is a Trinity in Unity. It must be remembered, and it is an important point to attend to, that fulness and openness of language, such as leaves no fair doubt as to meaning, is quite a different thing from formal precision, and regulated accuracy of language. It is in the former way and manner that we say Scripture is clear ; that it has a good free body of expression which declares its own meaning.

Although the word Trinity does not occur in the *Nicene Creed*, yet it would be an extraordinary assertion to make that the doctrine of the Trinity was not obviously contained in the Nicene Creed. It must be borne in mind that the Bible is addressed to, and designed for, the use of every individual Christian, to read with edification to himself, and with instruction to himself regarding the great truths of his religion. But it is difficult to see how the Bible can be an instructive and enlightening book to the individual on the subject of the great truths of revelation, if it does not declare those truths by its language, taken in its natural and grammatical sense. A book which admits of a number of alternatives of senses, and does not decide itself the right one of all these, may afford to a reader room for the exercise of his ingenuity in guessing at its meaning, but can hardly be said to instruct and edify him. For this purpose it is needful that there should be a sufficiently copious and obvious body of expression.

It is an important thing to consider too, that as a matter of fact a great variety of churches and communions do extract the same doctrinal meaning from Scripture, so far as relates to fundamental articles of belief. I do not see any reason why they should do so, except it is that the language of Scripture only admits properly of that meaning, and that that is the natural meaning of the language itself. I know that Tradition has great power in making people see that meaning in a book which Tradition makes them *expect* to see in it; but there is a limit to such a power; nor can we suppose that people could go on for ever saying that such and such language meant so and so, and did not mean anything else, if the language did not, according to ordinary rules, express that meaning. And these communions have some of them broken with Tradition on some things: why then should they be tied to it upon others? This unanimity and consensus then among different communions is certainly a tribute to the obviousness of that meaning of Scripture in which they agree. And when we find on the other hand that the matter of belief upon which they disagree is such as, being non-essential, Scripture is under no obligation to express, the evidence becomes strong for the acquittal of Scripture as an obscure book; for a book is not an obscure book because it omits certain subjects which do not come within its necessary scope, if it is adequately clear and open upon those subjects which do.

There is one great exception indeed to this unanimity in the interpretation of Scripture in fundamental matters of belief, namely, the Socinians; but is not their case one to which the saying, *exceptio probat regulam*, may fairly be applied? The uphill battle which this sect has to fight in interpreting Scripture, and the strain they apply to the words, is but too conspicuous.

Indeed, when we examine the case, as regards the mutual relations of Tradition and Scripture, it becomes difficult to see how Scripture could fulfil its necessary function of being a check *upon* Tradition, unless it expressed the revelation with which it was charged with an adequate openness and clearness. A book which admits of many alternatives of meanings may admit indeed of the *right meaning*, but cannot in the nature of the case be a check upon the *wrong ones*. Let us imagine Tradition having no check at all of a written word upon it. How would the case stand? Tradition then is undoubtedly a perfectly natural channel of the communication of truth; and we all depend upon it in a hundred different ways every day. But when people assert, as they have a full right to do, the natural use of Tradition, they sometimes forget its qualifications and its limits. It is evident that an oral tradition for twenty years, and an oral tradition for two thousand years, are very different things. We cannot argue because Tradition would be a guide for a certain length of time after the lifetime of the apostles, that it therefore would have been enough for the Church to depend upon up to the present day. Imagine, then, as I have said, for a moment, that there *was* no Bible, no written word at all, and that the Christian revelation had been committed to oral tradition, for men to hand down, generation after generation, by speech. It would be evident that such oral tradition would be only another name for corruption; and that, taking human nature as it is, such corruption of revelation would begin early, would expand largely, and would never stop. But if the absence of a written word altogether would leave Tradition an unchecked and uncontrolled course, a written word of which the language was ambiguous and only admitted of a true meaning, in common with erroneous ones, would not have a very different result. Such a dubious *litera scripta* would agree with wrong tradition as well as right, and the traditional principle would be the real master of the position; and would ever, at every step, determine on its own part the sense of the written word, instead of the written word exercising a true veto or check upon the traditional principle. It would have an unrestrained course. The Anglican doctrine of Tradition, which imposes scriptural limits upon it, and erects Scripture into a decisive Court of Appeal, thus requires for its working, *in limine*, an adequately clear and not an obscure Scripture : the doctrine provides by its very structure, for a free and open body of expression for the substance of the faith; because without this there would be no check upon Tradition.

It may be said that in the statement just given of the tendency of Tradition to corruption, it is forgotten that the theological writings of the Church in each successive age are a check upon the degeneracy of Tradition; inasmuch as they record the established doctrines of the Church in the age in which they are written, and so expose the late origin, and therefore falsehood, of the doctrines which rise up in a succeeding age. It might thus be said that Tradition, even without a written Bible to check it, is still coerced by the natural course of theological literature and the inevitable succession of writers in the Church; that it is hindered from having its full swing; and that its tendency to corruption is stopped from coming to a head. This argument of the check of theological writings upon Tradition is used in T. C.'s reply to Archbishop Laud's Relation of his Conference with Fisher: "Universal traditions," he says, "are recorded in *authors* of every succeeding age, and it seems more incident to have the Bible corrupted than *them*, because of its bulk and passing through the hands of particular men, whereas universal and immemorial traditions are openly practised and taken notice of by every one in all ages."[1]

Stillingfleet, in his Vindication of Laud, answers this argument by the reply that the traditions might corrupt the writings, rather than the writings test and authenticate the traditions: "You say, they are recorded in authors of every succeeding age; but if a book be written out of traditions, will the very traditions preserve it pure?"[2] The process of corruption of doctrine is so gradual that, supposing no original check provided for it, each succeeding age of writings would record an addition to the last step in the progress, rather than furnish an exposure and refutation of the next. In

---

[1] *Laud's Labyrinth*, by T. C. P. 98. Paris, 1658.
[2] Stillingfleet's *Vindication of Laud's Conference*, vol. i. p. 389; Oxford, 1844.

a very gradual process, each step authorises the next as *leading* to it, rather than disowns it as stopping short of it. And so without a written Scripture in the first instance to seal the genuineness of doctrine, the course of theological literature in the Church would only *reflect* the gradual change which busy and restless, or gross human, thought had wrought in Christian doctrine instead of convicting it; would express corruption instead of checking it.

The objection will perhaps be made : If Scripture is thus clear and open, if it sufficiently expresses its own meaning by its own words, what use is there in Tradition at all ? I reply that Tradition has an undoubted use and function still reserved for it. "The sixth Article," says Mr. Keble, "leaves ample scope for the province which Bishop Taylor assigned principally to Tradition : practical rules relating to the Church of Christ,"—rules respecting which he adds, "the doctrines or propositions concerning them would not be necessary,"[1] but which might still *as rules* be important. But even in fundamental matter of belief, and on the supposition that Scripture expresses and states this fully, a very important use is still left for Tradition. The Bible may express certain truths perfectly adequately as far as its own language is concerned; we may take it and say to ourselves, and have the right to say to ourselves, This means so and so : it can mean nothing else ; and yet there is that element of self-distrust in the human mind, that even when it sees a thing quite plainly, and sees nothing wanting to a conclusion, belief is still sensibly confirmed and invigorated by another's agreement. When we are quite sure of something from our observation or reasoning, we still rise to another level of assurance, when there is concurrence with it from without. Isolated reason is practically weak ; it wants courage ; it needs reinforcing from another principle. Such is the case with respect to the construction of Scripture. The individual may feel certain that his construction is a good, plain, natural construction of the words ; and yet the agreement of his fellow-Christians in that construction, the concurrence of the Christians of all ages—in other words, *Tradition*

---

[1] Postscript to Sermon on Tradition, p. 13. 1837.

gives a new character to this assurance, and lifts it up to a *kind* of strength which it wanted before. Faith is social; one man's belief is increased by seeing another's.

I turn now to another side of this subject. The obscurity of Scripture is sometimes alleged in the interest of a sceptical religious philosophy; but we may remark first that, in this quarter, it is not so much the obscurity of Scripture itself that is asserted, as the existence of some intercepting medium in ourselves, which hides the true idea of Scripture from us. This intercepting medium is regarded as being caused by the gradual growth and accumulation of a succession of traditional interpretations of Scripture, with which Christian society is penetrated; a series of coatings as it were of human thought, which must be peeled off, before we arrive at what is the real core :—this core is the true idea of Scripture, but before we reach it all is delusion and deception. The answer then to such a position as this is, that we cannot be called upon to entertain an hypothesis which is wholly gratuitous and without evidence. This notion that we are prevented from seeing the idea of the apostolical age by coatings of successive interpretations which have got incrusted upon it in our minds, is a mere assumption. I take up Scripture; I see that, like any other book, it professes to express something that it wants to tell us; I look at one or another statement or sentence in it; the grammar of it is plain: according to ordinary rules of construction it means so and so. You say that my thinking so is owing to the medium through which I look: you refer me to a succession of interpretative coatings; all I can say is, I know nothing about them; I have no reason to suppose that this is the case; and until I have some reason I shall go on thinking that I understand the passage so, because the words mean it.

Or again, the philosophic charge of obscurity begins at the other end, not with a veil upon the minds of the interpreters, but with a veil upon the idea which is interpreted. According to this latter method, the apostles themselves did not know their own idea, that is, did not know what the true *inner* idea was, which was the centre and essence of that general rough conception which they put into language, and which they borrowed from the ideas of the age; but which was the popular, contemporary clothing of the true idea rather than the true idea itself. The apostles stand, according to this hypothesis, somewhat in the same relation to the idea which their statements fundamentally mean, as one theory of prophecy makes the prophets stand to the subject of their own prophecies. The prophets, according to some, made prophecies the true nature of which they did not themselves understand, but which they expressed as Divine instruments and mouthpieces. So the apostles are supposed here to express, in the conceptional language of their own day, fundamental truths or ideas, which were not the ones actually present to their own minds; but which the philosophical evolution of Christianity was subsequently to bring out.

This hypothesis is not then strictly concerned at all with the obscurity of Scripture, as a book expressing the idea which it intends to express. If a book expresses those ideas which are in the minds of the writers, then I do not call it an obscure book. If you say that those ideas themselves must undergo a process, that those ideas themselves must be translated into other ideas, that is certainly an obscure and difficult proceeding, an and interminable one. But we are not concerned with it on the question of a book's obscurity. We have not here to do with the mysteriousness of the ideas or their peculiarity, but only with the fact, that in Scripture those ideas are expressed, and that Scripture does not fail in the statement of them. And though it may fairly be required that the ideas which a book expresses, if it is to be acquitted of obscurity, should not be mere caprices of individual mysticism,—mere eccentric and isolated fancies,—so much requirement as this is undoubtedly fulfilled in Scripture. The ideas of Scripture are large and generally received ideas, they are ideas which are embraced by the human race. The ideas of the Incarnation and the Atonement have a place in human nature and in the human mind; and though they are incapable of pure intellectual conception, that is, no clear image or outline of them can be raised in the mind, it would be absurd to say that on that account they were not genuine legitimate ideas; because otherwise we should have to say that the soul was an illegitimate idea, or that duty or "ought" was; as we can raise no clear conception of the soul, or of what we call "ought." Unless we admit ideas which are not spurious, yet at the same time do not allow of accurate conception, we cannot advance a step either in natural religion or morals.

In conclusion, I will draw attention to a distinction between the practical use of Tradition, for assuring our own individual faith, and the conversion of it into a controversial *fulcrum*. In controversy, and especially in an age of free thought like the present, which deals with fundamentals, after asking you what is your religion, the very next question is, Where is your religion? Now, with the greatest appreciation of the practical use of Tradition for confirming our faith, I must yet make the remark that for the controversial object just mentioned, the supposed office of Tradition to select, out of the various meanings of an ambiguous Scripture, the true one, is the most cumbrous instrument that can well be imagined. It virtually sets up Tradition as the seat of Revelation, without the simplicity of that theory; but accompanied with an unwieldy apparatus of selection of documentary senses. The true Anglican doctrine of Tradition relieves us of this difficulty. Having set aside for Tradition a compartment of secondary truth not decided in Scripture, and having thus cleared the ground, it then definitively asserts that there is in Scripture a clear, full, and satisfactory statement of fundamentals; that is, declares there is a manifest statement—according to the natural meaning of words—of the Christian Revelation in Scripture. This then is a compact and effective answer to him who asks, Where is your revelation?—It is in Scripture. Laud saw this, and he made the natural sense of Scripture in *our* system correspond to infallibility in the Roman, as the *indicator of Revelation*. It would be a great mistake to suppose that oral tradition is the indicator of revelation in the Roman system; it has for that purpose nothing so remote, so indefinite, so dim, so difficult to trace: a present infallible guide decides that question. That is the Church of Rome's controversial fulcrum. *Scripture*, according to Laud, is this fulcrum in our system. "Sure Christ our Lord," says his opponent Fisher, "hath provided some rule, some judge, to procure unity and certainty of belief." "I believe so too," says Laud, "for he hath left an infallible rule, the Scripture. Scripture, *by the manifest places in it which need no dispute, no external judge, is able to settle unity and certainty of belief in necessaries to salvation.* It hath both the conditions which Bellarmine requires for a rule, namely, that it be 'certain and that it be known,' for if it be not certain it is no rule, and if it be not known it is no rule to us. Now the Romanists dare not deny but the rule of Scripture is '*certain*,' and that it is sufficiently '*known*' in the *manifest places* thereof, and such as are necessary for salvation, none of the ancients did ever deny; so there is an infallible rule." By infallible it must not be supposed that Laud means anything mathematical, but such practical certainty as naturally convinces a rational person. He asserts that such practical certainty is to be found in the statements of fundamental truth in Scripture; and he claims for this practical certainty of Scripture a rank and authority higher than that of all councils. For "full church authority," he says, "is but church authority; and church authority, even where it is at full sea, is not simply divine; though no erring disputer may be endured to shake the foundation which the church in council lays. But plain Scripture *with evident sense*, or a full demonstrative argument, must have room where a wrangling and erring disputer may not be allowed it."[1] Such is Laud's conclusion. We may not assign, it would be unworthy and presumptuous to assign, poor polemical ends to Scripture; but I cannot but think that a great controversial object like this—to indicate concisely the place where our revelation is—comes clearly within the scope or design of Providence in giving the *written* Word. The divine dispensation has here put a strong compact assertion in our hands, and if we do not take advantage of it when we have it, if we do not wield it effectively, it is our own fault and our own weakness. It is indeed not seldom the case that powerful and effective assertions are also false ones. This is not to be denied. But I

[1] Laud's *Conference with Fisher*, p. 163. Oxford, 1839.

maintain here that the view of Scripture which represents it as *obscure*, as ambiguous and a mere recipient of alternatives of meaning—that *this* is the untrue, the artificial view of Scripture, and that the real fact is the other way. Scripture is indeed but too plain, its truths too express, if we are to judge by the extraordinary difficulty there is in explaining them away. Some minds, however, applying a really reverential spirit too narrowly, seem to have been afraid that it would be disloyal to tradition to admit openness and clearness in Scripture. And so there has been a tendency, if I may say so, to make out Scripture to be uncertain even against facts, in order to call in tradition to decide. But it is hard upon us if we cannot use a most valuable assertion when facts give it us, and if we must fall back instead upon a controversial position, which is unwieldy and also untrue.

## V.—ST. PAUL'S TEACHING AN INTEGRAL PART OF HOLY SCRIPTURE.[1]

THERE is a good deal of theological opinion now, which, though it may not express its decision openly, goes in the direction of regarding the Christian Revelation as stopping with the Gospels, and the doctrine of St. Paul as being only *one* exposition and interpretation of the real Revelation, not part of Revelation. It is needless to remark upon this tendency (and almost more than tendency) of thought in some quarters, that if men once begin to cut off parts of that whole Scripture which has come down to us as Divine Revelation it is difficult to see where such a process can stop. There is something so arbitrary in the summary disposal of large parts of Scripture without any evidence whatever that they stand upon different ground from the rest of the Bible, simply by act of the will, that it is impossible but that the whole of Scripture must feel the blow. No real faith can be left in the Bible generally, when such a step has been taken. It becomes then a mere matter of a man's own choice what he accepts of Scripture and what he does not; and all rests upon a footing, not of authority or command, but only of a man's taste and predilection, which he gives some parts of Scripture the benefit of, and does not give others.

What the Pelagian movement practically amounted to was a rejection of St. Paul, and an exclusion of him from the canon of Scripture. That whole body of thought and feeling which in St. Paul's mind stood as the very sense and signification of the Gospel Revelation was cast aside : that whole deep view of sin as rooted in man's nature here, and of the moral law as unfathomable and beyond fulfilment—leaving in the minds of the best a sense of void and gap, which no obedience man can give here can fill up—all this was renounced : in consequence

[1] Delivered in the Latin Chapel.

## St. Paul's Teaching an Integral Part of Scripture. 75

the faith in the sacrifice and obedience of Christ, as an atonement for the sins, not of the wicked only but of the good—as a filling up of the defects of the saints, as a great imputation of Another's righteousness to all who can lay hold of it;—this whole import and effect of the gospel revelation was abandoned. In a word, the whole inward mystery of sin and of the redemption was rejected, and what was reposed on and accepted was that part of the gospel which was identical with the law of nature,—the power of the will, the obligation of duty, the rule of natural piety, and the acknowledgment of the goodness of God. The Pelagian movement was thus virtually what the present movement, to which I refer, is;—a rejection of St. Paul from the Canon of Scripture.

And yet when we go into the grounds there are for thus making revelation stop with the Gospels, or I ought rather to say with the simple morality of the Gospels, for if we go to the depth of their teaching, we shall find that the Gospels contain the whole foundation of St. Paul's doctrine; but deferring this point, when we go into the grounds there are for limiting revelation to the Gospels, we shall find that such a supposition is not only without any grounds, but that it is in the very teeth of the plainest intimations and announcements of the Gospels themselves. The Gospels are explicit upon the very point that they are *not* final statements of revealed truth, that there is more to come after them, that there are reasons why the last part of the disclosure is withheld, and that, in short, that dispensation which is to crown the gospel revelation, the dispensation, that is, of the Holy Ghost, has not yet begun. Thus it is clearly and expressly stated in St. Luke that when He should have *departed* from them, there would be still a continuance of the revelation; and that an Invisible Spiritual Power would go on with the work which His visible teaching had begun. "And, behold, I send the promise of my Father upon you, but tarry ye in the city of Jerusalem, until ye be endued with power from on high" (Luke xxiv. 49). No words could declare more plainly that there was to be a continuation of supernatural influence and inspiration after the period which the Gospels covered was closed. And in St. John's Gospel our

Lord makes at greater length, and with more particulars, the same announcement when He tells His disciples that when He is gone He will send a successor who will continue the revelation, and carry on a special and fixed stage of it which could not have been accomplished in His own lifetime.

It must be borne in mind that the very structure of the new dispensation,—as requiring our Lord's atoning death before its very nature could be disclosed, and its very purpose known, —that this implies a new and second stage of revelation after the *first* stage. The dispensation could not be understood till it had been completed and consummated in act; but that act was the death of the accomplisher of the dispensation. The full enlightenment, therefore, of the mind of the Church upon the subject of the dispensation, must take place after our Lord had departed; yet that could not be carried on without a continuance of the revelation, and without the succession of a new Divine Power to impart it. Here, then, is a second revelation after the first, a revelation to illuminate man's understanding and disclose all the bearings of the great fact of the Atonement, *after* the accomplishment of that fact itself. Christ had announced the *fact* itself indeed when He was upon earth. "From that time forth," we read in St. Matthew (xvi. 21), "Jesus began to show unto His disciples, how that He must go unto Jerusalem, and suffer many things, . . . and be killed, and be raised again the third day." And to the two disciples after His resurrection, He expounded, "how Christ ought to have suffered these things and to enter into His glory" (Luke xxiv. 26). But this great event of the Death on the Cross had not as yet been brought out into its full meaning, and in the light of all its consequences and fruits. There was another Revelation required to bring out all that inner and hidden truth; for man could not show it to himself. And this fresh revelation was plainly announced by our Lord. "The Holy Ghost, whom the Father will send in my name, He shall teach you and bring all things to your remembrance, whatsoever I have said unto you," that is, shall throw a new light upon whatever I have told you in reference to myself and to my work; shall both bring back the words, and also teach you their deep and mysterious import. "When He"—the Holy Spirit of Truth—" is come, He will reprove the world of sin, and of righteousness, and of judgment. When He, the Spirit of Truth, is come, He will guide you into all truth. . . . He shall glorify me, for He shall receive of mine, and shall show it unto you" (John xvi.).

*If*, then, a new stage of the gospel Revelation was to begin upon the departure of our Lord from the world, *if* the Holy Spirit was, after the consummating act of the Atonement had taken place, to illuminate the understanding of the Church respecting that act, to seat it within the heart of the individual Christian, to inspire him with the inward sense of what had been done for him, and to implant in the individual soul its relations to a Saviour,—why should not St. Paul have been the great minister and mouthpiece of the Holy Spirit chosen for this work? To place the apostle outside of the office and channel of revelation, as if the revelation was over when he began, is contrary, of course, to the whole of ecclesiastical testimony, and is to subvert at one blow the whole of that basis of external evidence upon which the fabric of the Canon of Scripture stands. That, of course, is its immediate effect. But it must also be observed, as a most important addition, that it is to go against the whole force of internal evidence as well. The whole structure of the revelation made in the Gospels pointed to another and a further stage of that same revelation, when it had left the confines of our Lord's earthly life: the closing act of the great Sacrifice required to be brought out in its consequences, and the obligations it entailed upon the heart of the individual. It was actually announced that a further revelation, which would be an extraordinary illumination of the individual Christian, a guiding him into all truth, a revealing within his mind of the glory of our Saviour and His work, would be made. And this was what St. Paul so pre-eminently did, and what it was his peculiar office to do. To stop revelation with the Gospels, then, before it comes to the Epistles, is simply to divide two parts of a great whole; to break off prematurely at one portion, which with its own mouth announces itself as requiring continuation; to intercept the very professed adaptation by which the Gospels link on to the Epistles; and to impose on the former a finality which they disclaim, at the cost of withholding from the latter a significance which they demand.

What is it which St. Paul does in his Epistles? If one were to express it shortly, does he not establish in the individual Christian that connection with, and relation to, Christ as his Saviour, which the great act of Christ's sacrifice requires? All those expressions of St. Paul's which denote so completely an individual interest in Christ's death, an individual life in Christ, and a union of the individual with Him, as the source of his peace and favour with God here, and of salvation in the world to come, what are they but a bringing of the great act of Atonement, once performed upon the Cross publicly, into the inner sphere of the individual soul?—illuminating individual life with those regards and relations which come out of that great fact; giving that development to the truth of the Atonement which was necessary to its being the real source of the individual's hopes and prospects. In a word, was not that which was needed to plant the Sacrifice of Christ in the Christian soul, as the root of his individual spiritual life, *the doctrine of Justification?* The doctrine of Justification completely and decisively conducted the doctrine of the Atonement into the sphere of, and moulded it into the stay of, the individual spiritual life. There was no mistaking the nature of the doctrine of the Atonement, after it left St. Paul's teaching, so as to suppose that it was only, so to speak, a public doctrine, and not a private and personal one. It was stamped with the ineffaceable seal of individuality, in its application. The blood of the Atoning Sacrifice was applied to the individual soul, and it issued in those emotions of gratitude, joy, and hope which a rescued being must couple with that fountain of cleansing and renovation.

Let us imagine for an instant, if it be allowable for the sake of illustration to do so, what might have happened in the Church's mind with regard to the fact of the Atonement, had it been left simply in the form in which it leaves the gospel history, of a public and general mystery. Let us imagine,

I say, for the sake of illustration, what would have happened in the treatment of the general mystery, if St. Paul's teaching, which gave it so pre-eminently an individual application, had been omitted. Would not a tendency have been observed in the mass of men, instead of seating the Sacrifice of the Cross within the spiritual man, and giving it an operation in the inmost corners of the soul, to have converted it into an external commemorative spectacle? We can imagine the mysterious event celebrated in striking form, made into a great and solemn exhibition, and surrounded with grand and imposing imagery to feed the religious imagination, and minister to poetical emotion. We might conceive it to have been invested with the ceremonial of one of the ancient mysteries; while all this time,—in the lack of Inspiration fastening on the Church the idea of the individual soul as the sphere of the operation of Christ's Sacrifice,—no one of all the crowds that attended this striking celebration would have had any idea whatever of this sublime mystical event having taken place for him; and of him individually being the subject of a reconciliation by it; and of receiving pardon and peace through it. That it made all this difference to himself personally would be far from being conveyed to him by the general pomp of a mystical spectacle. It would be one thing to gaze at a grand commemorative ceremonial which celebrates some general mystery in the history of the world, and another to receive that mystery into yourself—to regard it as applying to you, and to look upon your own righteousness in God's eyes as depending wholly on it. It is in its application to the individual that the yoke of this mystery upon faith begins to be felt. It is not felt before. The mystery, if it is outside of you, lodged in an exhibition, in a ceremonial, in a picture, is no troublesome claimant upon faith; and therefore men who are without belief still often like religious spectacles; they are convenient; they ask no questions. It is when a mystery comes within the man that many a one feels, if he would openly say so, that he hardly knows what to do with it, and wishes it outside him. But St. Paul's *exposition* of the Great Sacrifice brings it within the individual soul, with its whole application and consequences. It then asks for belief, and asks in a way which cannot be put off. It confronts you; it comes face to face with you; it must be believed or disbelieved. And thus some who could easily, and with a certain moral pleasure, have thrown themselves upon the general symbolic spectacle I have been supposing, are sometimes troubled and disquieted by a statement of St. Paul's. They feel awkward, with his sentences in their mouths. The challenge to their belief is insupportable. They shrink from uttering them, and the words die away on their lips.

Hence then, and by this sign, we see the work which St. Paul was inspired to do in his Epistles, for the establishing and carrying out of the doctrine of the Atonement. It was just that application of the doctrine to the inward man which was wanted, if the revelation of the Atonement was to be saved from evaporating into a dream, and growing into an outside spectacular mystery, and an airy vision of the imagination; if it was to become anything more than this, it must be applied, as St. Paul did apply it, to the individual, it must be interwoven with all his spiritual longings, and intertwined with the purposes of life. The individual must feel that the truth belongs to him with all its comforts, all its stimulus, and all its obligations on affection and gratitude. The doctrine of Justification, then, is the revelation of the operation of the Atoning Sacrifice of Christ *in the individual*. He is dead when this Sacrifice is made for him; and he becomes alive by means of faith in it; when the Sacrifice becomes to him, not only forgiveness for the past, but strength for the future, a mysterious principle of life in him, inspiring him with new spiritual energy. Our Lord's death figures throughout St. Paul's Epistles not as an outside piece of history to affect masses, but as an inner moving cause in each man, to which he feels himself owing his religious zeal and affection.

Look at St. Paul's language. In it Christ has left the historical sphere of the Gospels, and has entered into the human soul, as its peace, righteousness, justification, and redemption. "There is no condemnation to them which are in Christ Jesus. . . . For the law of the Spirit of life in Christ Jesus hath made me free from the law of sin and death" (Rom. viii. 1, 2). ". . . If Christ be in you, the body is dead because of sin, but the spirit is life because of righteousness" (ver. 10). "Ye are in Christ Jesus, who of God is made unto us wisdom, and righteousness, and sanctification, and redemption" (1 Cor. i. 30). It is evident that all this is the Mystery of the Atonement, not kept outside as history necessarily represents it, but showing itself forth as a principle within the man; and it is evident too, that this development of the great fact of the Atonement in this inner world of man's soul was the very design of Scripture, and was made to follow under the dispensation of the Spirit, as soon as the Act itself of the Atonement was visibly completed; that as soon as the Gospels have done *their* work, the Epistles intentionally come in with theirs, applying the great Act of the Gospels to the individual.

This work of the Epistles could not have been done *before*,— that is, could not have been simultaneous with the period of the Gospels and with Christ's ministry on earth, in the very nature of the case. He must have died, He must have risen again and ascended, He must have finished His work and entered into His glory, before He could reign in men's hearts, and before the work He had done could become a living power within human souls. Were the disciples, even the apostles themselves, equal to entertaining such a spiritual view of our Lord while upon earth? In those intimate communications of our Lord with His apostles which mark the close of St. John's Gospel, we do indeed see the beginning of a disclosure of some inward connection between Christ and His disciples, which was not accounted for, or contained in His visible earthly intercourse with them. The relation of the Vine to the branches is more than that of any teacher, however influential, to his followers. "I am the vine, ye are the branches: he that abideth in me, and I in him, the same bringeth forth much fruit. Abide in me, and I in you. As the branch cannot bear fruit of itself except it abide in the vine, no more can ye except ye abide in me" (xv. 4, 5). This description of an inward and mysterious union with Christ, given by Himself while He was upon earth, is an anticipation of the fuller spiritual union of Christ with the individual Christian after he had left the world. Our Lord, if we may say so, uses the language of His own apostle St. Paul, but still not *fully*; it was only when Christ's earthly life was over, that the full relations of Christ to the individual soul could be disclosed; of which subsequent disclosure it was that He said:—" I have yet many things to say unto you, but ye cannot bear them now. Howbeit when He, the Spirit of truth, is come, He will guide you into all truth. . . . *He shall glorify me;* for He shall receive of mine, and shall show it unto you" (xvi. 12, 13). Is not this an intimation which in the natural course of Gospel development points to St. Paul?. It looks like a prophecy of that revelation of the inward connection of Christ with every true disciple, which it was St. Paul's office to make known, and which was the glorifying of Christ in the Church, and in every individual member of it. This subsequent revelation, our Lord specially says, was, among other things, to convince the world of His *righteousness,* "because I go to my Father, and ye see me no more." And what is more sounded throughout St. Paul's Epistles than Christ's righteousness? and that not in the way in which the righteousness of a living person is exhibited, which operates by way of example; but celebrated as a righteousness of a higher and more mystical power, as the righteousness of the Son of God, who had left this lower world, and had gone to sit at the Father's right hand:—as a righteousness which makes righteous—that righteousness of *one,* which became the gift of righteousness to *others;* that obedience of one which became the justification of others.

The teaching of St. Paul then not only rests upon exactly the same external evidence of inspiration upon which the rest of the New Testament rests, but it is incorporated in the New Testament by the very internal *structure* of the New Testament, and by the very framework of the Revelation; an earlier part of which pointed to a later and supplementary part. It is evident from the very language of the Gospels themselves, that the great Act in which the Gospels culminated, leaves the Gospels with the rays of a very imperfect illumination thrown upon them, and needing, after the Divine Actor has departed from earth, a continuation of the course of revelation, in order really to show the Church what had been done in the fact of our Lord's death. That this fact was to be an Atonement is indicated by the Gospels themselves, which say that He was to "save His people from their sins" (Matt. i. 21); that He was "to give His life a ransom for many" (xx. 28); "that He came to save that which was lost" (Luke xix. 10). His own application to Himself of "all which was written in the law of Moses, and in the Prophets" concerning Him, stamped His death as a sacrifice; as well as His own words, that "it behoved Christ to suffer, and to rise from the dead the third day, and that repentance and remission of sins should be preached in His name among all nations;" and the exclamation in St. John's Gospel—"Behold the Lamb of God, which taketh away the sin of the world." But though Christ was proclaimed a Saviour and a Sacrifice generally in the Gospels, what were the relations to the *individual* into which this developed, —how sinful man was to feel individually different from what he had been; what were the spiritual consequences and fruits within the man—this must be a subsequent revelation. And of this subsequent revelation St. Paul was the great instrument.

Unless indeed this supplement was given, how was the reality even of the Gospel truth to be kept up? Unless the Atonement of Christ was carried into the sphere of the individual soul, and that was made to see the interest it had in it, that His death was a remedy for sin, effacing the sting of it,—unless this action of the Sacrifice upon the inward man was revealed, and he was made to know it and feel it—what was the Crucifixion but an outward simulacrum and spectacle the meaning of which would vanish as the event receded into history? It was the entrance of this mystery into the human heart, and the proof of its power by its struggle with the human will, that made the difference between the Atoning Sacrifice of the Gospel and the paschal solemnity of the Jewish Law; which raised it above a solemn exhibition, a representation, a symbolic rite; which made it more than a type and shadow. Whence then arises that reluctance to use the language of St.

Paul on the subject of the Atonement as it affects the individual soul, which some feel; at the same time that they will throw themselves with fervour into the solemnity of a Eucharistic service, which celebrates only the same mystery in ritual which St. Paul's language does in the interior of man's heart? From St. Paul's language, if they would confess it, some feel themselves divided by a kind of chasm; they would rather not use it; if they do, they go through it as a trial, for which they have to nerve their utterance. But let the Atonement be celebrated under the form of a rite, and they are at home with it. This reluctance to use St. Paul's language may indeed be partly attributable to the abuse which this language has suffered in the mouths of extravagant zealots: but is this all the reason? I am afraid not. Language of many kinds is abused, and yet we are not shy of the authentic and true forms of it. It is some inward reluctance which makes them shrink from this language, while they like the rite. And yet there ought to be no division between rite and language which have one common object, no discord in our hearts respecting the two. If there is such a chasm there, is it not because the language commits them to some *positive truth*, which they only half believe, whereas the *rite* is only contemplated as vaguely symbolic? they feel a resistance therefore to the language which they do not to the rite. But this very difference which they feel between the two, between the Atonement of Christ as carried into the interior of the individual by St. Paul, and as expressed in an outward service or rite, shows that St. Paul's language was wanted in order to give reality to the truth. For the true difference between the language and the rite to them is that the rite is capable of being taken in a vaguer and less solid sense than the language; and that the use of it therefore does not test belief, so much as the sincere adoption of the language. Let no one suppose indeed that in itself the Eucharistic service does not demand the most profound assent to the doctrine of the Atonement: it is evident that it is based upon it, and that every prayer in it implies it: it is only that in the case of a service its external form gives the opportunity of avoiding its inner assertion, and that therefore as doctrine it sits easier upon many minds than religious statement does.

What Pelagianism practically did was to get rid of this language. Their position ignored and subverted St. Paul's teaching. All that idea of sin as a necessity of this mortal state, of nature groaning under the yoke of it, of the weakness of the will, and the void in the conscience,—all that inward groundwork upon which the relation of the individual to Christ as based in St. Paul's Epistles, was swept away by Pelagian doctrine; and with the premiss went the conclusion. The mystery of sin was abolished, and with it went the mystery of a Redeemer.

There being a tendency, then, in some quarters to consider this language as only one theological exposition of the Atonement, and not a real part of Scripture, I have given reasons why such a view appears altogether untenable, and incapable of being maintained without the entire disruption of Scripture. The external evidence of the Sacred·Canon only concurs with the internal structure of the New Testament in giving the full basis of inspiration and a genuine place in the Bible to St. Paul's teaching.

## VI.—*THE DOGMATIC OFFICE, ITS SCOPE AND METHOD.*[1]

*Dogmatism, dogmatising, dogmatical*, etc., are terms which have gradually contracted in common speech an unfavourable meaning : however, what is denoted by these terms is not in itself either good or bad ; not in itself either advantageous or disadvantageous ; whether it is to be praised or blamed depends entirely upon the object and end it has in view, and the judgment and discrimination with which it is conducted. It stands on a par in this respect with many other proceedings and lines of action, which are in themselves indifferent, and which are only proper or improper, serviceable or injurious, according to the temper and aim with which they are adopted. Is dogmatism good or bad ?—speaking of it generally and indefinitely—is a question which can no more be asked than whether arguing is good or bad ; or whether philosophy is good or bad ; or whether going to law is necessary or vexatious ; or whether going to war is politic or impolitic. All these processes and lines of action are neither one of these nor the other in themselves ; it depends upon the modes of them, whether they are right proceedings, or wrong ones. And so with respect to whether dogmatism is wise and salutary, or trivial and mischievous, all turns upon the particular occasion and the object to which it is applied.

The dogmatic office has been sometimes regarded as the creation or substantial development of theological truth ; and writers have used language as if Christianity started with but a seed or rudiment of that truth, which it subsequently, by the successive statements and definitions of councils, attained. The primitive Christian enjoyed, according to this view, a

[1] Delivered in the Latin Chapel.

comparatively meagre share of the whole Christian Revelation; he lived at its commencement, in the day of small things, in the possession only of an elementary knowledge; and what had been revealed to him was but the root of that tree of doctrine under the branches of which the world afterwards rested. This subsequent growth was the fruit of the dogmatic office; the truths originally revealed by the new dispensation waited to gain substance, expansion, and maturity upon this soil and by this culture. According to this interpretation, then, of the dogmatic function, all the successive definitions and dogmatic statements of Councils in connection with Gospel truth were actual additions to and enlargements of that truth; they increased the substance of the Christian Revelation; by the gradual accumulations of these decisions the whole structure of Divine knowledge advanced as well in its positive size as in its connections and proportions; and those who lived under this completed formation had the advantage of a really higher Christian light than those who preceded them. Fresh and fresh enlightening truth streamed in successive ages from these synodical sources, the heart of Christianity glowed with exact definitions, and the stock of Revelation was enlarged, and the current of its life-blood made stronger, every time theological accuracy advanced a step, and a formula gained in precision.

Such a view however of the purpose and effects of the dogmatic office as this must appear, upon examination, to be a very mistaken one; because, in truth, the stock of Revelation cannot be added to by any process short of a new Revelation; and because too, when we examine, we find that this is not in fact what the dogmatic office does, in dealing with doctrine. The dogmatic office guards from error, but does not create or reveal truth. Let us take the doctrine of the Incarnation, which is a fact of Revelation, and the very corner-stone of it. This doctrine came several successive times under the dogmatic office of the Church during the first centuries; but what was the purpose for which it came under it? and what was the manner in which it was actually dealt with? It was dealt with only in this way, namely, that certain false meanings which were from time to time given to the doctrine were taken notice of and condemned. The false meanings thus *excluded* left the original doctrine as it was; the revealed truth was not allowed to be interfered with, but this was all the result that took place; the revealed truth gained no addition to its own substance, but only a protection against an error and a misinterpretation. Nothing accrued in the way of augmentation, it was only enabled to remain itself; no fresh truth was created, but only that continued which before stood. For instance, the doctrine of the Incarnation implies *one Person*: for we mean by the Incarnation the *Union* of God and man; but if they are *two* Persons they are not *united*; they *are* two and not one; the union therefore implies the unity of person; and that is the very idea of the Incarnation. Upon what principle, then, can it be said that the decision of One Person in God Incarnate was *new* truth, *added* to the truth of the Incarnation, —an augmentation of the doctrine's substance? The doctrine only gained the advantage of standing as it was by it. It *was* the doctrine always of one person. Our Lord is in the Bible as plainly as possible One Person; no one thinks or conceives of Him otherwise. But there came up the sect of the Nestorians, who said He was *two* persons. That new idea then was excluded from the idea of the Incarnation, but the only effect of the exclusion was the old idea remaining, not any new one added. The defined idea was exactly the same as the undefined, the falsehood was warded off, but the truth was not added to. Nor was the dogma of two Natures any more addition of substance to the original idea of the Incarnation than the dogma of One Person. The dogmatic office preserved, by this definition, the truth of the two Beings that were united,—that God and Man existed in the Incarnation, and not any third nature which one middle Nature would be; but this was all that was done: and that two natures, divine and human, were joined in the Incarnation, was exactly the same as saying that God and man were joined in it. There was no fresh substance added to the truth: it remained exactly the same that it *was*, only protected from being made what it *was not*, and from being changed into another doctrine.

Nor was any fresh light thrown upon the doctrine any more

than any fresh substance added to it. No new knowledge was communicated in these definitions; no man could say, except indeed he had a very ignorant and blind mind, that he knew one iota more of the doctrine by these definitions than he did before; it remained exactly the same incomprehensible mystery that it was before, and just as inexplicable to the intellect. It was no *explanation* of God being made man to say that God and man were One Person, or that God and man were two natures: the new statement imparted no light to the intellect; all that the new statement did was to preserve the original idea, mystery as it was, unaltered, to keep truth as it stood.

It was a complete misrepresentation, then, of the use and of the effect of the dogmatic office to exhibit it as an actual growth of truth, and increase in the quantity of Revelation. Indeed, when we are told of such a result of the definitions of Councils, and congratulated on the treasure of Divine knowledge, and the fresh accession of Divine light which we acquire any time an accurate distinction is promulgated by a council, and a new piece of terminology is constructed, we are called on to believe a delusion. These erections are necessary as defences of revealed truth, but to speak of them as themselves radiating with Divine knowledge and celestial light, as fresh affluences of Divine truth, raising the level of the Christian believer, and filling the world with an increasing atmosphere of illumination—this is to make the fundamental mistake of confounding words with things, and imagining you have got a new truth every time you have got a new term. These defences are necessary to guard the original truth, as ramparts are wanted for a city; but the ramparts are not the city; nor are these terminological structures truth's *substance*. The Truth is the original revelation. There is a mystery upon which the Gospel is founded, which is that of the Incarnation—of God having become Man; which mystery has been supernaturally disclosed. This then is the truth. But this truth cannot be augmented by human definitions. It must ever remain what it was when it was communicated. No mysterious terminology which we construct can rise higher than the original mystery, as water cannot rise above its own level. Whatever we say, we are confined within the precincts of an incomprehensible idea which we cannot overstep. We may erect ever so great a quantity of verbal machinery, but the truth is still what it was at first; the truth of God becoming man; no more and no less. This is the first and this is the last illumination of man; the primitive Christian used it as *his* inspiration, and the latest generation of Christians must use it as theirs. All Christians must use the one same mystical and incomprehensible but inspiring truth, as it came from the fountain-head; for the dogmatic office only preserves it, and secures it remaining the same truth.

It is true, dogmatism is incidentally a polemical process, because it is only upon a theological difference arising when there is a wish in some quarter to tamper with the original revealed truth, that the necessity to protect it arises. Nevertheless the aim of the dogmatical process is simply to vindicate the idea, to clear it from disturbance, and to keep it as it was originally communicated and revealed.

And these observations furnish an answer to the question whether Theology is a science. If science is understood in the sense in which it is taken when we speak of science popularly, using the term alone, and without an annex, such a claim is of course utterly untenable. When we speak of Science thus absolutely, we mean physical science; and to claim scientific knowledge as the property of Theology, in the sense in which scientific is understood in Physics, would be an absurdity. In Physics Science is the observation of facts, and the observation of facts in certain relations and in a certain connection; so that some facts are made to appear the causes of other facts. The chain of knowledge is thus ever lengthening in physics as fresh facts are discovered, which stand in an antecedent or casual relation to facts previously known, and it is the triumph of science that systematised fact is ever gaining ground upon disorderly and undisciplined fact, so that knowledge is ever establishing fresh inroads upon the territory of ignorance. The network of causes extends, and includes more and more of the empire of nature within its grasp, as new facts are day after day observed, and observed in certain relations. Now all this is as inapplicable, as can be conceived, to a Revelation which communicates in the first place not facts of observation, but mysterious truths, and communicates these truths once for all, to be transmitted as they were given, and handed down to all subsequent generations, as they issued from the fountain-head. There is no discovery of new truths in Theology: the same creed which served for the apostolic age serves for every age after. Why should it not? However this world may develop, man's relations to the other world must always continue the same. The wants of the human soul must be ever the same. The capacity of man as a recipient of revelation cannot be altered or enlarged by progress in physical knowledge. If, then, God vouchsafed in a particular age to give man a revelation, there can be no reason why that revelation should not serve him in every age after. The analogy of progress in physical knowledge which depends upon the use of man's ordinary faculties, does not in the least apply when we come to a revelation from above, which our ordinary faculties cannot add to. We use then that inspiring opening into another world which is contained in the Gospel creed exactly in the same way in which the *Gospel age* used it: the intervening expansion of man's ordinary knowledge makes no difference. That creed continues to be the same revelation that it always was to everybody to whom it comes; it has exactly the same enlightening, the same elevating, the same stimulating or nerving power. It is the same vision that it always was, as fresh as ever to those who take it in.

Theology, then, may be called a science in the sense that its truths, whether those of revelation or those of nature, can be taught *methodically*, and with proper relation to each other. There is an order and system in Divine things which can be brought out and placed in the proper light, even with our limited powers. All truths, ideas, or facts which stand in mutual relation are capable of being treated with *reference* to this, and in this sense treated or laid out scientifically. Thus we speak of the science of morals, and of the science of the law, and in this sense of order and arrangement *Theology* may be placed on the basis of a science, but Theology is not a science in the sense that its truths admit of scientific proof or scientific increase. The hypotheses of Science admit of proof by experiment, or the observation of facts; but the truths of Theology, being truths of the invisible sphere, do not admit of present scientific proof and verification, but await a future one, when sight will supersede faith, and what are now mysteries will be facts.

The proper scope of dogmatism then being simply to defend truth, to preserve and maintain intact the original idea, we must still see that there is a great deal to prevent the dogmatical task from being executed properly and justly. And the reason is that amid the unavoidable passion and agitation which attends theological conflict, we may make a mistake as to what *does* actually interfere with an idea, *what does* conflict with a truth or doctrine. We may think that something *does* which does *not*. There is such a thing as a clear and indisputable contradiction; but it is possible also to imagine one where there is not: and so to exclude as inadmissible and as discordant with a truth of revelation something which is in reality not so—something which co-exists with the truth, and which is not inconsistent with it. It is not *every* modification of a truth and *every* distinction which can be drawn in the mode of carrying it out, which can make the difference of corrupting the integrity of that truth; it is only *some* importations into a truth which can occasion this result. And therefore it is the office of correct dogmatism to discriminate between those differences which positively conflict with a truth of revelation, and those which do not, but leave the substance of it unimpaired. Now this is an office in which dogmatism may fail; and where it does fail, it does an injustice to those members of the Church whom its decision affects; because it thrusts them out of the Church as holding an opinion which is in contradiction with a truth of Revelation; whereas the opinion which they hold is compatible with that truth.

There is a notion, indeed, entertained by some that the dogmatical principle acts mathematically, that it proceeds by a succession of steps, each of which follows the other by necessary sequence; and that if we once begin we must accept any fresh link of the chain of exposition, definition, and elucidation. Nothing can be further from the truth than such an account of it, if the principle at least is carried out in that way in which alone, consistently with truth and reason, it can be. The dogmatical office with which the Church is invested is especially one which is not conducted by mathematical proof and an infallible evolution; it is peculiarly based upon the practical kind of judgment which decides each case as it arises upon its own evidence and merits. All true dogmatism—for in lack of other terms I must use a popularly obnoxious one—is specially an appeal to common sense. You are summoned in it to compare one idea with another; an idea which revelation has communicated, with another idea which it is proposed in some quarter to combine with that revealed one; you are summoned to do this, in order simply to ascertain whether in plain reason they agree or disagree; whether the new idea is inconsistent with, is tenable together with, the old one, or is at discord with it. This is a kind of comparison which as much hangs upon a sound practical judgment as multitudes of cases in ordinary life, in which we have to compare two things together. But it is this comparison and none other which is repeated in every successive decision which is made in the course of the dogmatical defence of a sacred truth. There is a recurrence at every fresh dogmatic occasion to a fresh comparison of the original idea of revelation with some other idea brought forward; to see if they agree or disagree. There is a fresh recurrence every time to common sense and practical judgment. Does this article of faith which has been communicated to us, and which we naturally understand as such and such a truth and no other, admit of this proposed interpretation? Let us compare the two ideas, and see whether they can be held together, or whether one does not subvert and supplant the other. This is a matter of judgment. But in this comparison it is not certain that the judgment will be always successful and make no mistake. Nor will it follow that because truth has been secured, and correct decision made in many instances, that therefore an incorrect one will not be made in another case of comparison when it occurs.

The dogmatic decision, for example, which closed the Arian controversy, was the result of a comparison of two broad and clearly marked ideas, which obviously could not be combined or reconciled. One plainly clashed with the other, both could not be held together, and therefore if the first original idea was to be retained, it was a matter of necessity that the new and later idea must be excluded. The idea of Revelation was that our Lord was God. The Arian idea was that our Lord was not God, but a transcendent and super-angelic created Being, *made* at God's good pleasure before the world, upon the pattern of the attribute of Logos or Wisdom existing in the Divine Mind; gifted with the illumination of it, and in consequence called after it; the instrument of creation and revelation; and at length united to a human body, in the place of a soul, in the person of Jesus Christ. The Being which our Lord, upon this idea, was, had a *beginning of existence*—there was a time when He was not, and He was formed from what once *was* not.

Such a being was undoubtedly an extraordinary and perplexing and an ambitious conception of the department of mystical and speculative theology; but nothing can be more certain than that he was not God, as such a being was fundamentally different from the Divine Being at every point of the definition. The idea of Scripture then, and the Arian idea, were absolutely at variance. In Scripture, "The Word was God, and the Word was made flesh, and dwelt among us;" the two elements Scripture admits in the idea of the Incarnation are *God and Man;* no other being is recognised. But Arianism introduced into the structure of the Incarnation another being who displaced both—both God and Man; a being whose conception was drawn from a Pagan source, rather than a Scriptural one, and represented the monstrous imagination of oriental religions—who was midway between God and Man; less than God, and more than angel—a counterfeit Divine Being whom simple minds would confound with the true one; who, without being God, was creator of heaven and earth, and without being God or Man, was mediator between God and Man.

The final decision, then, which pronounced that the idea of Arianism was inconsistent with the Scriptural idea of the Incarnation was undoubtedly a correct exertion of dogmatic judgment; because the two were really mutually contradictory; and no other result could fairly be arrived at. *On the other hand*, we meet with a doctrine in the early and especially the ante-Nicene Fathers, which was concerned with and affected in a certain sense the Godhead of our Lord, and which in later ages brought down upon the earlier Fathers in some quarters the charge of Arianism, but which did not in reality disagree with our Lord's Godhead. I refer to the doctrine of the *subordinateness* of the Son to God the Father, as being the ἀρχή—the beginning and fountain-head of the Godhead— subordinateness to Him in that one respect, that the Son's was by its very nature a *derived Godhead*, which, though co-eternal with the Father's, flowed forth and emanated from it; whereas the Father's Godhead was that which it emanated and issued *from*—the source and fountain of the whole Divinity. The language of some of the early Fathers insisted strongly on this distinction, and even occasionally appeared, on a cursory glance, to imply an essential inferiority in the nature of the Son to that of the Father; though this inference was abundantly rectified by the *context* of the passages and by the whole general language of the writers; and it was obvious that the subordinateness meant by them was a subordinateness of derivation only, and not of nature or of power. The Church accordingly never touched this particular language, because there was no incongruity between our Lord's being a *derived* Divinity and being Divinity.

And so with respect to the doctrine of the Trinity and certain ideas which were introduced bearing upon the internal structure of the doctrine and relations of the Three Persons. When Sabellianism was submitted to the dogmatic office of the Church, it was condemned, because the idea of the Three Persons being only three characters or aspects of God was at plain variance with their personality as described in Scripture.

Whereas, on the other hand, the Procession question has never been dogmatised upon by the whole Church, because that did not, one way or another, interfere with the substantial idea of the Trinity. In these cases the dogmatic judgment of the Church pronounced in one of them a contradiction to the revealed idea, and in the other case refused to pronounce it.

We are here indeed upon the threshold of a great question. When a caution against an excess of dogmatism is given, when a limit is enjoined, and when distinctions which lie beyond that limit are condemned as subtleties and refinement, the reply often is that upon the assumption which is made of a mysterious truth to begin with, we are no judges of the limit of that mystery, of the extent to which it is to be carried out, or of the minutiæ and refinements of distinction which it is necessary should be applied to it, in order to maintain it in its integrity. A mysterious truth, it is said, is at the very commencement, by our own confession, beyond our reason. We therefore have committed ourselves to the abandonment of reason as our test in the *acceptance* of it; and therefore cannot claim the right to revert to reason for a limitation and check upon the exposition and interpretation of it. This is the argument, for instance, used in reply to the objection we urge to the doctrine of Transubstantiation upon this ground. We say that the Roman divines push a mystery too far; that they carry it into subtleties and extremes and particularities which were never contemplated in it, which are over rigorous and artificially literal; and that it is an unreasonable and extravagant explanation of the change of the bread and wine into the body and blood to suppose that it necessitates the actual abolition of the material substance of the former; and they reply that the original doctrine being a mystery and beyond reason, we have no right to appeal to reason for the mode of explaining it. What is this consequence, they say, that you call extravagant, more than a *mystery*, and you acknowledge a mystery to begin with?

Let us examine this position, then, that Reason is no judge

with respect to mysteries, and can therefore impose no check in the exposition of mysteries. When we examine this matter, it will not be found fairly possible, I think, to maintain such a position. It is quite true that mysterious truths are beyond reason, they are beyond by the very fact that they *are* mysterious. And yet it may be quite true too that reason has certain rights appertaining to these mysterious truths, and that we cannot possibly protect ourselves from the most extravagant and monstrous delusions, unless we are ready to assign to reason some substantial functions and some power of interpretation and check with respect to mysteries. In the first place, with respect to a great class of mysterious truths, which we call natural mysteries, reason has so much to do with them, that though they are beyond reason, reason herself is the very discoverer of them. We should know nothing of them without reason. It is reason that imparts these incomprehensible ideas to our minds; and that which lies beyond reason is still at the same time as much a *part* of reason itself as any other of the materials and contents of this high faculty. Thus the idea of Infinity, the idea of Cause, the idea of Right and Wrong, are utterly mysterious, inexplicable, and incomprehensible; and yet to say that Reason judges with respect to these ideas, judges respecting their validity, legitimacy, and truth, would be much short of the fact, because, indeed, they spring out of reason, and they enter into its very composition.

Nor when we come to supernatural mysteries can it be said that reason has no office or function with respect to them; that it has no accepting and satisfying power, that it has no concurring part to take, that it has no criterion by which it can adopt some mysteries as reasonable, and reject others—if they are proposed to it—as fanciful and monstrous. Unless we admit some such discriminating office as this in reason with respect to supernatural ideas communicated to us, we as good as confess that, as far as internal evidence is concerned, all mysteries are alike; that they all stand on the same ground as regards acceptance or rejection, and that they are all alike unmeaning and senseless enigmas. But surely to say that in respect of intrinsic acceptableness, propriety, suitableness, fitness,

G

agreement with man's sense and reason, there is no difference between the idea of the Incarnation and any other incomprehensible conception which can be presented to the imagination, is to say something at variance with the common sense of mankind. God being invested by religion with special relations to man, as being not only the creator and preserver of the race of man, but as its inspirer and moral guide, it has ever appeared a meet and congenial idea to the religious thought and sentiment of the human race, that God should come down from His high throne in heaven to assume a greater fellowship with man, and to take upon Him his nature. The idea of the Incarnation has thus always been a natural idea to man, it has been incorporated in the religious imagination; and though it has taken often extravagant and grotesque forms, the substance of the idea has united itself with the deepest poetry and philosophy.

It would not be right then to put the idea of the Incarnation on a par with any other inconceivable idea, however devoid of meaning, prodigious or frivolous, which might be proposed to the human mind. But to say this is to say that Reason is a judge of mysteries, and has a right of discrimination with regard to them. So the idea of an Atonement has approved itself to the religious mind of man in all ages; nor would any one be borne out by the general voice of the human race in saying that, because an atonement was an incomprehensible idea, it was therefore on a level with any other incomprehensible idea which human fancy could conceive. Yet to say this is to say again that reason is a judge of mysteries, a judge at the outset as to what it is in sympathy with, and what, by an inner verdict, it discards; what is a rational mystery and what is an irrational one.

And as Reason is not prevented by the incomprehensibleness of mysterious truths from having a voice at the outset in the acceptance and rejection of them, so it is not prevented, by the same fact, from having a right to exercise a check upon the mode of carrying out, developing, and interpreting mysterious truths. Reason does not *grasp* these truths; in the very nature of the case it does not: and yet it may have a sufficient practical insight into the meaning and scope of them to know when an explanation and interpretation of these truths agrees and coincides with this scope; and when it goes beyond it and runs into excess and minutiae irrelevant to the import and design of these mysteries;—to know when the substance of the truth is adhered to, and when the substance of truth is lost sight of, and the mind is diverted into inconsequent subtleties and fine-spun distinctions carried out beyond all the needs of truth, and therefore to the injury and misrepresentation of truth.

To say that a mystery is beyond reason, and that its exposition cannot be regulated by reason, is one of those abstract arguments which ought to have purely abstract premisses to deal with. In the present case we are dealing with nothing abstract, but with that actual relation in which we stand intellectually to mysterious truths. This is an actual matter of mental experience, and in examining it, we find that it is a divided state of things. We know and we do not know, we know in one sense, and we do not know in another. A mystery is an enigma, and yet it is not wholly an enigma. There are various truths which we partly conceive, and partly fail in conceiving. Reason falls short, but reason has still such an insight into the meaning of mysterious truths as serves the practical purposes of religion; and this measure of insight is enough to warrant her right to impose a check upon the dogmatic exposition of them,—to justify a discriminating function on the part of reason, to distinguish when explanation fulfils and when it exceeds its purpose.

I have thus endeavoured to explain the dogmatic office; *first*, the true scope of it, which is the preservation and defence of, as distinct from adding to, the stock of revealed truth; and *secondly*, the mode in which it acts, namely, by a comparison, —a comparison between some new proposed idea to interpret revelation and the original idea of revelation itself. If in the comparison it appears that one of these ideas is inconsistent with, and contradictory to, the other, it is the part of the dogmatic office to exclude the new idea, in order to preserve the original one. If, on the other, the two are tenable together, then the dogmatic office allows and admits the new idea. No guarantee, however, is given that the dogmatic office—whatever be the zeal of men, and the goodness of men's intention—will invariably be exercised with perfect accuracy; and the comparison, when made, lead to a correct result. The Church, as keeper and guardian of the deposit of the faith, has undoubtedly executed her trust with such a degree of fidelity, as that that deposit has been preserved against the attacks of enemies; and the faith once delivered to the saints has not been lost, or the gates of hell prevailed against it. But it would be a too flattering description of the dogmatic career of the Church to say that she has never erred on the side of over rigour and strained exactness; that while she has certainly secured the perpetuity of the faith, she has not sometimes excluded legitimate opinion; that while she has kept out what was contradictory to fundamental truth, she has not sometimes failed to include what was admissible.

It must not, however, be supposed that where the Church committed an error of judgment in the exercise of her dogmatic function, she always did it from despotic and arbitrary motives. Doubtless those motives mingled with others in determining her policy when it was too exclusive; and they became stronger as heresy advanced; but in the earlier ages at any rate such motives were tempered by more excusable ones. The ferment of theological intellect, the interminable agitation, the constant rise of heresies and the perpetual necessity of resistance, imparted a strained and eager jealousy to that watchfulness and guardianship which was, under all circumstances, the Church's duty: the protraction of the strife aggravated the temper of the defender, till the Church grew suspicious and apprehensive, and began to detect a heresy under every rising expression. It must be remembered that if spiritual ambition is pushing and coercing, love subject to human frailty is also fidgety and interfering. Such love may indulge in a too constant manipulation of the sacred deposit, may exult in new definitions, and show a sincere but still weak fondness in a too lively pugnacity and a too restless temperament in its defence. It is ever the natural tendency of love to suspect attacks which are not meant. Dogmatism, then, even when strained, is not necessarily strained in simple tyranny. The Creed was the joy, the hope, and the inspiration of the Church, it contained everything she cared for. The Truth was her one treasure; and if in her treatment and defence of it she occasionally erred on the side of an excessive watchfulness, her watchfulness was stimulated by affection; it is natural to be busy and active, even over-anxious and scrupulous about that which we love.

## VII.—*MYSTERIOUS TRUTHS.*[1]

CERTAIN truths or doctrines of Christianity are mysterious ones, and we appeal to this characteristic of their mysteriousness in order to defend them from the charge of injustice which is brought against them. Such are the doctrines of Original Sin and the Atonement. When the charge is brought against these doctrines that they are opposed to our natural idea of justice, we reply that they are truths of which we have not complete and distinct ideas, and that therefore we are not in a position to bring such a charge against these truths. They are truths with which the common sense and feeling of mankind have sympathised, and which human nature has adopted. They agree with human reason in a large and general way. On the other hand there are certain difficulties, and difficulties of a moral kind in them. What we say then is—these truths are mysterious truths; they are truths of which we have only an indistinct perception intellectually. We cannot attribute then any validity to the moral objections raised against them, because we must have a definite intellectual idea of the truths themselves, we must know distinctly what they are before we can say what objections they are open to.

But we cannot enter fully into the position that these truths are mysterious, that is, truths to which we have no distinct corresponding ideas in our minds, without our attention being awakened in the very act of embracing and dwelling on this characteristic of these truths, to certain objections which have arisen *on this very ground,* namely, on the ground of their mystery or incomprehensibleness; and especially to the imposition of them as articles of faith. For however necessary such

[1] Delivered in the Latin Chapel.

an explanation and statement of the mysteriousness of these doctrines may be for the purpose of defending their truth, or of guarding against particular objections, we cannot dwell forcibly on the consideration that these truths *are* mysterious, —in their own nature unknown or only half-known truths—we cannot set forth, I say, this whole characteristic of these truths without being aware that we are setting forth, and taking particular pains to impose, just that aspect of them of which objectors are most ready to lay hold, as a ground for rejecting them altogether, or at any rate for not imposing them as essential. This is the natural effect of endeavouring to steer a middle course between two extremes, that of rejecting mystery, and that of embracing it at the cost of reason. In arguing against a false conclusion from an article of faith, such as shocks our moral sense, it is necessary to show the incorrect manner of holding such an article of faith, from which such a conclusion arises; namely, that persons forget that they hold the article as a mystery, and that consequently they cannot build upon it as if it were an ordinarily intelligible truth. But this defence against erroneous inferences on one side exposes the truths themselves to the attack I have just mentioned on the other. For it may be asked, Why are these truths considered of so much importance, when those who think them so are obliged, in order to guard their own maintenance of them, not only to admit, but to press the consideration that they are truths at present incomprehensible to us, and that we have no idea fully and distinctly corresponding to them in our minds?

This use then which is made of the mysteriousness of these doctrines for setting aside the importance of them altogether must be considered in its place; but I shall begin with the general objections raised against this class of doctrines.

The first objection, then, usually brought against this class of doctrines by writers of the Socinian School, is that they are contrary to natural reason. But this cannot be justifiably said apart from considering the sense in which these doctrines are imposed. These doctrines are not imposed upon men to be held in any sense contrary to natural reason, but only as representations, accommodated to our limited faculties, of truths which are beyond our reason. Indeed, we cannot but regard this objection,—of these doctrines being contrary to reason,—as a misconception at the outset; a mistake as to a matter of fact, as to what the Church's intention in imposing these doctrines is; and the mode in which the Church supposes them to be received and entertained by believers. For can any one seriously think that the Church requires men to believe what is contrary to reason? Can there be in truth any controversy as to such a question, or will not any one admit at once that no one ought to believe what is contrary to natural reason? Our reason is as much the gift of God, and is as sacred, as revelation; to violate it therefore in any of our notions, in any belief entertained by us, would be plainly as wrong as to disbelieve any special revelation of God. Yet this mistake as to what is required from us for belief in these doctrines is perhaps the strongest, the most influential source of opposition to them. This appears to be the great practical argument which settles the question as regards them. The certainty of the principle itself, that nothing is to be believed that is contrary to reason, seems to prove its own application, and to supersede the necessity of inquiry as to whether this rule is really opposed in the case of belief in these doctrines. These truths do, indeed, in their mode of expression, contain difficulties, but we must not stop short at the outside, we must enter into the real substance of the case, the mode and the sense in which these truths are held, the real intellectual relations involved in this belief. From this whole real interior of the question, the objector's mind allows itself to be excluded by the bar of that mere necessary imperfection of language in which these truths are embodied. He satisfies himself with the truth of the general formula he has adopted—that we must not contradict reason—which is indeed unquestionable, without going into the evidence as to the matter of fact, or ascertaining whether we do contradict reason in the particular case. Indeed men are generally very apt to rest in the assertion of some maxim or principle, and think that that does everything for them; as if its intrinsic weight and strength were a pledge for the correctness of *their* application of it. That men, however, of great acuteness and much reflection should stop short in such impressions with regard to these doctrines, is somewhat surprising, and only shows what great force preliminary impressions have, and what obstructions they raise.

This mistake in the Socinian School with respect to these doctrines is not unlike some of those great current mistakes on particular subjects, which operate, on a much larger scale, upon whole portions of mankind; mistakes which, once established, sustain themselves by their own weight. One consolation, however, may perhaps be derived from such a state of the case, namely, that as all such mistakes as to matter of fact have really no ground in men's intellects, but only one of particular prevalence and tradition, *this* amongst others may some day recede to a considerable extent before the influence of clear and reasonable explanation; when, of those who believe in these doctrines, persons from time to time step forward to show in what manner they are really held by those who devoutly believe in them; and that this manner involves no opposition to reason, in which case we may hope that the objections of many to accept these doctrines will disappear. For certainly when one sees the serious and conscientious type on which the minds of some who have rejected and argued against these doctrines, as contrary to reason, are formed; their deep sense of moral truth, their acknowledgment of Divine influences, their strong religious instincts, and susceptibility to all the mysteries of natural religion, one cannot but think that it is some great misapprehension which keeps them from the truth, on the removal of which they would discover its real congeniality with their minds. For what objection—I mean what objection which operates to the positive rejection of these doctrines—is left when the ground of their repugnancy to reason is gone? There is none. All that can *then* be said is that they are beyond reason. And will any reasonable man deny the possibility of there being truths beyond our reason, or say that he certainly knows the human intellect is coincident with all being? And in the absence of all positive ground of reason against these doctrines, the evident witness—though not in the same precise terms in which they are expressed in our

Creeds and Articles—of Scripture to them, and their early and universal reception, must strike and impress all candid minds. For Scripture is at present interpreted by these minds according to a previous judgment that these doctrines are in themselves unreasonable; upon which judgment it is necessary, however strong the language of Scripture may apparently be in favour of such doctrines, to interpret it differently; upon the sound rule, that if Scripture appears to assert anything which is contrary to reason, such apparent meaning cannot be the real one. But if that judgment is displaced, then there will be room immediately for the natural interpretation of Scripture.

But supposing due attention paid to the manner in which these doctrines are held, and supposing it admitted in consequence that these doctrines are not contrary to reason, the very argument which has cleared them of opposition to reason exposes them to the other objection above mentioned, for it may be said, "If you do not hold anything contrary to reason, because you are holding what is not distinctly understood,—what is so dim and obscure that its meaning cannot be grasped,—are you not under a mistake in imagining you are holding anything at all? For what is the meaning of holding, embracing, entertaining a truth, except that you first know what that which is proposed to your acceptance is, and then decide, on whatever evidence, that it is true? Thus in believing that a particular event took place, you have an idea in the first instance of what such an event *is*, say a battle, an earthquake, or any particular thing that this or that person has said or done, and then you decide that such an event *took place*. You form a conception in some rough way of what takes place in a battle, or a convulsion of the earth's surface, or of a person's speech, or of a person's action; and the conception formed, you believe that of which it is the conception, to have occurred. But it may be said if you have no idea in your mind, in the first instance, of what a truth proposed to your acceptance is, you cannot believe it, because there is nothing to believe. Belief implies a subject of it, something with which it comes into contact, and in which it rests; and this subject can only be provided by your having the distinct idea of something or other, in which you believe. One state of mind can only differ intellectually from another by having some idea which the other has not; if a man holds a truth then without having the distinct idea of it, how does he differ from one who does not hold it? They are both in reality in the same state of mind, being alike without the idea of the truth in question; and they can only by some great inattention and mistake imagine themselves to differ."

Upon the defence and vindication, then, of these Christian doctrines on the ground of their mysteriousness, these doctrines become exposed to such reasoning as this; and it is objected in the case of the mysterious truths of the Trinity, the Incarnation, Original Sin, and the Atonement, that those who hold them are under a serious mistake and delusion in imagining they are really holding any truths at all, in holding truths of which they profess not to have the distinct ideas. A Trinity, for example, in the Unity of the Godhead is maintained, or, that in the One Divine Being there are three Personal Beings. It is objected that this is contrary to reason; the objection is met by the answer that terms are used here in an unknown sense, in which sense we cannot say it is impossible that this proposition can be true; for this simple reason, that the proposition itself is not known. But then, it is rejoined, if the truth is unknown we are holding nothing in holding it, and there is a simple void in our minds while we entertain this article of faith. So in the doctrine of the Incarnation, in which we hold that a Divine and a human being are but one Being, the same objection is made, and the same answer is returned, at the cost of the same rejoinder. In the doctrine of original sin, again, according as it is expressed, we hold an actual share in the sin of Adam taken by all mankind, or a responsibility for another's sin: to the objection that this is contrary to justice, we say that this is mysterious sin, mysterious responsibility. In the doctrine of the Atonement again we hold in the same way a mysterious substitution of one person's merit for another's. With respect to this whole class of mysterious truths, then, we are reminded that we are under a mistake if we suppose that we are really holding truths at all in holding them; that we have not the distinct ideas of them in our minds; and therefore our minds are, in the act of entertaining them, vacant, and devoid of ideas. Whatever importance then, it is said, custom or tradition may have given to these truths, however strong the habitual impression may be that our minds have hold of them, it is certain, on the simplest philosophical principles, that as we have not the distinct ideas of these truths, we do not and cannot hold these truths.

And if this is the case, it is added, if we cannot even in any true sense hold these truths at all, how *a fortiori* can we *impose* and enforce them as fundamental ones? How can we make them the very foundation of the Christian scheme, and build fundamental religious distinctions upon them? How can we draw a barrier of separation between those who accept and those who do not accept such truths as if there were the greatest possible difference in their belief, when all the time, if we examine the real state of mind of these two, we shall find that both are alike without the distinct idea of what these truths are?

The whole objection, then, which has been just described, calls for our notice, and, if we can give it one, for an answer. And the answer to it appears to me a very simple and plain one. This whole objection appears to rest on the assumption that we cannot entertain truths of which we have not the full idea or conception. Now, if by having no idea of a truth be meant having no idea at all bearing upon it,—having no thought of any kind in our minds regarding it, this assumption is true; but then this assumption does not apply to the case of these doctrines, for we plainly receive *some ideas or other* into our minds connected with them. But if by having no idea of these truths is only meant having no *distinct* or full idea of them, then it is not true that we cannot entertain truths of which we have no distinct idea; and those who suppose so have an incorrect and defective notion of the constitution of the human mind. The human mind is so constituted as to have relations to truth without the medium of distinct ideas or conceptions; and that in two ways.

First then, we encounter in nature a class of truths of which we have no distinct idea, truths of fundamental importance in philosophy. Besides the whole class of ordinary, distinct, and plain ideas which we have, whether in the sphere of sensation or of mathematics, we encounter also in our minds another and a different class of ideas, to which I wish to call attention here; the characteristic of which is their very imperfect, dim, and only incipient apprehension; while at the same time they are ideas to which we are constantly referring, and on which we depend for our most important conclusions in philosophy and religion. We know, and are convinced, that we are able to hold and do hold these truths. Our minds are so constituted that we have the knowledge of the existence of certain truths, of which truths themselves at the same time we have no distinct idea or representation in our minds. The constitution of our minds, I say, makes this mixed state of ignorance and knowledge possible to us. Were the alternative of pure ignorance or pure knowledge necessary, it is evident that, when we left the sensible world, which supplies the subject-matter of simple apprehension, and the sphere of demonstrative meaning, we should be immediately in a state of absolute ignorance and utter darkness; we should not only be ignorant of the nature of other truths, but should have no sort of idea what those truths were of which we were ignorant, and should be wholly unable to think of or discuss them on that account. We should be cut off from the greater part of that higher thought and philosophy which has occupied the human mind in all ages; and the science of metaphysics would not exist. But this alternative is not necessary. We have an idea of the existence of truths, of which truths themselves we cannot form a true conception; that is, we have *some* idea of truths, of which we have *no adequate or complete* idea. We are not entirely cut off from them; we have some kind of apprehension of them. I will instance the ideas of Substance, Cause, Mind or Spirit, Power, Infinity. We have evidently no distinct idea of them; at the same time we have some idea. We find that our rational nature then introduces us to a set of truths which are incomprehensible; truths to which we have no corresponding or proportionate ideas, though we have ideas just sufficient to acquaint us with them; that is to say, we find that our rational nature introduces us to a class of mysterious truths. We are conscious of various ideas and conceptions, which we cannot open out, or realise as whole and consistent ones; we feel ourselves reaching after what we cannot grasp, and moving onward in thought toward something which we cannot overtake. Mysterious truths are not confined to religion, but are extracted by my reason out of this world of sense. I move in the direction of a Substance in sensible Nature, which I cannot apprehend. I move in the direction of a Cause which I cannot apprehend. That very Space in which I am included is mysterious as soon as I extend it in thought to Infinity. What is an infinite number of stars which we believe to exist but a simple mystery to me? It is a wholly incomprehensible fact, though we are sure it is a fact, or at any rate have every reason to believe that it is.

Again, if the rational contemplation of simple nature leads us to mysterious truths, certainly Natural Religion is a system entirely based upon them. We cannot think for an instant of so stupendous a truth as that of an Infinite Omnipresent Being without seeing that in entertaining such a truth we are wholly in advance of all our clear conceptions, and that we are without the adequate idea or representation in our minds of that in which we believe. It is evident that, while our reason has just light enough to see its want of, and necessary movement toward, this conclusion, it is still excluded by a veil from the truth itself, unable to attain the vision of it, and entertaining it altogether in a way quite opposite to the mathematical, or to clearness of conception.

The Divine Personality is another cardinal truth of natural religion, and is a wholly incomprehensible one. Our reason, independently of moral considerations, points to one Supreme Intelligent Cause of the Universe, and intelligence implies personality; for we cannot think of a designing mind that forms and executes plans and adopts means to ends without attributing to it that kind of unity and individuality which we find in ourselves, and which is expressed by the word Personality. And natural religion brings in the important consideration of our moral nature, and the idea of God as the Moral Governor of the world; and this is a great addition of force and substance to the idea of His Personality; for God is represented as being of a particular character. Natural religion too, brings in the idea of Providence, and the constant superintendence of God over the actions and affairs of mankind. A God who takes an interest in all human events, who disapproves of the evil and loves the good, is especially a Personal Being; and therefore natural religion may be said to teach, in a way in which the contemplation of external nature does not, the Deity.

But such personality is wholly incomprehensible in an Infinite and Omnipresent Being, and we can form no conception of it. That idea of a personal being which we have in our minds is uniformly taken from that kind of personal existence with which we are acquainted; nor can we form a conception of any other. But the kind of personal existence with which we are acquainted is a limited and local one; it is included in a particular form and confined to place. We possess the idea of man as a person, as being bounded by a certain bodily shape and outline, and only existing in one place at a time. We can form no idea whatever of a person who pervades all space, and is in every part of the Universe; and to apply our thoughts to the Divine Omnipresence is always to diminish for the time our idea of the Divine Personality.

To those, then, who object to the mysterious truths of Christianity, who say that they are truths of which we have no definite idea, and that therefore we cannot apprehend them ourselves, and still less have the right to enforce them upon others as fundamental articles of faith, this is the answer which may be returned: Reason itself suggests and obliges us to entertain this mysterious class of truths: and so does Natural Religion; which is argument to those who admit Natural Religion.

But indeed, apart from reasoning, do not the plain and broad facts of the case appear to prove what is here maintained about these mysterious truths, and *dis*prove the assertion that these truths cannot be embraced and in a certain sense apprehended by the human mind? An acute person may doubt, upon metaphysical grounds, whether these truths can be really entertained, whether the mind can have really any hold of them; but the fact which meets us everywhere is that these truths do not only lay hold of the human mind in some way, but take the most powerful hold of it. It is a matter of fact that these doctrines have a most strong influence, that they are practically very impressive; that they appeal to the feelings, and mould the minds and tempers of mankind. Considering the great subtlety of philosophical reasoning, and its proportionate liability to error, we ought perhaps reasonably to doubt its conclusions, when they disagree with very strong apparent facts the other way. For the supposition that mankind in general are so mistaken as to their own ideas, as to suppose that they hold, and are strongly impressed by certain truths with respect to which all the time their minds are entirely void, is at any rate a difficult one.

The doctrine of the Trinity has indeed a place by itself, as concerned with a truth so infinitely remote from us as the nature of the Deity; though even that doctrine was not maintained in the early Church apart from a moral ground, a ground of natural feeling, and religious instinct. For when the Unity of the Deity was objected to by Pagan opponents of Christianity, on the ground that it involved a solitary state, and that a solitary state was not in agreement with our natural idea of happiness, the objection was admitted as a natural one, but the doctrine of the Trinity was adduced in answer to it; according to which the Deity was not represented as a solitary Being, but as having a kind of society within Himself. And certainly, whether we look to the popular or the esoteric ideas of the Deity in the ancient world, to the established religions, or to the theological systems of philosophical schools, the notion of a solitary Deity does not seem to have approved itself to the human mind. Those who asserted in opposition to the polytheism of the mass, the Unity of God, still qualified it; and it may safely perhaps be said that the doctrine of the Trinity had some kind of anticipation of it in ancient philosophy. The doctrine of the Trinity thus regarded, is rather a concession to our reasonable and intellectual nature, than a stumbling-block to it. Nor is it easy to understand how persons can really consider it philosophical to reduce the Unity of the Deity to such a Unity as we understand and attribute to human persons.

But if the doctrine of the Trinity has a place by itself, those doctrines which touch our own condition, the mysterious truths of the Incarnation, Original Sin, and the Atonement, do as a matter of fact appeal strongly to human feeling; they are truths to which mankind in their inmost spirits refer, and which actually serve for the rest, the food, the support and consolation of human souls. Original sin is felt within as a mysterious guilt, coeval with our first reflection upon ourselves, an unfathomable sinfulness, a condition of being which makes it absurd for us to adopt any but the humblest ground, and which alters our relations to, and our mode of approaching the Deity. The Incarnation is received into the believer's mind as an event which elevates him, and brings him into nearer relations to God. He reposes in the Atonement as a sovereign remedy and satisfaction for sin, a mystery of rectifying love. And it is remarkable that these doctrines are not to be found in Christianity alone, but, in some or other form, in most of the religions of the world. The idea of the Deity assuming the nature of man, and visiting the inhabitants of earth, has been and is a leading one in the history of religion; it has been taken in by the human mind with enthusiasm, and grasped with tenacity, as an idea of something of not merely external interest, as the rise of any extraordinary man might be, but of something which truly concerned us, and brought us into a new and high relationship. The Eastern and the classical religions have their respective modes of expressing this idea, and ancient poetry, with the true skill which poetry has always shown in detecting the deep instincts and yearnings of the human heart, was much occupied with it; conscious that such a theme did not appeal in vain, but kindled, while it gratified an innate longing, a noble spiritual ambition in man to connect himself with the Divine. And the same historical appeal to the actual working of the religious instinct shows us human nature groaning under the sense of a necessary and irremoveable sinfulness contracted by the soul on its very entrance into this visible world; and consoled by the doctrine of sacrifices, that is, holding, in some vague or corrupted form, the doctrine of Original Sin, and the Atonement. These doctrines, then, respond to some instinct in the human heart, some fundamental wants. And that instinct which they respond to in its turn embraces, apprehends, and practically understands them. The religious mind enters into, and unites itself with, these truths in the sense of religious sympathy, just as in science the mind sees truths in the way of clear perception. To suppose then that truths, which are in some form the creed of the whole human race, though only perfectly revealed in Christianity, and of which this is the power, effect, and actual working, are not really entertained by the human mind at all, and cannot be, because they are not represented by distinct ideas, is to put ourselves in opposition to all the apparent facts of the case. It is evident that there is some mode in which the human mind comes into contact with those ideas, or whatever we may call them, which these doctrines embody; though that mode may not be scientifically ascertainable, or capable of expression in formal language. These truths and doctrines show, by the general evidence of practical influence and effects, that they are taken in and apprehended,—though not with full intellectual grasp, still with a real solid perception of some kind, by the human mind; that though mysteries, they are in some sense understood; and that they are not words only, but words which have a true meaning, and which express strong and real, though indistinct, ideas.

If the question is asked then, why in religion we build upon what we cannot understand, why we make incomprehensible truths, truths of which we can form no accurate or clear idea, the very foundation of religion, the answer is, that those kind of truths are recognised by reason; and that these are the only truths which in the nature of the case admit of a place in religion. Truths which are clear and distinct, that is, the truths of sense, and the truths of mathematics, do not in their own nature admit of being a basis of religion. The truths which are at the bottom of all religion must in their own nature be mysterious and indistinct truths, which we feel and reach after rather than intellectually apprehend. Religion must essentially be founded upon such truths as these. We do not pretend that religion belongs to the sphere of sense or of demonstration. It is, rather, of its very essence in this present state of being, that it belongs to neither, but rests upon the ground of faith. But faith, reasonable faith, does not require full intellectual apprehension; it would not be faith if it did; it requires such insight only, such perception of truth, as practically influences and persuades us. The very truths that lie deepest in our nature are just of this character, they are not philosophically grasped, but they are taken in with an indefinite but a true and substantial perception. These are the truths upon which all our belief that we are anything more than material machines depends; upon these rests our hope for the future, our expectation of immortality; our spiritual nature rests entirely upon this kind of inward evidence, and unless we allow the witness and validity of mysterious truth, we cannot even say that we have souls.

## VIII.—'*OF CHRIST ALONE WITHOUT SIN.*'[2]

### A REPLY TO PROFESSOR TYNDALL.[1]

PROFESSOR TYNDALL, in his remarks upon the Bampton Lectures of 1865 in the *Fortnightly Review*, confined himself generally to a ground of science—a ground upon which he justly felt himself strong, and in connection with which he has won so high a name: though I should be disposed to draw a broad distinction between the most intimate, subtle, and even imaginative insight into the facts of science and—what the Professor appears to claim—an exclusive right to the inferences, whether physical or metaphysical, from them. Upon one occasion, however, the Professor enters upon special theological ground, and objects to miraculous evidence as applying to the doctrine of our Lord's sinlessness :—

"Mr. Mozley demands a miracle as a certificate of character. He will accept no other evidence of the perfect goodness of Christ. 'No outward life or conduct,' he says, 'however irreproachable, could prove his perfect sinlessness, because goodness depends upon the inward motive, and the perfection of the inward motive is not proved by the outward act.' But surely the miracle is an outward act, and to pass from it to the inner motive imposes a greater strain upon logic than that involved in our ordinary methods of estimating men. There is at least moral congruity between the outward goodness and the inner life, but there is no such congruity between the miracle and the life within. The test of moral goodness laid down

---

[1] Reprinted from the *Contemporary Review*, April 1868.
[2] The XVth Article.

by Mr. Mozley is not the test of John, who says, 'He that doeth righteousness is righteous;' nor is it the test of Jesus, 'By their fruits ye shall know them: do men gather grapes of thorns, or figs of thistles?' But it is the test of another: 'If thou be the Son of God, command that these stones be made bread.' . . .

"Accepting Mr. Mozley's test, it is evident that, in the demonstration of moral goodness, the *quantity* of the miraculous comes into play. Had Christ, for example, limited himself to the conversion of water into wine, He would have fallen short of the performance of Jannes and Jambres, for it is a smaller thing to convert one liquid into another than to convert a dead rod into a living serpent. But Jannes and Jambres, we are informed, were not good. Hence, if Mr. Mozley's test be a good one, a point must exist on the one side of which miraculous power demonstrates goodness, while on the other side it does not. How is this 'point of contrary flexure' to be determined? It must lie somewhere between the magicians and Moses: for within this space the power passed from the diabolical to the Divine. But how to make the passage—how, out of a purely *quantitative* difference in the visible manifestation of power, we are to infer a total inversion of quality—it is extremely difficult to see. . . . Let us not play fast and loose with the miraculous; either it is a demonstration of goodness in all cases or in none."

The question of evidence here discussed is one which, from the peculiar nature of the subject-matter of it, I approach with some reluctance. As, however, only a bare reference to the subject was made in the Lecture, and as the whole question of miraculous evidence, as applying to it, is so erroneously stated by Professor Tyndall, I will take this opportunity of going somewhat further into the statement of the Lecture, though at the cost of treading upon ground where Christian reverence is properly sensitive.

Professor Tyndall, then, here assumes that if miracles act at all as evidence of Christ's sinlessness, they can only do so by reason of the greater quantity of the miraculous in our Lord's case. And upon that assumption he may well ask, What is the quantity which decides sinlessness? Some men who had a certain amount of this power were bad men. "How is this point of contrary flexure to be determined? How out of a purely quantitative difference are we to infer a total inversion of quality?" But to make this assumption is to overlook the fundamental idea of a miracle as evidence. A miracle, regarded in its evidential function, is only a guarantee to an assertion. It depends, therefore, on what the assertion is, what that is which the miracle proves. Nobody before Christ asserted himself to be without sin. No miraculous powers, therefore, which were exerted before Christ, could be any evidence of the sinlessness of those who exerted them. No miracle of itself proves anything; no quantity of the miraculous proves anything; there must be an assertion made before there can be anything for the miracle to verify or guarantee. Between a miracle and a conclusion from it there is an important intervening term—namely, an asserted doctrine or fact.

Professor Tyndall says: "There is at least moral congruity between the outward goodness and the inner life." There is. We can place before ourselves in imagination a certain outward character between which and the supposition of inward sinlessness, assuming the latter to be revealed to us, there would be no disagreement. But between one of these being compatible with the other, supposing the latter to be known and revealed to us, and one of these being sufficient evidence or proof of the other, there is a vast, an immeasurable interval. Take, for example, our Lord's denunciatory language against the Scribes and Pharisees. To those who admit, upon the evidence which is laid before them, our Lord's sinlessness, there is not the slightest discord between such language and such sinlessness; but common reason tells us that had we to judge of such language without the assumption of our Lord's sinless character, we could not tell but that some element of imperfection, some shade of prejudice, some passionate excess, might enter into such censures,—such taint of mortal frailty as has entered into the speeches and judgments of the best and most pure-minded human reformers. The majesty, the integrity, the holiness of our Lord's character is indeed conspicuous and obvious upon the facts of the case; but when we attribute absolute sinlessness to Him, it is plain that by the laws of reason we must be going upon some further evidence than that which is contained in His outward life and deportment.

The statement in the Lecture that "we accept our Lord's perfect goodness upon the same evidence upon which we admit the rest of His supernatural character," assumes, indeed, that sinlessness *is* a supernatural characteristic; nor, when we examine what we mean by supernatural, can we avoid giving this designation to it. We do not, indeed, assert it to be a *Divine* characteristic, or that it necessitates a Divine nature in the possessor; for Christians hold a past or paradisal and a future or heavenly perfection of the simple man; and two very opposite schools have inserted even in this intermediate state of things, and in the actual existing condition of human nature, a sinless mere humanity: Socinians, that of a simply human Christ; a Roman school, that of the Virgin Mary. But though not necessarily a divine, it is a supernatural characteristic. Both these schools connect the sinlessness which they respectively attribute to two human personages with a supernatural cause, not even entertaining the idea of such a characteristic being a simply natural fact, or imagining the possibility of mere human nature, or the human nature of experience, producing it. The Racovian Catechism asks the question,—"Was, then, the Lord Jesus a mere or common man?" and answers, "By no means;" by reason of "his supernatural conception, his resurrection, his being sanctified by the Father, and separated from all other men, being distinguished by perfect holiness," etc. All divines treat our Lord's sinlessness as part of His supernatural character.

What, indeed, do we mean by supernatural or miraculous? We mean that which contradicts universal experience. But is the field of experience confined to material nature? Does it not include just as truly, and just as strictly, the moral nature of man, the region of his mind, his will, his conscience, his moral feeling, his moral action? Undoubtedly it does. But what does universal experience assert with respect to this moral nature, but that it never, as a matter of fact, does produce a perfect moral condition of the man; that it never produces any other state of the moral being, but that in which, together with whatever good he may be conscious of, he is also conscious of evil—evil which he has done, and evil which exists in his motives and springs of action? We only know man as such a being. Different accounts and rationales are given of this fact by different religions and different philosophies, ancient and modern. The doctrine of original sin is the Scriptural account of this fact; Manichæanism is another account of it; Hegelianism is another. But apart from any rationales of this fact, whether false ones or the true one, we are now concerned simply and solely with the fact itself. Using the term *law*, in this moral sphere, in the same sense in which we use it in the physical—viz., as uniform and constant fact—sin is the *law* of human nature, regarded as a field of experience. The presence of it in the individual is as much the law of human nature as gravitation is the law of matter. That is to say, it is always found there as a fact. The extent to which it is perceived by the individual in himself depends upon the cultivation of his conscience, but of its existence in him there is no doubt; the absence of the perception, if it is absent, only indicates the firmer root of the disorder, although it may safely be asserted that no single human being, however savage and rude his condition, is without some consciousness of it.

Again, no theoretical difference in the mode of describing sin, whether as positive, or as a negation and privation of good; no difference even in the moral estimate of sin, whether a latitudinarian view of such sin as is universal, which represents it as a less serious matter, or whether a profounder or more condemnatory view of it is adopted;—neither of these differences affects at all the universal fact of sin. The most latitudinarian doctrine of sin admits that every man has cause for moral regret; it admits a struggle in every human heart in which the will has often given way to temptation, and taken the worse side instead of the better; it confesses to an impediment to goodness in every man, which has been yielded to wrongly or sinfully. Even the Pantheistic Fatalist's view of sin does not in the least interfere with the universality of sin. He regards good and evil, indeed, as at bottom homogeneous facts, the growth of one root, one great impartial discharge from the machine and workshop of the universe; but though he explains away sin at the base, he admits the universal phenomenon; in spite of his own explanation, he cannot rid himself of the *sense* of sin, of the inward confession of it, of the burden of self-reproach, and the pains of conscience. The poet of Pantheism makes it a matter of charge against the constitution of the universe that he is subject to such a galling yoke:—

> "And who made terror, madness, crime, remorse . . .
> And self-contempt bitterer to drink than blood."[1]

But in the very complaint at the injustice of it he admits its inexorable pressure. In relief he turns accuser, and institutes the contrast between man and nature. Nature is beautiful and tender, majestic, sweet, elevating, calm, consoling; man is unjust, grasping, cruel, mean, proud; a hypocrite, and an oppressor. The Pantheist admits all the sensations, all the struggles, all the defeat of a sinful nature. He regards the moral law as a tyranny indeed, and he would wildly break through that tyranny; but he cannot help feeling himself condemned if he does so. His theory of conscience is inexplicable; he sees no promise in it, no augury, no anticipation of a future; he sees no meaning in it; it gives him no prospect and no hope; but he admits it as a blind force within him, and he expresses that force and its movements with a strength which is all but religious.

This is so sure a law of our conscience, indeed, that we count upon and expect a sense of sin and moral imperfection in the very best man, with the same absolute certainty with which we count upon the return of the equinoxes, the course of the sun through the zodiac, or the alternations of the tides; we expect from him the consciousness that he has done wrong actions, and that he has the element of evil clinging to his motives and feelings. Free from this condemnatory consciousness, we cannot conceive ourselves to be for a moment without being self-condemned for it; to imagine ourselves without it would be to imagine ourselves different beings from what we are; to escape from it is to escape from the consciousness of

---

[1] Shelley's *Prometheus Unbound*, Act II. Scene 4.

ourselves. Consider the principle of impulse in human nature, —how serviceable, how necessary it is to produce any sterling virtue in man! What man is worth anything without it? It is the root of all action; but, if so, action is disordered at the root. The very virtues of man have some obliquity or excess in them, so that we could not extract the evil without eviscerating the good. Whence it is that in works of fiction we reject "too perfect" characters, knowing that such portraiture is a delusion, and that strong virtue cannot grow up in man without some erroneous manifestation of his nature being produced in the very process. We want the fault, then, for the sake of the virtue; we need the shadow to express the brightness; we interpret perfection as a blank. And hence, again, the rule of Scripture: "Be not righteous over much;" which is directed, of course, not at real exactness of conduct, but at the motive which sometimes stimulates an outward exactness; when men make it apparent that they really have the idea that they can and will, by pursuing conduct into minutiæ, attain a perfection of character to which nothing will be wanting. Consider again the indomitable internal wildness of the human mind, its irrepressible volatility, which is a constant fount of *moral* disorder; when it is hurried off by a thought, fastened on by a retrospect, disturbed at a mere glance of some casual obnoxious image that flits across its horizon; and the involuntary evil excitation is present before the better can prevent it. This wild nature is a *law* of the mind, because there is no perfect cure for it, no discipline which quite corrects it.

It is thus the very law of the human conscience that the better a man is, the more alive he becomes to the fact of evil in his actions and motives; and a sense of sin is part of the morality of human nature. The very normal effect of goodness in the human heart is the revelation of evil. Can any apparent amount of goodness, any phenomenal sublimity of character that we can picture to ourselves, cancel this law? Let us make the supposition of a man exhibiting the richest and most splendid assemblage of virtues, the utmost purity of life, largeness of heart, active zeal, love for others; let us suppose the loftiest bearing, the most calm and imposing wisdom, the most benevolent services to mankind; but let us suppose also this man asserting that he was without the sense of sin. How should we regard such a character—I mean on simply human principles? Could we imagine it for an instant as real, we could not contemplate it without consternation. Such a man would be an enigma, and a portent to us; wholly unintelligible, but not the less condemned by the conscience of humanity; a rebel against the first law which is stamped on human hearts, and an outcast self-excommunicated from the society and fellowship of the righteous. Let the void within be covered by ever so luxuriant a growth of outward virtue, we could not believe in the reality of such a man's goodness; his character could only appal; and the one thing wanting would destroy the most majestic external moral fabric. It would be converted into an unsubstantial shadow; and the nobler the assemblage of virtues, the more portentous would be the illusion and deception of the structure.

It may be asked, indeed, is there not a type of goodness, different from and higher than any exhibited in human history, which is capable of being manifested to human eyes, and which would of itself prove sinlessness? But the reply to such a question is, that however high the type of goodness in the person himself, it must still manifest itself to those without by means of such expressions and modes of action as would be to the human eye common to a perfect and to the highest imperfect goodness. How, for example, could strong indignation be the evidence of its own perfection, when the same expression would suit it and also a high imperfection? The obstruction to the proof of sinlessness by outward life is thus the essential invisibility of inward motives; and to this we must add the inexorable law of human goodness, in consequence of which the higher the outward life of any one, the more we count upon the sense of sin in that person.

If exception is taken at regarding anything so impalpable, so inaccessible, so mysterious as right and wrong are in their own nature, as holding a parallel position to physical fact, the reply is that we are not here considering right and wrong in their own nature, but only as fixed feelings or impressions of the human mind. However mystical, transcendental, and beyond analysis right and wrong may be in themselves, that they exist as feelings and impressions of the human mind, and that the impression of having done wrong is universal in the human mind, is a plain and palpable fact. The pains of conscience are sensible inward phenomena, they are special known feelings, quite different from any other.

To return, then, to the point from which we started: if the presence of sin is an universal fact or law of our moral nature, regarded as a field of experience, it inevitably follows that the absence of it is a contradiction to law; that is to say, that it is of the nature of a miraculous or supernatural fact. To be without moral regrets, without sense of shortcoming; for the whole root of inordinateness and dissatisfaction to be extracted from the soul, to be an ideal to yourself, to possess that which the more it has been pursued the more has fled all human grasp—the Crown of a Supreme Righteous Self-approval—suppose this, and you certainly suppose a marvel. It is an unknown state of mind, totally unlike experience; an anomalous insulation in the self-convicting conscience of humanity. That pervading subtle ingredient of life—how are we to imagine the total clearance of it out of the human interior; the removal of that part of man's self, the ever-accompanying shadow, the unfavourable reflection upon himself? Christ was satisfied with Himself. That is, He witnessed to Himself that His conscience was what no human conscience had ever been; that is, He witnessed to a contradiction to a universal law of experience, or to a supernatural fact. When we realise under what conditions we ourselves and the whole human race are working out the problem of our moral being; and that these conditions as uniformly in fact involve in our case the consciousness of sin as the law of any species in nature involves any characteristic of that species; when we embrace, in short, what is the experimental character of the moral struggle of life in any human being; and then turn to that fulfilment of an ideal, that absolute purity, that immunity of an inward life from all mixture and alloy,—we must see that all that extraordinariness, that strangeness of type, that difficulty of reception, attaches to the sinless state that attaches to a miracle; that it has that, at first sight, unreality, incredibleness, effect of astonishing, which the violation of a law of physical nature has; and that it is in short a miracle, only a miracle of the inner world instead of the outer.

Christ's sinlessness did not indeed imply a freedom from the burden of resisting evil,—of maintaining a contest. But the law of sin in human nature is not the contest with evil, but the failure more or less under the contest. It is this which constitutes the subject of that self-reproach under which all human nature labours : the immunity from this was immunity from a law of human nature, a universal characteristic of it.

Let the test of the historical imagination,—I mean the principle of deciding at once against the truth of facts, if, when we realise what they are, we start at the unlikeness to, the opposition to the experimental type,—let this test, which has been applied to physical miracles, be applied to the sinlessness of Christ, and does it meet that test ? Is there anything more certain, more sensible, more palpable than this universal fact of evil, this imperfect struggle with evil ? Is any geographical fact, any historical fact, more absolutely taken for granted ? Is there anything imaginable wanting to the constancy of experience, to the rigorousness of fact here, that out of this vast mill of probation which the world is, all goodness comes forth mixed with the "ineradicable taint"?—that no human life is clear?—that if any one said his was, we should not for an instant believe him ? With this overpowering stamp, then, of the actual, the real, upon his mind, with this strength of assurance from the world of fact, let any one turn to the thought of the One Sinless Conscience, that marvellous interior of One Man. Does not that paradisal insulation in humanity, the section of the heavenly state crossing with the earthly, sinlessness coexisting with pain and resistance, challenge the same wonder, the same astonishment, the same instinctive questions—Is it real ? Is it possible ?—that a physical interruption of the order of nature does ? Does it not excite the same antagonistic instinct of custom, the same jar with the experimental touchstone of truth? Has the one fact less of the, at first sight, incredibility than the other? If the resurrection of Christ was an idea, was the sinlessness a fact? The same antipathy of *un*reason, or mechanical impression, to strange, unlike, unknown types, rejects both; the same cultivation of true reason retains both.

What I said, then, in the Lecture to which Professor Tyndall refers, was, that sinlessness being an internal and supernatural characteristic of our Lord, of which His outward life, sublime as that was, could not in the nature of the case be adequate proof, miracles were a guarantee to the truth of that assertion of our Lord respecting Himself, in the same way in which they were a guarantee to the rest of His supernatural character. Not that miracles could prove such an assertion without other conditions co-operating; but that they had an evidential force with those other conditions concurring. And certainly whatever theoretical difficulties may be raised with respect to the mode in which miracles operate as evidence of that of which they are alleged to be evidence, practically speaking, to say that the whole of the miraculous circumstances of Christ's life, supposed to be true, would operate in no way as evidence of the truth of His assertion of His own sinlessness, would be to contradict the common reason of mankind.

There are two corollaries which attach so naturally and unavoidably to this statement of the supernaturalness of Christ's sinlessness, that they should not be omitted.

1. The religious and philosophical position taken by the late Mr. Baden Powell was, that the denial of supernatural facts does not interfere with the doctrines or spiritual truths of Revelation. But here is a doctrine or spiritual truth, an essential part of the doctrine of the Atonement, which such a denial does touch immediately. The moral perfection of a future state is no exception to this present order of nature because it is not inserted in it; but if the fact of a sinless Person is inserted in this order of nature, it is an exception to it, or supernatural, and is therefore shut out by Mr. Baden Powell's barrier.

2. It appears to be the notion of many—indeed, I may call

it a tendency of thought in the present day—to accept the Gospel moral portrait of Christ, omitting His supernatural character. Such a ground must be distinguished from the liberty which Christian writers claim, to portray our Lord's humanity, as for the time contemplated apart from His divinity. The extent to which this may be done, the Incarnation being a complex doctrine, made up of two great truths, is what may be called an administrative question in theology, not capable of any rigid definition. The notion, however, to which I am referring is, that the Gospel moral portrait of Christ can be fully and completely preserved, although permanently separated from His supernatural character.

What I observe, then, is that upon this basis of omission of the supernatural the sinless character of our Lord must be omitted, as well as the physical supernatural attaching to Him. A person might at first sight suppose that this basis of omission would only apply to the body of outward miracles which glorified His birth and death, and accompanied His ministry; but, upon reflection, he must see that upon this basis he must also omit another asserted characteristic of Christ. For what are the contents of the supernatural? Do the physical miracles, do these and the mediatorial and atoning office of Christ together, constitute the whole of the supernatural? No: the sinlessness is supernatural. Upon the basis, then, of the omission of the supernatural, the sinlessness must be omitted.

But does the omission of the sinlessness make no difference in the moral portrait of our Lord? That would be a strange thing to say. Consider, the moral character of Christ was not a mere exhibition or procession of actions; it was not a mere succession of abstract virtues; it was not a mere external fabric of virtue. There was behind all this manifestation of action a Person. What was the moral condition of that Person? It must make a difference; it must make a fundamental difference in the moral portrait which we have in our minds of the Person whether He was with or without the consciousness of sin.

This is no metaphysical distinction, it must be seen; no

difference which can be set aside as belonging to the sphere of unintelligible dogma; it is the difference of a plain and palpable matter of fact. As I have said, whatever be the impenetrableness of the distinction of right and wrong in itself, the feelings, the impressions, the consciousness in human nature with regard to it are the most sensible facts possible; they are actual mental sensations; everybody knows what they are; all the motions and workings of these feelings are known; they are assumed in all conversation, in all history and biography. The alternative here, then, is between there having been the absence in that Person of a sensible known consciousness such as we all understand to our cost, or the presence of it in Him,—no speculative difference. The alternative lies between a sinless goodness, or (if the sinlessness is omitted) a mixed and alloyed goodness—the goodness of human experience. What is the universal portrait of man good with the goodness of experience? This is his portrait: a man who has moral regrets, who blames himself, who does not rise up to his own ideal, who did something yesterday, this hour, which fell short of a standard within him, who is not satisfied with himself. Was Christ—the argument compels me to ask the question—such a man? Unless sinlessness is attributed to Him, the only alternative, the only possible alternative, is, that He was. Of all goodness which is not exceptional, of all the goodness of experience, this unfavourable consciousness is the uniform, the infallible, the inexorable law; its attendance is as certain as the most certain physical conjunction in nature; it is as certain as the succession of the seasons, as the law of life and death, as the reproduction of animal and vegetable types; and we should as soon expect the earth to roll back upon its axis as look for a contradiction to this law in any human being. Upon the principle, therefore, of omission of the supernatural characteristics of Christ, it follows inevitably not only that He ceases to be God, not only that He ceases to be mediator between man and God, not only that He becomes only man, but that He becomes sinful man. Sin must enter with the withdrawal of sinlessness, and sinlessness must be withdrawn with the withdrawal of the supernatural. But this is a fundamental subversion of the moral portrait.

For—and it is necessary to state this distinctly, it is by no means a superfluous thing to state, though it is a truism—there is no medium between "no sin" in a man and sin. We are apt to look upon the outside of goodness and to forget the inside, the human interior out of which it proceeds, and the conditions which accompanied it in the actual inward person himself. So suppose a generous or a condescending unbeliever drawing, as Rousseau and several have done, a portrait of Christ, and describing His course here; how it was characterised by consummate benevolence, patience, moral dignity, etc. Would he attribute to Christ a sinless character because he thus described Him? No. Yet neither on the other hand would he contemplate Him as having moral evil. He would stop short at the outside of his picture. What he has in his mind is a personification, an assemblage of various virtues, a spectacle, a superficies. But was not the centre of that whole outward erection of virtue a real Person? And was there not a real interior of that Person? There was; and we know with certainty what that conscious interior, *if* it was not sinless, was: that it was the sphere of moral regret, sense of shortcoming, sense of failure, etc. Here, then, is a subversion of the moral portrait. A person might say, indeed, I do not know what this mystical sinlessness is; I cannot form to myself a clear conception of it; therefore the absence of it is to me no absence of a positive intellectually apprehended part of the portrait. But to such a person I would say, Stop. Even supposing—for I need not enter into that question here—that you do not know intellectually what sinlessness is, you know the alternative very well which exists in man, if he is not sinless. You know that alternative intellectually; you know it by experience; you know it by the most sensible and palpable experience. This alternative is the difference of a broad fact; because there can be no neutral state: if not sinless, the man must have the consciousness of sin and its concomitants.

It is the tendency of the historical school among us to exhibit our Lord as a life without a Personality. They describe a great moral spectacle, a great exhibition of the virtues, a great procession of the highest attributes of humanity. But we want a centre of all this fabric and edifice of high action—an Agent, a Person, the Being who has inward life, soul, consciousness, conscience. This is not included in the description; and yet to exclude it is to transgress against the historical principle. That inward Man, the conscience of that Man, was as much a fact as His outward life. Was it a sinless conscience, or—I am obliged argumentatively to state the alternative—had it a history of self-reproach and dissatisfaction? Its condition must have been either the one or the other; either the former, which is supernatural, or the latter, which is a confession of sin. The alternative between a Supernatural Christ and a sin-conscious Christ cannot really be avoided; yet the historical school stops short of this point, does not approach it, and draws the moral portrait of Christ without the question being settled. It avoids the inward Personality, and confines itself to manifestations; yet the centre of this whole outward moral erection was not a void or cavity, like the Christ of the Docetæ.

The moral estimate even of the *manifestations* must be deeply affected by the rank of the person from whom they proceed. Were the benevolent, the compassionate manifestations, the condescensions of a Great One, a Superior, to frail, weak, and miserable man; or did they represent the active benevolence of a philanthropist to his fellows? Upon the latter supposition there would be an immediate difference in the moral impression which those actions produce. They would still be good, but their goodness would be different. There would be a fall in the type; a solemnity, a beauty, a depth of moral interest would have vanished; they would have ceased to be what they are. Any common poor man would be sensible of the alteration, as he read the Gospels. The acts of mercy and sympathy as they come upon him make a peculiar moral impression, and embody a higher moral type in his eyes, in consequence of something in their background, in their basis; that they come from an Agent who is lifted up in the nature of His goodness above mankind,—from an exalted Personage. The love which descends from a mysterious height is the greater and profounder love; because it is connected with the supernatural, it is higher morally. The moral type gains from the loftiness of the Agent, and the actions rise with their fountain-head. They are the acts of the Unknown One —unknown, though known as well; the unknown moral state from which they come gives an untold weight and meaning to them. The philanthropy *in* our Lord's actions, supposed to proceed from a philanthropist only, would fall flat upon the mind.

The omission of the supernatural, therefore, would be the subversion of the moral portrait too, as being the omission of the inward sinlessness. But, again, upon this basis not only is the great internal characteristic of Christ abstracted, but there is the total demolition of an actual, visible, outward portrait; for if the sinlessness is omitted, the next step is inevitable— namely, that the *assumption* of it must be omitted too. But although the characteristic itself is internal and supernatural— that He *professed* to be sinless, that He made this pretension, that He used this language, is part of the visible and external character, as portrayed in the Gospels. The assumption pervades His acts and speech; it is as much a portion of the Gospel biography as His benevolence, His compassion, His purity, His courage, His resignation; as much as His judging the scribes and Pharisees, instructing the poor, suffering for righteousness' sake, witnessing to the truth, and delivering Himself to death in behalf of His mission. What a man thinks or says of himself, his view of himself, his estimate of himself, is a most important characteristic of the man, in secular biography. The writers of the life of Christ have transmitted, as an essential portion of Him, this great act of self-assertion, this tone about Himself, which was quite unique, and to which there was no approach in human history. Nor can this characteristic be removed without a complete destruction of the whole portrait, and the substitution of another Christ for the Christ of the Gospels; whose profound statement respecting Himself reappears in the Epistles, as believed and bowed to by the Apostles, and made the foundation of a new message to mankind.

Let us place side by side this Character and another. In St. Paul we have a participation in the lot of humanity, an experience of a struggle, a sense of disappointment and shortcoming, a sense of weakness joined to a triumphant sense of strength; we have the beauty and the interest of the simply human character. He is akin to that "whole creation which groaneth and travaileth in pain together until now,"—to that nature which says, "to will is present with me, but how to perform that which is good, I know not." This is the goodness proper to man. The sense of weakness, the humility of confession, the self-condemning type, is a fundamental requisite for man's goodness; without it no apparent grandeur or sublimity can satisfy us. No strength of will, no greatness, no calmness of the philosopher, no zeal of the philanthropist, without this, can gain our moral affections. It is impossible to love a man because he is majestic, because he is wise, because he is calm, because he is active, because, even, he is philanthropical. We demand from him first a participation in the lot of humanity, a fellowship with it in confession of sin and weakness—not the mere sympathy of a human benevolence upon a high condescending ground with humanity;— that will not do; that is not enough; we must have confession. St. Paul makes this confession, and acknowledges fellowship with weakness and frailty. Now take the other Character. There stands One, erect and unconfounded before the throne of God. He casts off from Himself that whole fabric of language toward God which the sense of sin had formed; He throws off for Himself the whole penitential type. His humility is the humility of condescension, of magnanimity, of patience, of long-suffering innocence, of dignity undisturbed by mockery and insult; it is the humility of good desert; it is not the humility of imperfection and frailty which is the characteristic humility of man. The normal effect of sanctity is reversed, and it reveals in Him no sin—righteousness only; and that while His own moral criterion searched the inmost corners of the heart. A man may fulfil to the letter an outward ceremonial code; but Christ's code was, "Ye have heard it said, Thou shalt not kill; but I say unto you," etc.; "Ye have heard it said, Thou shalt love thy neighbour and hate thine enemy; but I say unto you," etc. The more inward the touchstone, the greater enigma the assumption of perfectly standing it; the more astounding the profession that the law was not death but life to Him, because He fulfilled it wholly. Yet this Man *preached* confession of sins; He preached it as the very criterion of an accepted state, and denounced self-justification as the condemnation of man. The publican was justified, because he smote upon his breast and owned himself a sinner; the Pharisee was condemned, because he thanked God he was not like that sinner. The very form of prayer which he put forth as the prayer of all mankind involved confession of sin. But the same Man who laid down the law of self-abasement for sin for every other human being disowned it for Himself; He condemned the Pharisee, and He did what the Pharisee did, justify Himself; He praised the publican, and declined to do what the publican did, condemn Himself; His prayer made all mankind sue for pardon, but He Himself did not pray to be forgiven. He said to others, "Repent;" but He Himself *explained* why He submitted to the baptism of repentance. That He disowned the confession of sin for Himself is the fact it is, because the confession of it in others constituted them the first objects of His love. There may have been philosophical philanthropists who did not bow their necks to the penitential yoke; but then they were men who did not accept the penitential type—who did not admit the truth of that moral standard which imposes it—whose idea of morals superseded it both for themselves and others—who thought it imbecile and weak, and below the dignity of human nature. But Christ's sympathy was with the penitential type solely; He abhorred the righteous in their own sight, He loved those to whom much was forgiven.

Now it is evident that these two characters cannot both be right, except upon the assumption of some entire difference in the basement or pedestal upon which each stands. They are opposed in fundamental type. If both characters are attributed then to the same ordinary humanity, if one is right the other is wrong. It might appear at first sight that a criticism of a character upon one basis was perilously near to a criticism of it upon another; but in truth no two acts of criticism are wider apart; we are never further off from a character upon its own appropriate basis than when we regard it upon another and improper one. We have never a more different character than when we have the same pretensions with different rights. The latter of these two characters is plainly enormous and monstrous, except upon the supposition of a humanity morally higher than all experience,—or supernatural.

But this *is* the claim and the assumption of the Christ of the Gospels; it is the basis of the whole moral portraiture in the Gospels. This character has never indeed from the first stood but upon one foundation; the portrait has never, from the time it was first drawn, belonged to any other than a supernatural personage, it is given *as* the character of such a Being; that is its explanation; that is historically its connection. Removed from this basis, it does not correspond to our moral sense, but this is its basis. The portrait that was drawn as a *contrast* to human saintly characters cannot be proper *as* a human saintly character; but then it was drawn as a contrast. Scripture is a succession of saintly biographies all upon one type, the penitential. By a sudden transition there springs up one solitary instance of a completely opposite type, which vanishes, and never reappears. But the solitary and insulated unpenitential type makes also a solitary assumption of worth, and the assumption is part of the portrait.

There is, then, a total demolition and destruction of this visible Gospel portrait upon the principle now commented on, because with the omission of the supernatural sinlessness must go, and with the fact of sinlessness the pretension to it must go—that is, the whole of that high and majestic assumption which constitutes the peculiarity of the character of Christ in the Gospels. For what is the character in the Gospels without this claim? Particular features might be left, but the whole would be gone. We should have a different character. The supernatural in Him goes deeper than into His outward miraculous life—namely, into the structure of His moral character.

One remark in conclusion. The liberty of permanently omitting any elements in the Gospel life of Christ must assume the spuriousness of those parts of the Gospels which contain those elements. The liberty to omit the outward miracles must assume the spuriousness of the miraculous record. The liberty to omit the supernatural offices of Christ must assume the spuriousness of those parts which contain the mention of those offices. The liberty to omit *all* the supernatural must assume the spuriousness of all those parts in which a claim to and assumption of the supernatural appears. And according to the foregoing observations, the high moral assumption of our Lord about Himself would be included under this head. The Gospel *moral* portrait of Christ, considered in the light of a whole, would thus have to be pronounced spurious. The whole, therefore, of this subject belongs to, and must be handed over to the jurisdiction of the department of Christian Evidences.

## IX.—*ORIGINAL SIN.*[1]

THE doctrine of Original Sin is sometimes stated as the transmission of the sin of Adam, or hereditary sin; or as the corruption of nature, and other equivalent phrases. These are attempts at expressing the mode in which original sin operates in the human race. But before we come to the mode of operation on the part of original sin, there is a previous and much more fundamental point to be stated, namely, what is the fact which is involved in original sin, and which is at once its actual *substance* and its *evidence?* When we have got the fact of the sin, the mode of it is another and further consideration not of such fundamental importance.

Original sin then is, fundamentally, simply *universal* sin. That is the fact which is at once the evidence and the substance of it. We know that if sin is universal, and if there is no instance of a human being without it, universal sin must receive the same interpretation that any other universal does, namely, that it implies a *law*, in consequence of which it *is* universal. Nobody supposes that anything takes place universally by chance, accident, or what we call curious coincidence. We know that there must be some law working in the case. That is the reason why we talk of the laws of Nature. The laws of nature are only, in their foundation, facts—facts which always happen in certain circumstances; but because they are universal we invariably, and by the very construction of our minds, infer that there is a cause for this universality; we cannot imagine that a thing occurs universally by chance. A person may throw the same number two or three times running by chance; but if he threw it fifty times running, we should be perfectly certain that it was not by chance, but that there was a cause for it, or that it came up thus invariably by a *law*. And so, before the physical cause of the different

[1] Delivered in the Latin Chapel.

seasons of the year was found out by astronomical discovery, people knew that there must be a cause for this uniform succession, or that it was by a *law* that the seasons always followed each other in the same order. And so now, when certain sequences in nature are universal, though the discovery of the cause may not yet have taken place, we know there must be a cause; that these sequences take place by a *law*, and not by chance.

And this consequence applies just as much to the fact of *sin* in the human race, if it is universal. If it is universal, if no man who ever lived was without it, and not only his whole life without it, but if no man was ever without it altogether in any moment of his life,—if not in act or word, still in thought or some inner and latent desire and inclination of his mind;—if sin is thus universal, it must be so by some *law*. And this *law* we call Original Sin : we say it is the fault or corruption of the nature of every man; that it is an inclination to evil belonging to the nature. But before original sin becomes a law it is a fact —it is the fact of universal sin. That is its visible and tangible shape,—the shape in which we meet original sin actually. We first observe the fact of universal sin; and thence, as in other cases of universal *fact*, we infer a *law* of sin. It is evident, indeed, that there can be no ground for a law, unless there is a universal fact of some kind in the first place. We should feel no need for a law, and no dispute could arise about original sin at all. Supposing the facts of the case were that a few men only were sinners; such a fact as this would be accounted for by the ordinary action of free-will—that men had free-will, and that some used it for good and others for evil. There would be nothing but what could be explained upon the common principle of contingency or an even chance. We should feel, therefore, no need for a law. But if the facts of the case are that all men are sinners, and that nobody could be believed who said he was not, then we say there is a law on the subject. There must be some cause. The universal fact cannot be by chance, or by the mere contingent action of men's own wills. Supposing we knew nothing of the existing facts of human nature, and were only told that a race of beings was created who had the power of acting well or ill, according as they chose, and that the side each individual would take was beforehand a contingency, could we prophesy that all would be sinners? We should have no ground for such a prophecy. Beforehand each man would be as likely to avoid sin as to fall into it. When then in matter of fact we find that all men *are* under sin, and that nobody gets free from it, we find a state of things that could not have been calculated upon, on the sole hypothesis of a contingent action of free-will in each.

Let us take the old heathen proverb—οἱ πλείονες κακοί—can we account for this result upon mere chance or contingency? The heathen saying did not of course mean that the majority were wicked in the sense of committing crimes and gross offences which the civil law or society took notice of; but only that there was a taint in their aim and scope in life, a low standard, an indifference to virtue. But why should there be a much larger number of this sort than of the other sort? Why should those whose minds espouse virtue and are congenial to it be the few, and those who are of the other character be the great mass? Why should it be *so*, rather than that it should be equal both ways? Upon the hypothesis of simple contingency to start with,—a free-will in everybody, and nothing more to take into consideration, the chances are as much one way as the other. The existing state of things then is not accounted for by mere free-will; and mankind are in a condition in which they would not be upon the doctrine of mere contingency. There must therefore be a reason for this. The proverb of οἱ πλείονες κακοί implies a law in operation.

Such is the foundation upon which the doctrine of Original Sin arises; there is first the universal fact of sin; and then the interpretation, which always follows, of a general and acknowledged fact into a law. What we call that law is a secondary question; the great thing is to see that there is a law. If all the individuals who come under the head of a certain nature have sin in them, then one mode of expressing this law is to say that it *belongs to the nature;* the nature being the common property and ground in which all meet. If all are descended from a common *stock*, then another form of expressing this law is that of transmission or descent—and we call it hereditary sin, or birth-sin. But the acknowledgment of there *being* a law is the first and most important matter; the particular way in which to express the law is, though not unimportant, a subordinate question.

Now, then, let us turn to St. Paul's mode of treating the subject, and to the order in which he proceeds. It is a characteristic of St. Paul that he writes without outward method; and yet in the midst of the free and informal and broken epistolary language of his letters, there is an order very easily perceptible in his flow of thought on this subject; and that is the order which has been just spoken of, namely, that there is first laid down by him the fact of universal sin, and then and upon that fact is established a law of sin or what we call original sin. St. Paul's broad statement of the facts of the case, at the beginning of the Epistle to the Romans, will immediately occur to us. The first thing he does, on entering upon the subject of that Epistle, is to look around him simply, and see what the facts are.

He puts himself into the position of a spectator, and directs his eye to the great trunk lines of human action and forms of human character that have occupied the ground in all ages, and under the Divine dispensation and covenant as well as outside it. He looks on all sides of him, and he sees that mankind as a mass have always acted in a way to offend their Maker and violate their own consciences. All, both the Jews and Gentiles, are proved under sin. "By the deeds of the law there shall no flesh be justified" (Rom. iii. 20);—"*all* have sinned and come short of the glory of God" (ver. 23);—"death passed upon *all* men, for that all have sinned" (Rom. v. 12);— "If one died for all men, then were all dead" (2 Cor. v. 14). We can discern the universal assertion indirectly under other forms. Thus: "the law worketh wrath" (Rom. iv. 15); that is, no man fulfils the law, but is self-condemned under it; which is an assertion of the universal law of sin. Again: "while we were yet sinners, Christ died for us" (Rom. v. 8);—"*you* who were dead in sins" (Eph. ii. 1);—"who hath delivered *us* from the power of darkness" (Col. i. 13);—"we" and "you" are universals, meaning *all* of us; because those whom he addresses are only samples of all mankind.

And while this is the broad historical view of mankind, the great conclusion of observation, St. Paul also goes within, and finds a universal consciousness of sin in the inward experience of the soul as well; that no man fulfils the law to his own satisfaction; but that there is a falling-off, a shortcoming for which he reproaches himself. This is a universal fact of inward experience: "when I would do good, evil is present with me; . . . that which I do I allow not; . . . for what I would, that do I not; but what I hate that do I" (Rom. vii. 21, 15).

It is, then, upon the great and broad ground of experience and observation that St. Paul founds the doctrine of Original Sin. He first appeals to history and then to conscience for a universal fact; first comes the observation of what is without, and then the examination of what goes on within the soul of man. On the great stage of the world and history was open, triumphant, and unresisted sin; in the interior scene of the human heart, where conscience has come into action, was sin resisted, but still not subdued; in both was sin, and both together make the universal fact of sin; and when he has got the universal *fact* he lays down and expresses the *law*.

With respect then to this Law of sin, it must be observed that St. Paul at first calls it simply a law—as in the remarkable passage Rom. vii., using the word in a sense somewhat analogous to the modern, namely, that of an unknown cause at work, which is shown by universality of experience. "I find then a law, that when I would do good, evil is present with me;"—"I see another law in my members;"—"the law of sin which is in my members." But when he expresses that law, which universal fact shows, more specifically and descriptively, he expresses it under the form of a connection between ourselves and the first man, as the head of our race and its representative, and this connection again either takes the form of the first man's sin being imputed to us, or of the first man's sin descending to us:—"By one man sin entered into the world, and death by sin;"—"for if through the offence of one many be dead;"—"the judgment was by one to condemnation"

(Rom. v.);—"by one man's offence death reigned by one;" —by the offence of one judgment came upon all men to condemnation;"—"by one man's disobedience many were made sinners" (Rom. v. 18, 19);—"in Adam all die" (1 Cor. xv. 22). This is the language which describes the law, and figures what kind of a law that is which the universal fact of sin proves the existence of. It gives a certain specific shape and outline to the law; but that there *is* a law, he has said implicitly before in the whole Epistle, in saying that sin is universal. That is his staple mode of declaring and asserting the existence of a law; of maintaining and laying down the principle of Original Sin. It is sometimes said,—St. Paul only makes mention of original sin in four or five texts—as if it was a slight exceptional and casual basis in the apostle's language on which the Church had founded the *doctrine* of Original Sin. But when we examine—although the actual law itself is seldom laid down in terms, in reality and implicitly every *universal* of St. Paul's is a law; for you cannot assert a universal without tacitly asserting a law. In truth then the doctrine of Original Sin is contained in that whole language in which St. Paul asserts the universal fact of sin.

The language of St. Paul, then, which described the law of sin which universal fact evidenced—which described this law as the sin of the race *in* the first man, or the imputation of the first man's sin to the race, was adopted and exemplified by the Church. Original Sin indeed did not always stand, either in the apostle's language or in patristic language, in special or definite connection with Adam. The phrases which St. Paul employs often have reference only to our nature generally, without the mention of the person of Adam at all: "we are by *nature* the children of wrath:" and the expression the "natural man" implies the same general form of the law of sin as adhering to the *nature*. And the Fathers employ the general phrases of "The Apostasy," "The Captivity," "Naturæ corruptio," and the like, which contain no reference to a personal source of original sin. So Tatian says generally—ἡ ψυχή χαμαιπετής: Athanasius—ἡ ψυχή ἀποστᾶσα. Basil—ἡ ψυχή παρατραπεῖσα. Tatian again ἡ πρώτη γένεσις—ἡ παλαιά γένεσις without express reference to Adam. But still the idea of *transmission* of *hereditary* sin was very prominent in the patristic mode of describing Original Sin. "Fuit Adam et in illo fuimus omnes," says St. Ambrose. "In lumbis Adam fuimus," says Augustine.—"Unus quisque homo cum primo nascitur"—"In illo qui hoc fecit, quando id egit, omnes eramus" —"Ipsi atque ille adhuc unus fuerunt." He calls Original Sin originis vitium, originis contagium, and explains—"Hoc delictum *alienum* obnoxia *successione* fit *nostrum*."—"Cujus male reatus non innocentibus, ut dicis, sed reis *imputatur*."

Original sin then is here described in language which is a sort of paraphrase and amplification of the language of St. Paul, and which puts the sin before us sometimes simply as the sin of our nature, sometimes as sin contracted at our birth and by our descent from Adam, who first sinned. But it must be observed that all this was only a mode of describing a *law*, the *nature* of which in itself is utterly unknown to us, but the existence of which is implied in the fact of Universal Sin.

When a great philosopher of this country, Samuel Taylor Coleridge, came to consider the subject of Original Sin in his *Aids to Reflection*—a book which has had great influence in forming the religious philosophical mind of this country, he undertook the office of forming a new language to express that law of sin in the human race of which we have been speaking, and it appeared of great importance to him entirely to cut out of the description of Original Sin all reference to the person of the first *man*—all idea of transmission or hereditary sin; all idea of an imputation, or of Adam's sin being charged and reckoned as sin to his posterity. The idea which he aimed at expressing was that of an *apostasy of* the *will*—the whole and universal will of the human race. He considered Adam's fall only as representing a fall in every individual will, or in the Universal will of man; and not as having any actual effect peculiar to itself by transmission or imputation.

When we come then to the examination of Coleridge's philosophy on the subject of Original Sin, we find in the first place, that original sin is founded in his idea, as *St. Paul* represents it as being, upon the universal fact of sin; and is only a law representing that fact. He says, "Sin is evil, having an *origin*. But inasmuch as it is evil, it cannot originate in God; and yet in some *Spirit* it *must*. Sin therefore is spiritual Evil; but the spiritual in Man is the Will. Now when we do not refer to any particular sins, but to that state and constitution of the will which is the cause of *all sins* . . . in this case, we may with no less propriety than force entitle this dire spiritual evil, and source of all evil, —Original Sin."[1] Here Coleridge in truth primarily calls Original Sin simply *universal* sin. He says it is evil in the will, only evil not in a particular will only, but in *all* will—that is, not in any one man's will, but in all men's wills. This is to say, he only speaks of it as a universal *fact*. But from the fact he infers the law: from universal evil in men's wills, original sin.

"Let the grounds," he says, "on which the fact of an Evil inherent in the Will is affirmable in the instance of any one Man, be supposed equally applicable in every instance, and concerning all men: so that the fact is asserted of the individual, *not* because he has committed this or that crime, or because he has shown himself to be this or that man, but simply because he is *a* man. Let the evil be supposed such as to imply the impossibility of an individual's referring to any particular time at which it might be conceived to have commenced, or to any period of his existence at which it was not existing. Let it be supposed, in short, that the subject stands in no relation whatever to Time, can neither be called *in* time nor out of time; but that all relations of Time are as alien and heterogeneous in this question, as the relations or attributes of Space (north or south, round or square, thick or thin) are to our Affections and Moral Feelings. Let the reader suppose this, and he will have before him the precise import of the Scriptural doctrine—or rather of the fact acknowledged in all ages, and recognised, but not originating, in the Christian Scriptures—of Original Sin."[2] Again, "The actual existence of moral evil we are bound in conscience to admit; and that there is an Evil common to all is a *fact;* and this Evil must therefore have a common ground. Now this evil ground cannot originate

---

[1] *Aids to Reflection*, 2d edition, p. 263.   [2] *Ibid.* p. 179.

in the Divine Will; it must therefore be referred to the Will of Man. And this evil ground we call " Original Sin."[1]

The philosopher thus entirely agrees in the substantial doctrine of Original Sin; nor can we be otherwise than struck with his deep sense of the unfathomable mystery of sin and of the absolute necessity there is of acknowledging the existence of a law of sin in human nature, which must be expressed in some way or other. What he differs from the patristic and received doctrine in is only the form of expression; he objects to considering original sin a transmission from one person to another, and insists on having it regarded as the vice and corruption of all Will in common,—all human wills, which have concurred in contracting this nature, in bringing down upon themselves this yoke, and in subjecting themselves by some universal, inexplicable, and mystical act to the law of sin. The corrupt nature of the will, Coleridge argues, must in some sense or other be considered its own act, that is to say, the corruption must have been self-originated. This he considers to be a conclusion which follows from the very nature of the case, because it would not have been the corruption of the will if it had sprung from any other origin than the will. But this act, in the case of a universal corruption, must be a universal one, and such an act is a mystery and an enigma just as much as sin by transmission is. It is true the law is exemplified perpetually in human conduct, that the will can by its own acts make a sinful nature for itself, can subject itself to a law of sin which then domineers over and dictates to it. We have not to go far for the proof of such a liability in the will, for in truth every sinful habit a man contracts is to a certain extent an instance of it. Habit is a second nature, and in proportion as a man falls under the power of a bad habit, in that proportion he loses the freedom of his will. And our experience shows that bad habits once contracted may become so strong, and may secure so deep a foundation in the man, that practically he loses his free will, and becomes the slave of his habit, bound to an irresistible law of sin within him: while at the same time the slavery under which he has fallen

---

[1] *Aids to Reflection*, 2d edition, p. 281.

is strictly the consequence of his acts, and of the bad use of his own free-will. The rule to which Augustine is so often referring—of *Peccatum pœna peccati*—that the punishment of sin is sin, the punishment of sinful acts, a sinful habit, and sometimes ultimately an irresistible sinful habit, is verified constantly in the facts that come under our eyes.

But this, though it is a common-sense explanation of one individual will contracting a sinful nature, such as we call an irresistible bad habit, fails entirely as a solution of *all* wills having done so. The difficulty now is the universality of the action in the will, which brought on its corruption and degradation. How is it that *all* wills have done this act—have done that which issued in a sinful nature? If all wills have gone wrong, that cannot be by chance or mere coincidence; it must be by a law. Thus what you want to account for is a law of sin in the will; and what you account for this law of sin *by*, is a law too. The difficulty is thus as far from a solution as ever.

Coleridge's mode of expressing the doctrine of original sin then has no advantage over that of the Fathers, and over the ordinary language of the Church, in respect of being at all less mysterious and incomprehensible. There cannot be a more unfathomable and inexplicable mystery than what he assumes —a universal act of self-corruption and self-degradation in the will of the human race. The usual theological mode of expressing the doctrine of Original Sin is by the supposition of a transmission of sin from one person to another, or a descent of sin through successive generations. Coleridge says not that one will has inoculated another will, not that contagion has spread from one being to another; but that all will has gone wrong; that universal will has, by a universal act, originated its own corruption. But this act he describes himself as a wholly mystical idea, and entirely out of the sphere of reason's cognisance. It is an act, he says, which cannot be referred to any particular time; which "stands in no relation to Time, can neither be called *in* time nor *out of* time," and to which "all relations of Time are as alien and heterogeneous as the relations and attributes of space are to our affections and moral feelings."[1]

[1] *Aids to Reflection*, 2d edition, p. 279.

This is profound mysticism; and so he himself concludes, "The fact," he says, "of a law in the nature of man resisting the law of God" has been universally acknowledged as "a mystery, and one which, by the nature of the subject, must ever remain such,"[1]—a problem of which any other solution than the statement of the fact itself is demonstrably impossible. The reason why Coleridge prefers fixing the source of original sin in the unfathomable abyss of universal created will to the ordinary theological language of *transmission,* is that the statement does not involve any difficulty on the score of justice, as the common notion of transmission does. In this new philosophical language, it is its own evil act for which all evil is punished—punished with a law of evil. It is true that this act is out of the sphere of time, is in no relation to time, and is totally incomprehensible; but the form of statement, the mode of speaking, as such, avoids the collision with justice; which collision attaches *prima facie* to the arrangement of one individual receiving his sin from another. He supposes therefore that he gains an advantage by superseding this arrangement; which is exposed to a charge of injustice which one common universal lapse escapes.

In estimating the value of this difference, however, we must consider to what extent we regard the ordinary theological mode of describing original sin as really open to this charge. It is a charge which only touches the mere surface of the language, and not its substance. The surface of the language is indeed open to the charge that one man is punished for the sin of another; but that is a language which we use with the acknowledged understanding that we only use it to express an unknown truth of which we have no actual idea. We are not committed to an injustice by it, but only to a mystery. This alone is the substance of the language.

But whatever perplexity attaches to the article of original sin, or the corrupt and sinful *nature* of the human will, the philosopher explains in a passage[2] which I will quote at length, "This is no tenet—and it will remove a world of error to hear it—that was first introduced and imposed by Christianity, and which, should a man see reason to disclaim

[1] *Aids to Reflection,* 2d edition, p. 277.     [2] Pp. 275, 276.

the authority of the Gospel, would no longer have any claim on his attention. It is no perplexity that a man may get rid of by ceasing to be a Christian, and which has no existence for a philosophic Deist. It is a FACT, affirmed, indeed, in the Christian Scriptures alone with the force and frequency proportioned to its consummate importance; but a fact acknowledged in every religion that retains the least glimmering of the patriarchal faith in a God infinite, yet *personal!* A fact assumed or implied as the basis of every religion, of which any relics remain of earlier date than the last and total apostasy of the pagan world, when the faith in the great I AM, the *Creator*, was extinguished in the sensual polytheism which is inevitably the final result of Pantheism or the worship of Nature. . . . Thus in the most ancient books of the Brahmans, the deep sense of this fact, and the doctrines grounded on obscure traditions of the promised remedy, are seen struggling, and now gleaming, now flashing, through the mist of Pantheism, and producing the incongruities and gross contradictions of the Brahman Mythology. . . . From the remote East turn to the mythology of Minor Asia, to the descendants of Javan, who dwelt in the tents of Shem, and possessed the Isles. Here again, and in the usual form of an historic solution, we find the same fact, and as characteristic of the human race, stated in that earliest and most venerable Mythus (or symbolic parable) of Prometheus—that truly wonderful fable, in which the characters of the rebellious spirit and of the Divine Friend of mankind are united in the same Person: and thus in the most striking manner noting the forced amalgamation of the Patriarchal Tradition with the incongruous scheme of Pantheism. . . . The fact of a moral corruption con-natural with the human race was, however, recognised; and in the assertion of Original Sin the Greek Mythology rose and set."

Such is the position of Coleridge with reference to Original Sin. I will conclude with the reflection that it is when we view the consciousness of sin as the law of our nature in this life, that the sinlessness of Christ appears in its true light as a supernatural fact—an inward invisible miracle surpassing in wonder any of the visible miracles which He wrought.

## X.—ORIGINAL SIN ASSERTED BY WORLDLY PHILOSOPHERS AND POETS.

THE great characteristic of St. Paul's teaching is that he brings out so prominently the mystery of Original Sin. It is remarkable, and a circumstance which deserves notice, that in this, the foundation mystery in St. Paul's teaching, St. Paul has the support of the modern intellect; and that modern analysis of character—that singular and deep fruit of the *recent* mind of the world, as dated from the era of the Renaissance and the Reformation—is in extraordinary sympathy with St. Paul's leading doctrine. It is singular to observe that upon the subject of this law of sin in our nature, this root of evil in humanity, the thought of modern times, so far from diverging or loosening itself from the great Apostolic position, rather fastens itself the more upon it; and that there has been a most remarkable development of this deep view of human life and man's nature; that the modern mind of the world has in its way plunged far down into the mysterious idea of some insoluble original mischief and corruption which lies at the bottom of this whole visible system of the world and human life.

The Satirists of the ancient world commented on the vices, faults, and errors of mankind, but their view of human nature was altogether below that of the modern school of satire in acuteness, depth, and the power of seeing facts as a whole. Horace, drawing with vivid fidelity the portrait of mankind—that part of it which came in his way,—and representing with consummate lightness of touch, dexterity, and skill the levity and folly of men; yet but skimmed the surface of society, and did not go any way into the darker part of man, and the underground of the structure. Juvenal denounced the criminal classes, the slaves of luxury, intemperance, pride, and lust, the court, the world of fashion, and the low adventurous life of Rome.

But when Satire was taken up under Christianity, and under a later philosophical influence, it certainly penetrated much deeper. It assumed a new function and office. It not only censured, not only branded, not only denounced and stigmatised men and classes of men, but it professed to lay bare the foundations of human nature. Vices, meannesses, vanities, were not single features, they belonged to a whole. There was something wrong in man, whence all his thoughts proceeded. It was accidental what particular line this radical wrongness took; it was there, and sometimes it manifested itself in one way, and sometimes in another. Sin was Protean, it slided into different shapes, it went from one opposite to another; the outward figure it took was not the important thing, but the inner substance; the symptoms were various, but they were only various as signs of the original disease, which was one and the same. "In the human heart," said the philosopher, "there is a perpetual generation of passions, so that the ruin of one is almost always the foundation of another. Passions often produce their contraries; avarice sometimes leads to prodigality, and prodigality to avarice; we are often obstinate through weakness, and daring through timidity." But again, what was very important, and showed a far deeper and more subtle power, satire in this new stage entered into the structure and probed the root of human virtues. It tried them by a test never tried at least with system and determination before—the test of motive. The strength of this test is in proportion to the knowledge which he who applies it has of the springs of action in man; of the foundations of character; of the power of latent wishes; and the secret force of certain aims and objects which adhere to man in spite of professions, and mingle intimately even with his best actions. The modern school of analysis of character dragged all this to light; a deep knowledge of human nature enabled it to detect fundamental motives, which it then proceeded to fasten upon human conduct, and even to append to the man's virtues. Such was Rochefoucauld's philosophy of sin. He held that there was a sort of sin in man which produced various outward forms of sin, and particular vices, but which was in itself the substantial vice of man. And in this view human nature always carried about this original fault with it; that however it might appear to be raised above low aims, a taint was still inherent in man's motives, and a secret selfishness insinuated itself into his most splendid actions.[1] He probes with frigid accuracy the soundness of the foundation, and his book is a succession of maxims which remove the mask from human pretensions and professions. We identify him with what is called the Cynical Philosophy. His name is indeed a proverb: it stands for an utter disbelief in the purity and simplicity of human nature, for a complete scepticism as to the genuineness and sincerity of men's virtues. But he was not this disbeliever in human goodness from mere acrimony, from passion, from violence, and a vituperative spirit. He had a philosophy, a theory of human action; he analysed its motives, and upon this analysis he came to the result he did—that all human virtue had for its motive some latent and refined form of selfishness.

When we enter, then, into this philosophy, it appears to us to go into the error which many other philosophies do, namely, that it is too complete and systematic, and consults unity at the expense of truth. It is the ambition of theories to possess simplicity. What this theory does, is that it lays down a uniform root of human action; not only this, but it represents this root as acting with uniformity. It has somewhat of the rigidity as regards virtues, that the Stoic rule had as regards vices—*omnia peccata paria*—all virtues are alike as Rochefoucauld portrays them; alike under the stimulus of a radical selfish motive. The mode, then, in which the great men, who conducted this analysis of human character, applied their discovery, admits of criticism; they applied it roughly and indiscriminately, without exactness, and without those adaptations and accommodations with which all great maxims must be applied. They applied their principle with a certain passion, as men use a watchword, which calls forth some powerful

---

[1] "L'amour propre fait tous les vices et toutes les vertus morales selon qu'il est bien ou mal entendu."—*Reflexions Morales*, p. 75, ed. 1743.

sentiment and forcible association. The passionate mode of the promulgation of this principle, as a truth respecting this system of things, was indeed in the case of some of the remarkable preachers of it vehement almost to madness. They looked upon the whole face of human society as a disguise, which hid, underneath its high professions, a servile and vain egotism—there was deception at the bottom of human life; and the original delusion, as it worked itself out, only added to its intricacy, and multiplied the labyrinth of a fraud. Rabelais wrote in a state of furious scorn and indignation, which he expressed by a boundless laughter. And he has his echo in our own literature, in him who drew in bitterness of soul, and with lacerated heart, that picture of man which, except to himself, gave mirth to the whole world.

Such is the disturbance and excitement with which the perception of the root of evil in human society has operated upon some minds, producing a commotion of the spirits like that with which one hears some frightful news, or sees some repulsive spectacle. Even Rochefoucauld's calm and imperturbable precision of statement rather disguises passion than suppresses it. It is *in* him; he keeps it under, and does not allow it to come up to the surface, but it is there, underneath the polished brevity of maxim, underneath the oracular form of judgment, underneath all his gravity and all his sententiousness.

In the mode, then, of *applying* their analysis of man, this school went wrong; it erred in the uniformity and sameness of the result; and the rule wanted flexibility and elasticity. They omitted the important distinction in applying the ordeal of motive;—that while the mass of mankind were blind to the motive on which they acted, and received into their character the full depravation of its hidden working, in some (though it acted by the faults of nature, which was too weak to shake it off), it acted still under a protest. It had not that dominion which a motive has when the man is utterly unconscious that he is influenced by it: it then plays havoc indeed in the soul, and is under no check. It was seen, the man was conscious of it; he confessed it, and that was in itself a kind of disowning of it. Sin then did not reign over him, and though every action was alloyed by the taint of some inward aim which would not stand the test of open day, and shrank from inspection; still the conscience, by its confession, relieved itself of the guilt and condemnation of it.

But without entering at present into the rigours and extravagances of this philosophy, it is enough, for the purpose before us, if it maintained in any shape the principle it did, namely, that human conduct, even human virtue, was invariably accompanied by certain latent motives proceeding from self-love; and these motives always mingled with, and corrupted the actions of the man. For this, undoubtedly, is to assert original sin. The alloy of the motive is represented by this school as universal; to attach to every man; it therefore exists by a law; it belongs to the nature; it is therefore the sin of nature; that is, original sin. Indeed, if a universal falsity, or taint in the motive is so uniform that you may be certain that a man, simply because he is a man, has it, if those who teach *this* do not teach original sin, then St. Paul himself did not teach it either.

We have, then, risen up in modern times, as the product of a large observation and a keen philosophy, a school of analysis of character which has had enormous influence, and whose maxims have been incorporated with the world's wisdom; and this school turns out to be the unconscious disciple, though at the same time distorter, of St. Paul; and its system in a new language, and under a peculiar philosophical dress, a republication of original sin. Its maxims have been, to the extent which is necessary to the present argument, received into the whole of society. Its rigid extremes of statement may have been avoided, but residuum enough has been adopted to establish that truth. It cannot then be said that the doctrine of St. Paul has become obsolete: it is new, it is fresh, it is living, it mingles with the intellect of the modern world, and comes out expressed anew from the search of modern analysis. It falls in with the lines of modern thought, it unites with man's introspection of himself in a new era of philosophy.

So with respect to the doctrine of perfectibility, by which

we mean man's perfectibility in this life—the philosophy of this school entirely ratified the scriptural position. In the eye of Scripture, as we know, any mere man, fancying himself sinless, is a rebel against the law of his present being; or is deprived of his reason, and is under captivity to some strong delusion. And yet men have been deceived into the idea that they have attained perfection,—that they are in a state pure from all sin. Even the language of the first ages of the Church was not wholly free from concessions to this feeling; and sects have from time to time been carried away by the hallucination. Even very recent times show instances of it, and have placed the attainment of perfection within their system;—only, as might have been foreseen, as the sad prognostics of terrible downfalls. How would the philosophy we have been considering treat such an assumption? It would hardly condescend to argue with it, but would set it down at once among the delusions and madnesses of mankind. And thus the old truth of Scripture collects, as it descends to this modern era of the world, the suffrages of modern thought: the latest maxims of philosophy concur with it, and it mingles with the whole vein of recent search and analytical investigation into man.

We have nothing here to do with the characteristics of those leading men themselves who thus analysed the action of mankind, and formed the school of modern philosophical satire. The wildness and extravagance with which some wrote gave their philosophy the look of an enthusiasm; nor were they men whose lives corresponded with the antagonism in which they stood to the corruption and selfishness of society. And in this point of view, the scope of their philosophy totally differed from the scriptural writer's. The latter saw through the corruption and fall of man to a recovery beyond; and only insisted on the evil to direct to a restoration and redemption; but these philosophers only analysed human nature as naturalists examine some species, to report the facts; they had nothing to do with religious hope. But this did not make them the less true witnesses. They had gifts—extraordinary faculties of insight and acuteness of perception; but gifts never have gone, and never will necessarily, go along with a life ennobled by them. True prophets have been faulty men. These men have done their part;—we do not take them for patterns;—they had endowments; they were enabled to see deeper into human nature than ordinary people can. They saw that men professed to be better than they were, and they took off the disguise. They would not be deceived; they would see things as they were: "*Decipi turpe est*" was their motto. As a school of teachers they brought man to his senses, they estimated him at his value, and by determinate exposure of the root of evil, they overthrew the whole perfectionist view of human nature.

It is very remarkable, again, that in this latter age of the world, when the mysterious truths of Scripture have been subjected to intellectual analysis, and, upon not answering to the test, have been thrown aside by so many, that a school of *poets* should have arisen who should particularly have taken up and been arrested by the incomprehensible spectacle of a fallen world and a sinful nature. The very doctrine which the sceptical intellect has ever criticised as an inconsistent, self-contradictory one, not agreeing with itself, and therefore such as reason must discard, was—enigmatical as it was—the very truth which this school of poets, which I am speaking of, saw. They looked within and without them, into themselves and into society, and they saw a root of sin in human nature which they could not explain; and became the involuntary witnesses to a great mystery on this subject. And thus arose the remarkable spectacle of a school of infidel poetry giving complete loose to its own thoughts, and yet issuing in an agreement with the scriptural oracle upon this great subject. It is remarkable, I say, that at the very commencement of a sceptical age, such a school should, in matter of fact, have taken up and adopted this very mystical truth of original sin, with all its sadness and perplexity, as its great subject;—the cardinal material at once of all its fretful pangs of anger and irritation, and of its gloom and despondence—and that the great fact which elicited that torrent of emotion, and furnished that grand scale of sentiment and passion, grief, and indignation which characterised their poetry, and gave it its hold upon the popular mind, should have been the very fact which St. Paul saw—" the whole creation groaning, and travailing in pain together until now "—a world under a law of *sin*, and, as a consequence, of *misery*. To say that Shelley's or Byron's poetry is penetrated with a doctrine of original sin, may be an assertion that will sound strange and incongruous: certainly they had no intention of supporting and seconding St. Paul: that is clear enough; but, however, that was what they *did* do in fact; if unconsciously and without knowing what they did, and what auxiliaries they were to the doctrine of Scripture, so much the more valuable their evidence. What they did do in fact was to proclaim human nature as involved in some inextricable labyrinth of evil; of which alike the source and the issue was inscrutable. They did not see this law of sin as reconcileable with a good God, as Scripture sees it; but in the acknowledgment of a law of evil itself—that the world was under a yoke, and that human nature was under a cloud; that conscience at the best was restless and dissatisfied; that as human nature came out and its faculties and tendencies developed in strength, they revealed a native corruption and alloy; and that a scene of enmity, of collision, of discord and grief was the expansion of the original seed of human life;— in this they were at one with St. Paul; and with him they said, "The whole creation groaneth, and travaileth in pain together until now." Had they been actual disciples of St. Paul they could not have embraced more tenaciously the idea of some universal evil in humanity which was moral and touched the heart; of some law, that is, of sin, in consequence of which sin came up by a uniform emergence in the character of mankind. A canker disclosed itself in the motive, a treachery in the affection, there was an antagonism to good, working within; and the consequence was a universal disfigurement and disorder, an embroilment of relations and a war of selfish interests, which composed a moral chaos, and stamped degeneracy and corruption in the human race. What is their view of history then, but that of St. Paul? What is their sad interior of the human soul, with its unequal strife, and languishing will, but that of St. Paul? In their own language then, and in the midst of wild outbreaks and desperate complaints, these poets substantially preach with St. Paul the doctrine of original sin. They declare an original deflexion in the human race from right, and a divergence into error and vanity. They appear in the unconscious character of witnesses to the truth of Scripture, and to the profound depth of that law of sin which Scripture has proclaimed. Everything has, they say, gone wrong here; we are in a maze of falsehood and deception. Wherever they go they see before them a scene which disturbs, confounds, and envenoms them—the sight of a fallen world.

The idea of original sin which we meet with in these poets, is indeed fatalism; but it agrees with St. Paul's idea so far as this point is concerned, which is the principal one in the doctrine of original sin;—that of sin attaching to nature. This has been the objection, as we have seen, to that doctrine; that a man cannot help his nature, and that if he cannot help it there is not sin. Now, however neat an argument this may sound in naked philosophy, you may see how completely it is brushed aside as soon as men come to actual facts—to the facts of internal nature and moral sensation. Sin attaching to nature appears as a regular and thoroughly recognised combination in these poets. They see a great law of sin in mankind, a seed of moral evil which develops into a corrupt world, but do they, because sin is a law and a nature, regard it not as sin? By no means. It remains sin. It is because it *is* sin that they complain. That is their grievance;—that there is this fount of evil and corruption in nature, and that it is felt to *be* evil and corruption. They see that there is consciousness of sin in man as such; that he cannot rid himself of it, he cannot get over it;—that there is this sin in his nature; and yet they feel it is sin. Could the poet vote it not sin, he would have nothing to murmur about; there would be nothing to excite his rebellion and sense of grievance as far as this point is concerned; it is because he feels it to be sin, and cannot dismiss it, that he murmurs and rebels. So, I repeat, sin is recognised by him in the nature of man, and still it is recognised as sin. That is to say, the mysterious combination which rationalism discards, Pelagian rationalism, and modern rationalism—the fundamental mystery of Scripture—has been adopted by an infidel school of poets. Lord Byron says :—

> " Our life is a false nature—'tis not in
> The harmony of things,—this hard decree,
> This uneradicable taint of sin,
> This boundless upas, this all-blasting tree,
> Whose root is earth, whose leaves and branches be
> The skies which rain their plagues on men like dew—
> Disease, death, bondage—all the woes we see—
> And, worse, the woes we see not—which throb through
> The immedicable soul, with heart-aches ever new."[1]

Again :—

> " How beautiful is all this visible world!
> How glorious in its action and itself;
> But we, who name ourselves its sovereigns, we,
> Half dust, half deity, alike unfit
> To sink or soar, with our mix'd essence make
> A conflict of its elements, and breathe
> The breath of degradation and of pride,
> Contending with low wants and lofty will,
> Till our mortality predominates,
> And men are—what they name not to themselves,
> And trust not to each other."[2]

Byron then shows obviously enough, and by sufficiently loud demonstrations, that the sense of sin which he feels is not a mock sensation, though he regards it all the time as part of a law which attaches to his being. He regards his life as a chain which has wound round and round him with the force of an irresistible fate, which he could not conquer, but at the same time hated.

> " For he through Sin's long labyrinth had run."[3]

It was a labyrinth out of the mazes and windings of which he could not extricate himself, yet he had contracted the guilt of it; it was destiny, and yet it was sin. Any one indeed who is at all acquainted with the life of Lord Byron knows the state of

---

[1] *Childe Harold*, Canto iv. 126.   [2] *Manfred*, Act I. Sc. 2.
[3] *Childe Harold*, Canto i. 5.

almost furious anger which the remarks of society in this country upon his profligate and disorderly life, produced in him. And yet the remarks that were made were only observations of the plainest facts, which he could not deny; they were patent and known to all the world. But it was because they were facts, and undeniable facts, that the allusion to them was so infuriating. He had, however, his own point of view, in which this criticism appeared to him unfair. His life had been, in his own view, the winding of a fatal chain round him, coil after coil had fastened him in its odious grasp, till he was its complete prisoner. He was miserable, he was tormented with himself, he was full of discord, and torn with self-reproach—not profitable self-reproach indeed, but still such as embittered his whole life. Why, then, when he was thus torn inwardly, was he to be the butt of the animadversions of a commonplace world—more glad of an object of easy censure than watchful over itself? This was his point of view, and it was like every attitude he took in his whole career—a rebellious one. But one thing certainly was shown by it, namely, that however he regarded sin as a hard decree, an uneradicable taint, this boundless upas, this all-blasting tree, whose root is earth,—however, that is, he regarded it fixed in nature, he still regarded it as sin, otherwise it would not have goaded him. When we come across the outbursts of the peculiar feeling just described, which is nothing less than a denunciation of all judgment and observation upon him, the remark indeed is obvious that if a man acts quite publicly and openly in contradiction to morality, he has no right to object to the world at large, at any rate, seeing what he does. We are only, however, concerned here to extract out of this whole agitation and demonstration of feeling, that ingredient in it which bears upon the doctrinal subject on which we are engaged. The poet believes in a great root of evil in nature—in original sin; but he is conscious that, though in nature, it is real sin. This is a combination which Pelagianism resisted, but which St. Paul preached.

The other great poet of this school—Shelley—would seem at first to deny a law of sin in the world, and to attribute the whole of man's sin to false teaching, and the ideas put into his head by interested men, rulers and superiors; he spurns the doctrine of a sin of nature in terms as taught by the Church, and says it is all owing to a bad education. But when we take his philosophy as a whole, and see what it is, apart from words that he teaches, what is the fact he maintains? we find that it is some evil and moral evil in man as a race which is equivalent to a sin of nature, though he does not call it such. He says as Byron does :

> " The universe
> In Nature's silent eloquence declares
> That all fulfil the works of love and joy,
> *All but the outcast man.*"[1]

In behalf of the whole human race he complains of the consciousness of sin as a yoke which has been imposed upon him as a hard necessity :—

> "And who made terror, madness, crime, *remorse,*
> Which from the links of the great chain of things
> To every thought within the mind of man
> Sway and drag heavily, and each one reels
> Under the load towards the pit of death,
> Abandoned hope and love that turns to hate;
> And *self-contempt* bitterer to drink than blood?"[2]

Now then examine this language, "Who made self-contempt?" That is a remarkable question to ask. The whole phrase is extraordinary. The phrase implies that man did not make it for himself, but that it is annexed to his nature. Translate this into religious language. There is a law of our nature by which we never can gain self-approval; we try, but cannot; we find ourselves obliged to condemn ourselves. The human spirit pursues moral self-approbation in one stage of action after another; but the more man pursues it the more it flies away from him, he cannot get up to it, reach it, or grasp it. It is a will-of-the-wisp, which ever retreats, as the pursuer advances. What the poet asserts then is that self-disapprobation, a consciousness of sin, "self-contempt and remorse," he calls it—cleaves to man as such, to the race; but if this is not to assert original sin, I know not what is.

[1] *Queen Mab*, iii. p. 17.  [2] *Prometheus*, Act II. Sc. 4, p. 216.

Thus again :—

> "Monarch of Gods and Demons and all Spirits
> But one, who throng these bright and rolling worlds,
> Which Thou and I alone of living things
> Behold with sleepless eyes! regard this earth,
> Made multitudinous with thy slaves, whom Thou
> Requitest for knee-worship, prayer, and praise,
> With fear, and self-contempt, and barren hope." [1]

Here again is the same complaint—that self-contempt is annexed to human nature. It is the poet's term for that self-disapprobation which figures as a law of conscience so prominently in the language of St. Paul.

It must be observed indeed that when Shelley makes this assertion of original sin, he does not make it in the spirit and temper of, or in concurrence with, the *philosophy* of Scripture. Shelley's fierce and vehement fatalism makes sin not only a part of this world, but actually a part of God. Our nature inherits it, not only as something inherent in itself, but as something inherent in the universe and in the Divine nature itself. The doctrine of original sin in Scripture, as we know, is guarded by checks on all sides from committing the Divine Being, and implicating the Divine design in the creation. Shelley too says there is original sin, but so far from guarding or checking the doctrine, or wishing to do so, he includes all the universe in it, together with its author. His system is that absolute Pantheism which deifies and incorporates in God *all fact* of whatever kind, good or bad; and he sees in the universe an absolute chain of evil, the links of which hang on inextricably to each other, including the deceived and the deceiver, the corrupted and the corrupter, the oppressed and the oppressor, the despot and the slave, all in one dire embrace and one fatal coil of necessity :—

> "No atom of this turbulence fulfils
> A vague and unnecessitated task,
> Or acts but as it must and ought to act.
> . . . . .
> Even the minutest molecule of light
> Fulfils its destined, though invisible work :

[1] *Prometheus*, Act I., Opening Speech.

> The Universal Spirit guides : nor less
> When merciless ambition or mad zeal
> Has led two hosts of dupes to battle-field.
>
> . . . .
>
> Necessity, thou mother of the world,
> . . . . the poison tree
> Beneath whose shade all life is withered up,
> And the fair oak whose leafy dome affords
> A temple where the vows of happy love
> Are registered, are equal in thy sight."[1]

Now, then, separate from this philosophy all that is peculiar to the blasphemy of Pantheism and the rebellion of fatalism; separate from it all that charge against the Divine Being, of being a hard master whom it is impossible to please, and who has unjustly implanted in man this root of evil, whereby man is made a self-condemning being, displeasing to himself; eliminate its impiety, and you have in the residuum the recognition of original sin. There is a root of evil in the world and in man, and though it is sin in nature it is still in the poet's eyes real sin, otherwise he would not care about it. It is that very consciousness which is the torment and the grievance. He finds he cannot escape the consciousness of sin by appealing to a law of sin that does not deaden or nullify it. He calls self-contempt a law of our nature, but the very wrong which he attaches to it still implies that the man bows to the verdict; the very yoke of sin assumes the fact that it is felt as such. That is to say, he flings to the winds the cardinal argument of the Pelagian and the rationalist, that sin in a nature cannot be sin. Were the sense of sin a false sense, were it a deception, he would not mind it; it is because it is a *true* sense that it frets and irritates, and embitters and envenoms. And so the other great poet, though he regards sin as a law, shows obviously enough, and by sufficiently loud demonstrations, that he does not regard it as a mock sensation.

We have thus, while examining the sentiment and feeling of one remarkable infidel school of poetry, had before us an extraordinary and striking phenomenon, namely, a great and unconscious testimony borne by that school to the profound oracle

[1] *Queen Mab*, vi. pp. 32, 33.

which speaks out of the sanctuary of Scripture. Throwing aside their collateral points of view, they agree with the voice of inspiration, in declaring a root of evil and corruption in man which is involved in an abyss of mystery. And it may be said that this sad and painful mystery is a considerable part of the inspiration of their poetry—of the serious and strong-feeling part of it. It is viewed indeed as an inexplicable injustice, which demands their protest and indignant complaint, but still it is there, and though they complain of it they cannot rid their own conscience of it. It is indeed remarkable to see such a theme of poetry. Other great poets have taken the heroic for their subject. The great medieval poet took for his subject the last Judgment on Man, and our own poet took the first Judgment on Man. But the subject of these two great modern poets which penetrates their mind, and runs through all their thought, is original evil—the sin of nature and of the world, in which all present visible existence is implicated.

There is thus something in St. Paul which is ever fresh and never can be obsolete, which is in sympathy with the modern intellect as well as the old mind of the Church. New schools of thought, new inspirations of poetry, unconsciously acknowledge him, and he is a living oracle equal to all ages of the world.

## XI.—*PERFECTIBILITY.*

[In the Lent Term of 1874, Dr. Mozley gave a Course of Lectures to Graduates—delivered in his study—on the three great controversies conducted and finished by St. Augustine; the Manichæan, the Pelagian, and the Donatist; the first of which—*The Manichæans and the Jewish Fathers*—concludes the volume of *Lectures on the Old Testament*, delivered in 1875. The series being mainly occupied with the subjects treated in the author's *Augustinian doctrine of Predestination*, and illustrated by frequent extracts from that exhaustive work, was not designed for publication, but one Lecture dealing with the view of Perfectibility held by the great founder of Methodism is not open to this objection, and is therefore given here, introduced by a portion of the previous lecture on the Pelagian doctrine of Perfectibility as refuted by St. Augustine.]

. . . . . . . .

THE absolute power which the Pelagian set up of man to act without sin, and be morally perfect, was evidently a fiction, based on an abstract idea and not on the experienced faculty of free-will; and when he followed with his list of perfect men, he simply trifled, and showed how absurd, fantastic, and unsubstantial his position was. Human nature is too seriously alive to the law of sin under which it at present acts, not to feel the mockery of such assertions. Every one knows immediately that if these men were perfect, they were dolls and not men; they had not the passions, the impulses, the forces and wants of humanity; that action was in them a totally different thing from what it is in the mankind of experience, and was without the stimulus and motive which produces action in the real man. In all real men the same vigorous impulse which is essential to strong action, is also sure to go beyond the mark, and engender more or less of disorder. It is, practically speaking, impossible to help these excesses, greater or less, and disturbances which accompany action. Nobody does *exactly* what he ought, nothing more or less. Every one leaves the region of action with a sense of sin in his mind; he has gone further, or he has stopped short; he halted here, he was precipitate there. "It takes a great many particulars," says the author of the *Religio Medici*, "to make a good action." A good action is presented to our mind at first as much a unity as the number 1 in Arithmetic; but if we once examine it, it turns into a thousand things. In this intricate labyrinth of motions, who is not conscious of distinct faults? If a man says he is faultless, we do not know what he means; it is an unintelligible assertion; action is necessary for man, and all the modes we have experience of are connected with faults, slide into faults, and go out into what is a declination from the straight line.

If such an assertion of sinlessness, lying within the natural power of man, had any scope or tendency beyond the mere boast of it, it tended to a Socinian morality. People must suppose that if this perfect state were in the natural power of the will, it must be exemplified not with such absolute matchless rarity; that it is an instance of a power which exists in nature, and that when a power exists regularly in nature, it may be expected to come out in a certain number of cases; how many we cannot say beforehand, but in a sufficient number to answer to the expectation which we form when we know that the facts in question spring out of the operation of a natural principle; it is a human characteristic; everybody has the source of it within him. We might therefore not unreasonably expect that the quality of perfection would not be confined to Enoch and Melchisedek, and a few patriarchs; that it will have its instances in all generations; nay, and that these instances would not be wholly wanting in number. It is difficult to see upon what reason we can impose any rigid limit upon the number of examples of it. Thus it ought not to surprise or startle us if we met several perfect men in course of a morning's walk; if three or four sat opposite to us at a party, or we were between two sinless men in a railway carriage, or in a public room; it ought not to astonish us if there were several perfect men in the House of Commons, several on the London Exchange, several in the large Corporations. This, if we retain the old religious sense of the word perfection, would be a rather astonishing fact. But if we invent a new sense of perfection—if we make it mean a high state of public virtue, an exemplary discharge of a man's social relations, an eminent possession of the useful and philanthropical class of good qualities—then such perfection is not impossible as a largely prevailing characteristic, even though springing entirely from the force of the human will. The general tendency of the position of the Pelagians was to a secular and Socinian idea of perfection. If this moral condition was simply a natural growth, and came by the law of nature, as applying to the will, then a considerable quantity of persons of this condition was to be anticipated; but if a considerable quantity of perfect men were to be expected, then it must be perfection in this lower sense, and with a Socinian interpretation explaining it.

The theology of the early ages is not altogether free from that superficial view of the law of sin, which maintains that it can be shaken off in this life by remarkable saints, who can attain to a freedom altogether from sin. It was a conception of the law of sin which approaches to a childish one—thinking that this deep root of sin in which human nature was founded could ever be extracted out of it, leaving human nature behind it. Writers speak of perfect men as if sin could be drawn out of man without any radical revolution in his nature, leaving him just what he was before, sin only being taken away. But this removal is such an utter change in man, that one does not know how one can contemplate it, but in accompaniment with a totally different and new condition of his whole being.

Augustine's view was a great modification of this assertion, and expressed itself rather in suggesting possibilities, and proposing questions on the subject, than in any actual assertion. First he denied absolutely and *in toto* that any one of the human race has been or can be without sin from the first, all being born in sin; and that the only question is whether some have not attained to sinlessness in the course of their lives. Non legitur sine peccato esse nisi Filius Hominis.¹ Second, he denied that anybody had in fact attained to a sinless state in the course of his life, and as change from a sinful state. Si autem quaeratur utrum *sit*, magis credo Scripturæ dicenti, Ne intres in judicium, etc.² "If we collect," he says, "into one assembly all the saintly men and saintly women who have ever lived, would they not with one voice cry out, 'If we say we have no sin we deceive ourselves, and the truth is not in us'?"³ Having got this fact he then shuts up the question in this dilemma, in which he destroys and refutes altogether the supposition that they could make this confession humbly, but not truly. "These men do not make it a part of humility to speak falsehood. But either way they have sin. If they say this truly, they have sin, because they say they have sin, and the truth *is in* them. If they say this falsely, they have sin too, because the truth is *not in* them."⁴ He reserves, however, the liberty of excepting the Virgin Mary from this general assertion,— "De qua, propter honorem Domini, nullam prorsus, cum de peccatis agitur, haberi volo quaestionem."⁵ Thirdly, though he denied the fact, he admitted the possibility of attaining to a sinless state in this life, but this possibility is through the Divine grace or power, and through a miraculous exertion of that power. "Et ideo ejus perfectionem etiam in hac vita esse possibilem negare non possumus, quia omnia possibilia sunt Deo."⁶ He denied any example of perfection having existed, and yet he maintained the possibility of it: "Ecce quemadmodum sine exemplo est in hominibus perfecta justitia, et tamen impossibilis non est."⁷ "Fierit enim si tanta voluntas adhiberetur quanta sufficit tantæ rei."⁸ "Let them," he says again, "if they can, find any one living to whom God has not something to pardon. Truly they cannot; yet it is by no means to be said that in God there is not the power of so assisting the human will, that not only that portion which is of faith, but also that according to which we shall live in eternity, can be fulfilled in us."⁹ Fourthly, Augustine thinks that to assert

¹ *De Perfect. Just.* n. 29.
² *Pecc. Merit.* 2. 8.
³ *De Nat. et Grat.* n. 42.
⁴ *Ibid.*   ⁵ *Ibid.*
⁶ *De Spiritu et Litera*, n. 7.
⁷ *Ibid.* n. 67.
⁸ *Ibid.* n. 63.
⁹ *Ibid.* n. 66.

that there have been persons in this life who have attained to the sinless state though an error is a venial error, an error as to fact rather than to doctrine: " Quinetiam si nemo est aut fuit, aut erit, quod magis credo, tali puritate perfectus; et tamen esse aut fuisse aut fore defenditur et putatur, non multum erratur nec perniciose cum quadam quis *benevolentia fallitur*: si tamen qui [hoc] putat *seipsum talem* esse non putet, nisi revera et liquido talem se esse perspexerit [1]—an excellent piece of advice, but one which does not throw much light on the doctrinal question. Again, "whether there *has* been or *is* or *can* be," he says, "*in this world*, any one living so justly as to be wholly without sin, is a point which can be left a question among true and pious Christians. Yet any one is foolish who doubts that there *can* be *after this life.*" . . . [Nobody disputed this, and therefore the assertion is not to the purpose.] "But I do not wish," he adds, "to raise a dispute even about *this life*. For though I cannot understand in any other sense the text, 'No flesh shall be justified in thy sight' and others like it, still would that it could be shown that these texts could be otherwise understood." [2]

Both St. Augustine and Pelagius had abundant power in their respective theories to produce individual perfection in this life: the one an unlimited strength in the human will, the other an unlimited divine power or grace. But Pelagius in his assertion of human perfectibility was met by a fact which he could not oppose—the fact, namely, how very few there were to whom that attribute could with any show of probability be allowed. Thus common sense withdrew what theory maintained. Yet he stuck to his theory, and dealt with common sense as he could: he upheld his theory by the assertion of an unlimited will, and deferred to common sense by contenting himself with a small list of perfect men; whereas either his theory strictly implied and carried a much larger list of men, or the smallness of his list confuted his theory of an unlimited will. Augustine, again, was provided with ample means for insuring human perfection in this life, by the infinite Divine Power which had direct control of the human will, and which could bend it to good. But when he came to examine how this Divine power

[1] *De Spiritu et Lit.* n. 3.     [2] *De Nat. e Grat.* n. 70.

acted on fact, and what was its matter-of-fact relations to the human will, he saw that the Divine Being did not in fact use His power to produce this effect: and that though the power existed to produce any amount of perfection, as a matter of fact the perfection itself did not exist. He drew in then, as Pelagius did, only with much greater decision and more of principle. He admitted a strong and rooted impediment to perfection in human nature—an impediment which resided in the nature in its present state. He talked, indeed, of the possibility of it, and deferred to old language which had been used by Fathers before his time; but he denied the fact past, present, or to come; and so left the possibility of it a name rather than a reality. He even found a kind of reason for it, in the admirable effect of the sense of sin upon the character— that it created a humility which compensated for the source and occasion of it, and founded a character which was a sort of perfection based on imperfection.

## XII.—*MODERN DOCTRINE OF PERFECTIBILITY.*

THE subject of perfectibility in this life was discussed at some Conferences of the early Methodist Society in 1760, and subsequently; and we have contained in the Reports of them the opinions of John Wesley upon Christian Perfection, as a state and habit of mind capable of being, and actually being, arrived at in this life, by a certain proportion of Christians. It was indeed unanimously agreed that every one must have this spiritual perfection, that is to say, entire sanctification, at *the hour of death;* that it was necessary to be purified from all sin at the time of death, and that there was Scripture promise for this. But while this was held to be necessary, it was also maintained that a state of perfection was *possible* at any time of a person's life; and that that state might be entered upon instantaneously, if it pleased God to bestow the gift by an immediate act; but that it was more generally a gradual process. The way in which it is entered upon, when it is gradually attained, is described as follows. The first step is the sense of justification, "knowing they are justified freely through His blood they have peace with God through Jesus Christ. . . . In this peace they remain for days, weeks, or months, and commonly suppose they shall not know war any more, till some of their old enemies, their bosom sins . . . assault them again, and thrust sore at them, that they may fall. Then arises fear that they shall not endure to the end." Then the Lord comforts them. Then together with this comfort "for the first time do they see the ground of their heart, which God at first would not disclose unto them, lest the soul should fail before Him, and the spirit which He had made. Now they see all the hidden abominations there." Then there arises an "inexpressible hunger after a full renewal in His image, in righteousness and true holiness. Then God is mindful of the desire of them that fear Him, and gives them a single eye and a pure heart; He stamps upon them His own image and superscription, He createth them anew in Jesus Christ, . . . and bringeth them to the rest which remaineth for the people of God."[1] Such are the steps to a state of perfection. The state itself is thus described: "They are freed from self-will, as desiring nothing but the holy and perfect will of God; not supplies in want, not ease in pain, nor life, nor death, nor any creature, but continually crying in their inmost soul, Father, thy will be done. They are freed from evil thoughts so that they cannot enter into them, no not for a moment. Aforetime, when an evil thought came in, they looked up and it vanished away. But now it does not come in, there being no room for it in a soul which is full of God. They are free from wanderings in prayer. Whensoever they pour out their thoughts in a more immediate manner before God, they have no thought of anything past, or absent, or to come, but of God alone. In times past they had wandering thoughts which darted in, which yet fled away like smoke; but now that smoke does not rise at all. They have no fear or doubt as to their state in general, or as to any particular action. . . . They are in one sense freed from temptations, for though numberless temptations fly about, yet they trouble them not. At all times their souls are even and calm, their hearts are steadfast and immoveable."[2]

A state of perfection is thus a state of sinlessness—of deliverance from inward as well as from outward sin. Simply not to commit sin is the privilege of a babe in Christ, but to be without inward sin is a very high privilege.

But now is there any set-off of human infirmities and defects in these persons, which, though not sins—for they are by the supposition freed from sins—still interfere with the impression which this perfection makes upon others? There are: "They are not perfect in knowledge," says Wesley. They are not free from ignorance, no, nor from mistakes. We are no more to expect anything living to be infallible than to be omniscient. They are not free from infirmities, such as weakness or slow-

[1] Wesley's Works, vol. xi. p. 381, ed. 1829.     [2] *Ibid.* p. 379.

ness of understanding, irregular quickness or heaviness of imagination. Such are impropriety of language, ungracefulness of pronunciation, to which one might add a thousand *nameless* defects, " either in conversation or behaviour."

This list of extra-moral faults seems to have produced such a strong impression on the mind of Gibson, Bishop of London, that he would appear to have decided that such a list of exceptions to Perfection was enough to make it a very attainable condition. "He asked me," says Wesley, "what I meant by perfection. I told him without any disguise or reserve. When I ceased speaking he said, 'Mr. Wesley, if this be all you mean, publish it to all the world.'" It is possible that Bishop Gibson may have considered that this list of defects practically involved some that were great disturbances to the completeness of perfection; and that therefore Perfection might be allowed, with this list of irregularities to weight it, without conceding anything which a Christian need object to conceding. Still it may be doubted whether, when Wesley allowed this list of imperfections and defects, he meant to concede quite enough deduction from perfection to lower it into being an attainable state in the common judgment of Christians. A slow understanding, a heaviness of imagination, and an ungraceful pronunciation can hardly be called sins; and therefore if the admission is made that a man in a state of perfection may still possibly labour under these defects, no great admission is made. Bishop Gibson, however, might possibly think that an unlimited dispensation for making mistakes was a dangerous liberty to concede to the Perfect man, and that in practice such a licence did border upon what jarred with our ideas of perfection. For how much of conduct depends upon a man forming, to begin with, a sound judgment on the facts of the case? Thus a man in a state of perfection may blame another wrongly, and use strong language, upon the supposition of a mistake which he has unblamably made as to some action of the person censured, or as to his character generally. Still if these mistakes are often made, and if the privilege is used beyond a certain point, it must be seen that the impression that will be made on other peoples' minds will not be favourable to the belief in the man's perfection. The question of mistakes is more particularly discussed under the form of question and answer.

*Q.*—" What is Christian Perfection ?

*A.*—The loving God with all our heart, mind, soul, and strength. This implies that no wrong temper, none contrary to love, remains in the soul; and that all the thoughts, words, and actions are governed by pure love.

*Q.*—Do you affirm that this perfection excludes all infirmities, ignorance, and mistake ?

*A.*—I continually affirm quite the contrary, and always have done so.

*Q.*—But how can every thought, word, and work be governed by pure love, and the man be subject the same time to ignorance and mistake ?"

"*A.*—I see no contradiction here: a man may be filled with pure love, and still be liable to mistake. . . . I believe this to be a natural consequence of the soul's dwelling in flesh and blood. . . . We may carry this thought further. A mistake in judgment may possibly occasion a mistake in practice. For instance, Mr. De Renty's mistake touching the nature of mortification arising from prejudice of education. . . . Every one may make a mistake as long as he lives. Yet where every word and action springs from love, such a mistake is not properly a sin. *However it cannot bear the rigour of God's justice, but needs the atoning blood.* . . Every mistake is a transgression of the perfect law : therefore every mistake, were it not for the Blood of the Atonement, would expose to eternal damnation. . . . The most perfect . . . may they say for themselves —Forgive us our trespasses. . . . This easily accounts for what might seem otherwise unaccountable, namely, that those who are not offended when we speak of the highest degree of love, yet will not hear of living without sin. The reason is they *know* all men are liable to mistake. . . . But they do *not* know, or do not observe, that this is *not sin*, if love is the sole principle of action."[1]

This was the judgment of all the brethren who met at

[1] Wesley's Works, vol. xi. pp. 394, 395.

Bristol in 1758. The question whether man could be perfect or not in this life was thus reduced to the question whether mistakes are sins or not. All people made mistakes, but it was maintained that it was improper to call mistakes sins. "Mistakes," it was said, "and whatever infirmities necessarily flow from the corruptible state of the body, are no way contrary to love; nor, therefore, in the scriptural sense, are they sin. . . . They are deviations indeed from the perfect law, and consequently need an atonement; yet they are not properly sins. . . ."[1]

Nevertheless, though perfection admits of mistakes, and mistakes are not properly sins, still Wesley informs us that, in order to be quite safe, he never speaks of "sinless perfection." He goes a little further into the question: Mistakes are involuntary transgressions. Involuntary transgressions "need the atoning blood," but are improperly called sins. "I believe a person filled with the love of God is still liable to involuntary transgressions. Such transgressions you may call sins if you please: I do not, for the reasons above mentioned." And he concludes with a judgment in which he mediates between the two sides on this question. "Let those who do *not* call them sins, never think that themselves or any other persons are in such a state as that they can stand before infinite justice without a Mediator. Let those who *do* call them so, beware how they confound these defects with sins properly so called."[1] It is evident throughout these observations that Wesley is taking part with both sides, giving each encouragement to think that he belongs to it, and so retaining a hold upon both. With one side, he says, a man may be in such a state in this life as to have only involuntary transgressions; with the other side he says, he will still have transgressions which require the atoning blood of Christ: with one side he says, he will not have sins; with another side he says, he will have what may be called sins, though he does not admit quite properly; with one side he admits perfection; with the other he does not admit sinless perfection. It is plain, however, that a complicated state of the question like this, full of artificial and fine distinctions, and of balks to, and checks upon, both sides, is not one in

[1] *Ibid.* vol. xi. p. 396.

which a doctrine of perfection can properly be put forward. A doctrine of perfection ought to be a simple transparent doctrine, otherwise it is not worth having. It is not worth while calling a man a perfect man, only to be told immediately he commits innumerable transgressions which require the atoning blood of Christ to efface: perfection must disappoint if it cannot be taken in its obvious sense;—if though it does not admit of sins, it admits of what may be improperly called sins; if though it is perfection, still it is dangerous to call it sinless perfection: and he, Wesley, always cautiously avoids calling it so. This may be a very diplomatic and sagacious settlement of a controversy which has broken out in the Wesleyan body, threatening a disturbance, and requiring the calming and settling hand of a religious politician. But it is impossible that such a perfection as that which raises an endless discussion upon the nature of the transgressions it commits, —which, though not properly sins, are still "deviations from perfect law, and need an atonement,"—can satisfy the aspirations of those who want a real perfection; while it offends the scruples of others who deny boldly the possibility of a state of perfection in this life.

We see the distinction here between Augustine's judgment on the subject of Christian perfection in this life and Wesley's. Between Augustine's facts and Wesley's facts there is not so much difference. One would like, indeed, to know what authority Wesley has for saying that a man can arrive at a state of perfection in this life, in which he only makes mistakes. The great experience of human nature certainly is that there is a sort of positive evil in human nature, which works in the most perfected minds. Wesley may say this is involuntary working, and therefore is not itself *sin* properly so called; but I am not aware that the working is so involuntary after all, but that it implicates in some degree the responsibility of the person himself. Old faults continue in men, they may be good men, they may be saintly men, but we certainly see that natural frailties continue, and they continue with a certain identification of the man with them; and his errors are not all mere mistakes, but have something wrong about them. Yet on the whole one may say that Augustine's facts and Wesley's facts are much the same. But what a difference in the judgment which is formed upon them! Augustine, with a slight reserve occasioned by deference to former writers, says that what these facts amount to, is that human nature is under a law of sin, and cannot wholly get free from it. Wesley draws distinctions between perfection and sinless perfection, between transgressions which require the blood of Christ to atone for them, and sins. His judgment on the question is an obscure and perplexed one, and obviously tempered by diplomacy.

And there is this difference between Wesley's and Augustine's theory, namely, that Augustine regards the perfect state in this life, should it ever be realised, as a miracle, and contrary to all the ordinary laws of God's working; Wesley regards it as only in keeping with, and consistently carrying out the natural growth of Christian grace. It is the natural conclusion of the proofs of sanctification. In the Conference of 1745, it is asked when does inward sanctification begin? And the answer is, In the moment a man is justified. From that time a believer gradually dies to sin and grows in grace. Yet sin remains in him till he is sanctified throughout.

" *Q.*—Is this ordinarily given till a little before death?

*A.*—It is not to those who expect it no sooner.

*Q.*—But may we not expect it sooner?"[1]

Here the perfect state is made a necessity a little before death, and as naturally to belong to a Christian at that time, as ordinary sanctification does at any other time. The perfect state, instead of being a supernatural fact, as it figures as in Augustine's view, is the natural ascent of every Christian. But upon what scriptural evidence does this supposition rest that every Christian must be perfect before he dies? Why is it necessary that people should be perfect just before they die? What is the meaning or sense of a momentary perfection like this? Is it that they must be prepared for heaven? But that need not be here. This is a gratuitous and arbitrary idea, as if God could not supply in a future life what was wanting in this, and purify the soul so as to prepare it for heaven. It is

[1] Wesley's Works, vol. xi. p. 387.

not to be wondered at, that having made a perfect state necessary a little before death, it should have occurred to the Methodist that, after all, this was a very arbitrary time to have assigned to it; and that, if universal among Christians a little before death, perfection should be at any rate rather prevalent at a somewhat earlier date in life. So they think that "a believer ought to come daily nearer and nearer to perfection, that he ought to be continually pressing after it," until he actually reaches it, which of course he will do, if he is a Christian at all, some time before death, but which it is better he should do sooner. "Before you die," says Wesley, "will that content you? Nay, but ask that it may be done now, to-day, while it is called to-day. . . . Certainly to-day is His time, as well as to-morrow. Make haste, man, make haste!"[1] This is a coarse application of the Scripture precept to aim at perfection; as if because you aimed at, and did not leave off aiming at it, you must therefore be lodged in it some time while you are alive here; and had the right to say, There, now you are perfect; you have been aiming at it, and you have got it. Here is an argument which just shows the rough texture of the fabric of enthusiasm,—of what coarse earthenware it is composed. It cannot treat any subject except in a hard technical way, and its flights and extravagances are from its dry shallowness. The aim at perfection goes on and on; but to say you must get it at last, and make yourself believe you have got it, because God would not expect you to follow after it unless you could get it, is a sort of bargaining logic which is utterly out of place in such a mysterious matter. Yet when the Methodists come to deal with Perfection, they quite forget the utterly mystical state of being which it must be; that it must be a contradiction to all known states of mind; they deal with it as if they could map it out, examine it, and make a report upon it; they make it quite common; they append it to their system, and make it follow its rules; it is a gift of God which is received by faith, and which may be received "instantaneously in one moment; and that we are not to expect it at death only, but at every moment; that now is the accepted time, that now is the day of salvation."[2] Thus they sound the trumpet, pro-

[1] Wesley's Works, vol. xi. p. 403.     [2] *Ibid.* p. 393.

claiming the gift, and making anybody expect it in his own case. It is his right as a Christian. This is to vulgarise and degrade the very standard idea of perfection altogether, and convert it into a different thing from that which Scripture and moral sense pronounce of it.

But now for the tests of Perfection and of men being *in* the Perfect State. It appears to me that Wesley is very unfair upon the criticising public in the case of perfect men, that is, those who profess to have entered into the state of perfection. It seems to me that the public have a right to require a good deal from perfect men. Yet Wesley is always checking the public in its demands, and forcing his perfect men upon it; insisting on their swallowing them whole, blindly, and suppressing remorselessly any suspicions and recalcitrations which may be felt, after a certain number of tests have been fulfilled in the opinion of the persons themselves. Thus—

"*Q.*—When may a person judge himself to have attained this?

*A.*—When, after being fully convinced of inbred sin by a far deeper and clearer conviction than that he experienced before justification, and after having experienced a gradual *mortification* of it, he experiences a *total death* to sin, and an entire renewal in the love and image of God, so as to rejoice evermore, to pray without ceasing, and in everything to give thanks."[1] Yes, but how are we to believe that all this has taken place, and what are the outward signs by which we are to judge that it has? Wesley evades this question, and still refers us to the man's own testimony to himself. A man can only be deceived, he says, if he limits his attention to some of these points; if he attends to them all, he cannot be. "I know of no instance of a person attending to them all, and yet deceived in this matter," says Wesley, "and I believe there can be none in this world."[2]

Wesley is indeed wonderfully content with assertions on the part of those who profess to be perfect. "I rejoice that this soul is happy in Christ. I rejoice that he feels no unholy temper, but the pure love of God continually."

"*Q.*—Is there no danger, then, in a man being thus deceived?

[1] Wesley's Works, vol. xi. p. 401.     [2] *Ibid.* p. 402.

*A.*—Not at the time he *feels* no sin; so long as he *feels* nothing but love animating all his thoughts, words, and actions, he is in no danger."[1]

But this after all only relates to the *man's own* satisfaction as to the fact. What is to satisfy other people? I see no answer given to this question; no test given by which other people are to be assured that certain persons are in a state of perfection.

"*Q.*—How should we treat those who think they have attained?

*A.*—Examine them candidly, and exhort them to pray fervently that God would show them all that is in their hearts . . . with the most earnest exhortations to abound in every grace, which are given in the New Testament to those who are in the highest state of grace."[2]

Others, then, are not *obliged* to believe those who tell them that they are in a state of perfection: for an "examination" of them certainly implies a right to doubt their assertion. Wesley indeed admits that whether a man is free from sin and perfect cannot be certainly known to another.

"*Q.*—How may we certainly know one that is saved from all sin?

*A.*—We cannot infallibly know one that is thus saved, unless it should please God to endow us with miraculous discernment of spirits."[3]

Still Wesley protects the professors of perfection with great care against positive doubt, and critical remarks upon them.

"*Q.*—But what does the perfect man do more than others?

*A.*—Perhaps nothing; so may the Providence of God have hedged him in by outward circumstances: perhaps not so much, though he longs to spend and be spent for God . . .

*Q.*—But is not this proof against him—I feel no power either in his words or prayer?

*A.*—It is not; for perhaps that is your own fault."[4]

Certainly it is possible it may be. And yet why is a man to be allowed not only to believe himself to be perfect, which nobody can prevent him doing, but to tell others that he is perfect, and divulge his belief to the world, unless he can show some signs and manifestations of so high a state? A man says

[1] Wesley's Works, vol. xi. p. 405. [2] *Ibid.* p. 403. [3] *Ibid.* p. 398. [4] *Ibid.* p. 400.

he is perfect: another man says—"but he does not come up to my idea of a perfect Christian." Well, and that is a very natural observation for any one to make to whose idea of a perfect Christian he does not come up. How does Wesley meet it? "He does not perhaps come up to your idea; and perhaps no one ever did or ever will . . . *Scripture perfection is pure love*, filling the heart . . . If your idea includes anything more than this, it is not scriptural."[1] But the critic may say, My idea *is* no more than this, and still I am not satisfied with him; he does not come up to my idea of a man whose heart is filled by pure love. Wesley, however, has nothing more than a caution, which is half a rebuke, for the critic. He supposes him to be animated by jealousy in his examination of the case. He says—"Suppose he is weighed in the balance and found wanting, is this a matter of joy?[2] Ought we not rather to grieve, or be deeply concerned, to let our eyes run down with tears?" And though he says we cannot infallibly know that a man is perfect, still, he adds, "we apprehend those (meaning that list of tests to which we have referred) would be sufficient proofs to any reasonable man, and such as would leave little room to doubt." (1.) Exemplary conduct for a certain time. (2.) If he could give a distinct account of the time and manner wherein the change was wrought. (3.) If his subsequent works and actions were holy and unblameable.[3]

Upon this general treatment of criticism on the claims of this professor of perfection, it is enough to say, there is no necessity why those men should divulge the secret of their sinless state; it may remain a secret between God and themselves; if then they make it public, if they tell others about it, they must expect that their claims to this high and privileged state should be fully examined. And therefore a strong opinion seems to have been expressed by some of the less enthusiastic members of the Methodist body, that these persons should keep their high and gifted condition to themselves, and not divulge it.

"*Q.*—But would it not be better to be entirely silent, not to speak of it at all?"

Wesley, however, discarded immediately and would not hear of this yoke of silence. It was quite true that perfect men them-

[1] Wesley's Works, vol. xi. p. 401.    [2] *Ibid.* p. 405.    [3] *Ibid.* p. 398.

selves might suffer from the disclosure of their own high and singularly privileged state to the world; they might shrink from the publication of it; but then the glory of God must be thought of. They must sacrifice themselves for the Divine honour, which would be advanced so largely, and gain so conspicuous an accession to itself, as soon as the exalted endowments of these men were known. The question is asked, Would you advise him, one of this elevated class, to *speak of it*, and the answer is—He could hardly refrain: his desire to declare the loving-kindness of the Lord would carry him away like a torrent. But afterwards he might shrink; and then it would be advisable not to speak of it to them who know not God, nor to others *without some particular reason*. But if he had particular reason then he must speak of it.

"*A.*—By silence, he might indeed avoid many crosses which will ensue necessarily, if he simply declares even among believers what God has wrought in his soul. If, therefore, such a one were to confer with flesh and blood, he would be entirely silent. But this could not be done with a clear conscience, for undoubtedly he ought to speak. Men do not light a candle to put it under a bushel; much less does the all-wise God. He does not raise such a monument of His power and love to hide it from all mankind . . . His will is 'that many shall see it' and rejoice, 'and shall put their trust in the Lord.'" . . .

"*Q.*—But is there no way to prevent those crosses, which usually fall on those who speak of being thus saved from sin?

*A.*—It seems it cannot be prevented altogether while so much of nature remains even in believers."

Wesley then would not hear of a yoke of silence being imposed upon this privileged class. They spoke then, and when they spoke, one naturally expects to hear that the believing public shall have the right, the full right allowed them of judging their pretensions to the unique grace which they profess to possess. But no, says Wesley practically: you must believe such a person; he says he has it; he conducts himself piously; his behaviour is exemplary; it is not likely he should lie for God, but speak as he felt; I have abundant reason to believe this person will not lie; he testifies before me, I feel no sin, but all love; . . . now, if I have nothing to oppose to this plain testimony, I ought in reason to believe it."[1] That is the way in which Wesley settles the question. But this virtually gives any man whatever the right of declaring himself a perfect man, and throwing the *onus probandi* that he is not perfect upon others. They must prove some definite sin against him. But they have a right to say: No; he has laid claim to a unique character, and he must show it by a unique manifestation. I have a right to require that *he* should prove it by impressing me in a unique way, not that I should be bound to disprove it by a special proof to the contrary. If he does not bring this perfection home to me, I shall go on disbelieving it. Of course a disbeliever in perfection altogether could use a much more summary argument, but I assume here a member of the Methodist body who believes in the possibility of perfection. Wesley puts the society at the mercy of individual professions. A man objects: This man does not *pray* like a perfect man, he does not come up to my *idea* of a perfect man. That is all nonsense, says Wesley. "It is your hardness of soul," perhaps, that prevents your appreciating his prayer; and as for your *idea* of a perfect man, it is derived from all quarters in the world but Scripture. The objector is prevented then from all power of disproving the man's perfection, provided he only abstains from open sins, and behaves with general fervour. The gift is vulgarised and degraded by the low standard of proof which is required for it. Wesley throws this whole class of pretenders, in short, upon the society, to make what of them they can; not compelling them indeed to believe them, but insisting upon the most favourable construction of their claims. They were doubtless a class to whom it was worth while accommodating things; men of enthusiasm and power, who, if their claims had been treated in a summary way, might have taken themselves off elsewhere, and deprived the Methodist body of so much strength. It was necessary, therefore, to please them to a certain extent. Wesley put down in his community all "prejudice," as he calls it, against them, and provides them with an indulgent form of proof, acting in favour of their pretensions; his principle being that if the man is deceived in

[1] Wesley's Works, vol. xi. p. 398.

his estimate of himself no harm is done, if the mistake is made through fervour.

"But he is deceived. What then? It is a harmless mistake while he feels nothing but love in his heart. It is a mistake which generally argues great grace, a high degree of holiness and happiness. This should be a matter of real joy to all that are simple of heart; not the mistake itself, but *the height of grace which for the time occasions it.*"[1]

This is a somewhat different estimate of the mistake of a man thinking himself without sin from that which the Apostle formed. Wesley says: "It is the height of grace which for the time occasions it." The Apostle says: "If we say we have no sin, we deceive ourselves, and the truth is not in us."

But there is another point in this treatment of Perfection, which vulgarises and empties the gift of reality.

"*Q.*—Can they fall from a state of perfection?

*A.*—I am well assured they can; matter of fact puts this beyond dispute. Formerly we thought one saved from sin could not fall; now we know the contrary. We are surrounded by instances of those who lately experienced all that I mean by perfection; they had both the fruit of the Spirit and the witness, but now they have lost both. . . . There is no such height or strength of holiness as it is impossible to fall from."[2]

Thus the state of perfection is one which, it appears, it is quite common to fall from. But what *is* the state of perfection when it is thus fallen from; when a person has it this week, and loses it next? Is it not of the first elements of morality that if a man turns out bad, he must have the seeds of that badness in him now; that he cannot be absolutely perfect now and start from a fresh root to-morrow. There must be a line of continuity in the human character. It cannot be thus broken up. It is part of the technicality of Wesley's mind that he can regard man as split into so many pieces—perfect to-day, and withered to-morrow. It is a travesty of perfection —supposing it is nothing but a feeling for the moment, or set of formalities performed, and stopping when these are over. Christian perfection cannot be made an alternative of good conduct with bad.

[1] Wesley's Works, vol. xi. p. 405.  [2] *Ibid.* p. 426.

## XIII.—*THE ATHANASIAN CREED.*

So much attention has been drawn lately to the subject of the Athanasian Creed, that it is not unsuitable to give it a place in the course of these Lectures;[1] to notice the objections that are made to some statements in it, and to explain the relations in which the Creed stands to Scripture, as well as to other parts of our formularies.

And the first thing we observe in the Creed is the important point that men are condemned in it on account of their belief. We need not just at present examine the exact nature of that belief, but only attend to the general fact that a right belief is assumed in this Creed to be a matter for which men are responsible, and that men are exposed to Divine punishment and condemnation for the want of it. Before we go into particulars of faith, this is the first and preliminary law which is assumed in what are called the Damnatory Clauses; but to this principle, that men can incur Divine punishment for their religious belief, great objection is made. How then does Scripture stand with respect to this general principle of punishableness for belief?

In examining Scripture, then, we can hardly fail to see that not only does Scripture make express statements that men will be condemned for their belief, but that the principle of men being divinely punishable for their belief penetrates the whole of the Bible from first to last, and is assumed in the whole teaching of the Bible. It is evident, in the first place, that this principle is at the bottom of the whole of the old Dispensation. The old dispensation is founded upon the assumption that a belief in the unity of the Divine nature was necessary for enjoying

[1] Those delivered in the Latin Chapel.

the Divine favour. A man was punished with death for idolatry. The civil penalty was indeed a part of the Jewish law which was not intended for permanence; but the Divine condemnation of the idolater, of which this was the temporary expression, is a permanent and fundamental truth of Scripture. But idolatry is an offence upon a point of faith, rather than of morals. The worship of God and the worship of Him as a Spirit and not embodied in any material object or form, is an article connected with the nature of the Deity; and the nature of the Deity falls under the head of matter of faith.

The whole of the Old Testament dispensation, then, was founded upon the principle that men are responsible for their belief, and that false religious belief subjected them to Divine punishment. Now it may be said, that when we come to the New Testament we shall find all this altered, and this principle given up as an obsolete part of the old Law. But is it so? As the belief in the Unity of God had been imposed at the cost of Divine wrath in the Old Testament, so in the New the belief in Jesus Christ as the Son of God was imposed at the same cost. We have thus express damnatory language: "He that rejecteth me, and receiveth not my words, hath one that judgeth him."[1] "He that believeth not is condemned already, because he hath not believed in the name of the only begotten Son of God."[2] St. Paul adopts from the old dispensation the form of the Anathema—"Though we, or an angel from heaven, preach any other gospel to you than that we have preached unto you, let him be accursed."[3] "If any man love not the Lord Jesus Christ, let him be Anathema: Maran-atha."[4] What St. Paul demands is not love in general, the moral affection, but the love of Christ, which requires to begin with the article of belief to have been received that He *is* Christ; and thus in the latter text as well as in the former, faith is guarded by an Anathema. But indeed that faith is necessary for salvation is so completely the basis of the New Testament that if we take away this principle the whole fabric of the Gospel falls to the ground; and the whole language of the New

---

[1] John xii. 48.  [2] John iii. 18.
[3] Gal. i. 8.  [4] 1 Cor. xvi. 22.

Testament becomes an unintelligible riddle. "Believe on the Lord Jesus Christ and thou shalt be saved;"[1]—this was the necessary condition of salvation and of entering into the kingdom of heaven. The whole of St. Paul's Epistles would be unmeaning, if he did not mean to assert and to teach in them that faith in Jesus Christ was necessary for our justification, without which justification we still remain under condemnation.

So far, then, as regards the objection to the Athanasian Creed of condemning men for their belief, here is a clear and distinct answer for those who acknowledge Scripture. It is plain that Scripture makes a particular religious belief necessary for salvation. An unbeliever would indeed deal shortly and summarily with this language of Scripture, and would treat it as an antiquated part of religious language, which had ceased with growing philosophy and civilisation: but we who accept Scripture cannot treat this language as obsolete, while at the same time we must see the fact of the language. We must see that Revelation not only declares its truth to the world, but imposes that truth upon the world; that it not only communicates itself, but asserts itself; that it claims as of absolute right the belief of mankind, and makes that belief the condition of salvation. The strongest damnatory language is applied to those who do not believe—that they "shall be judged at the last day;" that they are "condemned already;" and that "he that believeth not shall be damned;"[2] that they who preach any other Gospel are accursed. Our Church then could not possibly admit any objection to the Athanasian Creed, founded upon the principle that it made a particular faith, as distinct from mere morals, indispensable for salvation, without coming into collision with the plainest and most direct statements of Scripture, the constant assumptions of Scripture, and the foundation of the whole doctrine and scheme of Scripture.

The condemnatory language of the Athanasian Creed is regarded indeed by many as isolated language which can be

---

[1] Acts xvi. 31.
[2] Mark xvi. 16 ["he that disbelieveth shall be condemned." Revised Version, 1881].

cut whole out of the Creed without entailing any consequences, and leaving all the surrounding ground untouched. But though doubtless the introduction of these clauses into the Creed was not in the first instance necessary, and the Apostles' and Nicene Creeds are without them; when they are once in the Creed, to turn them out on the ground that such statements are wrong, and ought not to be made, is to entangle ourselves in consequences, and to expose ourselves to encounter difficulties upon surrounding ground, which will begin to open out upon us as soon as ever the obnoxious matter has been removed from the Creed. These condemnatory statements have indeed their root deeper than in the Athanasian Creed; and when we come to extract them, we shall find that the process of extrication will involve more unsettlement and tearing up than we anticipated. For in truth these condemnatory statements are substantially in Scripture: that is, we have in Scripture plain universal condemnations which cannot be separated in principle from these condemnations;—general judicial sentences which involve the same difficulties, moral and speculative, which these do. We shall not find it easy then to do what we want without doing more than we want; to accomplish the extraction from the Creed without touching the doctrine of Scripture too.

If an objection is to be maintained and made good against the damnatory clauses, it must be, not upon the ground of their adopting belief as the necessary condition of salvation, but upon the ground of the particular belief which they adopt as that condition. It must be said: Scripture undoubtedly asserts the condemnation of those who disbelieve the doctrine of Scripture; but this is *not* the doctrine of Scripture, as Scripture communicates it to us, and as Scripture states and expresses it; this is a human exposition of the doctrine of revelation, adopted indeed by the Church, and applied for the purpose of explanation and instruction, but it is *not* the original and genuine doctrine of Scripture itself.

Undoubtedly, then, nothing less than a real difference between the two doctrines, that of Scripture, and that of the Creed, would justify the distinction between the respective disbelief in the two doctrines; would justify the contrast that the doctrine of Scripture must be believed at the cost of Divine condemnation, but the doctrine of the Creed need not be. But when we come to investigate this question, and ascertain whether the doctrine of the Athanasian Creed is the same with or different from that of Scripture, we immediately find that point decided by one of our Articles, which says of the Athanasian Creed, that "its doctrine may be proved by most certain warrant of Holy Scripture." What then is the state of the case? Scripture says that belief in the doctrine of Scripture is necessary to salvation; the Article says, this *is* the doctrine of Scripture :—Scripture condemns for rejecting the faith; the Article says, this *is* the faith;—Scripture is answerable for the judicial principle, the Article for its subject-matter, and the case to which it applies. Those who hold Scripture, then, and do not hold the Article, are not prohibited from saying that the Bible condemns for rejecting the faith, but that this is *not* the faith. But it is not so easy to see how we, who admit both the Article and Scripture, can take that course; how we can say that Scripture is right in asserting the necessity of holding the doctrine of Scripture, the Article right in saying this is the doctrine of Scripture; and the Creed wrong in asserting the necessity of holding it.

A great deal indeed is thrown upon the distinction, which was just noticed, that the Creed is an exposition of the doctrine of Revelation, adopted and sanctioned by the Church, but not that doctrine itself. The doctrine of the Trinity in Unity does indeed, it is said, lie at the bottom of the Christian dispensation, but this is not only the doctrine of the Trinity in Unity, but it is that doctrine with something else added to it, other terms and other language and phraseology.

But when we make a distinction between a *doctrine* and the *exposition* of a doctrine, it must be remembered that an exposition is not at all necessarily, not identical with the doctrine, because it is an exposition of it. It would be extraordinary if this were so. It is, indeed, quite possible that an exposition may diverge in substance and meaning from the doctrine which it professes to expound; that it *may* introduce foreign matter, and that it may misinterpret a doctrine instead of representing it faithfully. But, on the other hand, there is no reason whatever why an exposition may not be the same identical set of assertions with the doctrine, so that it would be impossible to establish any difference of truth or meaning between the two. It is assumed that as soon as ever there is a *succession* of statements there must be alien matter. But this is a very erroneous and irrelevant test of alien matter. The criterion of an exposition adhering to revealed doctrine or departing from it is not a test of length, but of meaning; one statement may diverge from the doctrine and ten may keep to it, one sentence may introduce foreign matter and human conjecture, and ten may never give up their pure hold of the original truth.

When then we take the doctrine, as ordinarily received and stated, of the Trinity, on the one side, and the exposition in the Creed on the other, we certainly find in every successive statement of the latter what looks like a very complete identity of the two, the exposition and the doctrine. Let us take the doctrine as expressed in our first Article: that "there is but one living and true God," and that "in the unity of this Godhead there be three Persons, of one substance, power, and eternity; the Father, the Son, and the Holy Ghost." The doctrine then is, that these Three are Three Persons, each of whom is God, and there is only one God. What does the exposition then say? 1. We must not confound the Persons, or divide the one substance of the Godhead. Is this an addition to the doctrine? No, it is exactly the same with it; for if the Persons are confounded they cease to be Three, and if the Substance is divided it ceases to be One. Again, "the glory is equal, the majesty co-eternal." Is *that* an addition? Or is it possible that one Godhead can either be unequal to itself, or not co-eternal with itself? Again, "Such as the Father is, such is the Son, and such is the Holy Ghost." This is the doctrine simply, and nothing more; for this must be so, if each is God. Again, "In this Trinity none is afore or after other, none is greater or less than another." This, too, is the doctrine simply, and no addition to it; for if each is God, how can God be greater or less than God, prior or posterior to God?

There has been a supposition then that the Athanasian Confession is metaphysical; and this supposition has so completely occupied the very entrance of the subject that it has been regarded as the simplest fact; and no aspect but that of a chain of metaphysics has been allowed for this Creed. But though there are doubtless metaphysics in this Creed, in the sense in which there must be metaphysics in everything which has to do with the Divine nature, in the sense in which there are metaphysics in those parts of Scripture which relate to the Divine Being, His incomprehensible attributes and mode of existence; in no other sense do there appear to be metaphysics in this Creed. The Creed is metaphysical in the sense in which the doctrine of the Trinity itself is metaphysical; but the doctrine of the Trinity once assumed, there is nothing added to it, and the exposition adheres as closely as words can do to the original truth, only carrying it through different forms of language. If Father, Son, and Holy Ghost are each God, it can be no addition to say that each is uncreated, that each is incomprehensible, that each is eternal, that each is Almighty, that each is Lord, that the Three are equal in majesty and glory, that such as the One is, such is the Other. And again, if these Three Persons are one God, it can be no addition to say that there is but one uncreate, one eternal, one incomprehensible, one Almighty, one Lord. Any one sentence in this whole succession involves every other. I cannot conceive a mind so constituted as to believe really that there are Three Persons, but that they ought to be confounded; and One Substance, but that it ought to be divided. I cannot conceive such a type of reasoning power as would admit that the Son was God, and the Holy Ghost God, and yet not allow them the attributes of God. If a person, then, disbelieves the doctrine of the Trinity, he has the best of all reasons for disbelieving the Athanasian Creed; but if he believes it, then I do not see what else he has to believe in the Athanasian Creed but this. After lengthening by reduplication, and unfolding by equivalent terms, after affirming the positives of the truth, and denying the negatives, the Creed shuts up into one assertion, namely, that of the Trinity in Unity.

What purpose, indeed, would it have answered to have clothed and clogged an article of faith with philosophy? None at all; on the contrary, philosophy would have been a great deal in the way. It is plain, what is wanted in this Creed is to fix the orthodox doctrine of the Trinity upon men's minds, keeping them as close as possible to it from first to last; sustaining and prolonging the one great doctrinal assertion by forms of statement; heightening the dignity and solemnity of it, but not interfering with, but only exhibiting, the original truth. But this would have been *prevented* by the introduction of metaphysics. It would have just disturbed the single scope, the uniform impress, the determinate march of the Creed. Thus it was the very interest of the Creed, if I may say so, to avoid metaphysics. Speculation was foreign to its aim. The orthodox doctrine of the Trinity assumed, every clause in the exposition must simply coincide with it, purely echo it. *That* was the object; and if that was the object, it is the Creed's best guarantee that that one doctrine was all that was expressed and contained in it. I do not know that it would make any difference in this respect, even had the Creed been composed, as a hostile writer has suggested, for a warning against the Visigoths. For whomsoever it was composed, it was composed for persons who wanted their ears to ring with the doctrine of the Trinity, and did not much care to hear anything that would clash with the singleness of that appeal. It would be to the last degree improbable that the Franks would have understood one word of a scholastic argument; it was highly advisable therefore that any one who wanted to influence their religion should abstain from metaphysics, and adhere as closely as possible to a doctrine.

On one point, indeed, namely, that of the Procession question, the Creed gives the relations within the Trinity in the sense of the Western, and not in that of the Eastern Church. But the whole form of the Creed shows that what it insists on, and what it guards by damnatory language, is the main doctrine of the Trinity, and not any subordinate controverted distinction.

The step which was lately demanded from the Church is, in substance, a judicial step; it is a judgment upon, and against, the damnatory clauses, in effect declaring them to be illegitimate and wrong. I know that the act is not in form judicial; the Church is only asked to withdraw them, and not to *say* anything. She is only asked to divest the Creed of statements which it might without error have been made without. There was no necessity that the damnatory clauses should have been attached to the Creed in the first instance, no Church rule made it obligatory, and the Apostles' and Nicene Creeds are without them. But though no act would be done in form judicial, it must be seen that when these clauses are in the Creed, and have been in ever since it was made; to remove them now could be no other than a condemnatory act on the part of the Church. Had the Creed been made without these clauses, that would have been no judgment at all on the part of the Church upon the condemnatory clauses themselves; it would only have been to say that there was no necessity to introduce them in that particular place; the Nicene Creed being without them was no reflection upon them, because the Council proclaimed them in another place. But the place in the Creed once given, and held for ages, cannot be taken away without a judicial act on the part of the Church upon and against the clauses themselves.

And though in some days such an act as this might be performed by a Church without having its strict intrepretation pressed home to the actors, and without having any strong consequences drawn out of it, such could not be expected to be the case now. The American Church a century ago shelved the Athanasian Creed, but it was at a time when people did not go very accurately into the meaning of what they did, and only aimed at a certain convenience in excluding anything which had an explanation wanted for it. It would be impossible now to do the same act in the same easy and negative spirit in which it was done in America at the end of the last century. When two stormy currents, of religious belief on the one hand, and unbelief on the other, have set in, each side at once sees such an act illuminated by the powerful rays of an intellectual focus. The undogmatic school will interpret the Church as giving up doctrine, when she no longer dare annex a condemnation to the rejection of doctrine; and this school will prize the result. The dogmatic school will see the act in the same light, and will reprobate the result.

The act, then, which was lately required from the Church, being a judicial act, condemning the damnatory clauses as wrong and mistaken, the first question is, Can the Church do this consistently? It must be seen that the Church cannot entertain a proposition like this without at the same time having regard to the whole existing fabric of her belief. Our Church has a constitution, formularies, and a declared body of religious doctrine. A Church cannot act in an insulated way, but must consider what she is asked to do with a reference to what is her own basis of teaching, and structure of faith.

Upon what ground, then, could our Church take her stand, in condemning the damnatory clauses of this Creed? We have seen that it could not be upon the ground that Scripture did not condemn for a wrong belief, and that it could not be upon the ground that the doctrine of the Creed was not that of Scripture. She herself declares that it "may be proved by most certain warrants of Holy Scripture;" and when we take the doctrine of the Trinity laid down in the first Article, and compare it with the Creed, we find that the Creed is *nothing but* that doctrine carried through a series of identical forms of statement.

Although our Church, then, could indeed, by a special insulated act, condemn as erroneous these clauses, what she cannot do is take the step consistently, and in agreement with her own premisses, with her own express body of teaching, with her own declared fabric of doctrine; with her articles and formularies of faith. It would be a single inconsistent act on her part.

But we are not confined to the *Articles* for the place which our Church gives to the doctrine of the Trinity. It is in the Prayer-book more than in the Articles. The three Persons in the Trinity stand forth in our Prayer-book as the Objects of every Christian's faith; to Whom we are placed in the most intimate relations, as Creator, Redeemer, and Sanctifier. We know no God in the Prayer-book but that God who is Three in One. We pray to the three Persons; we address them; we speak to them; we petition them; we ask them for mercy, we adore them, and we give glory to them.

Our Prayer-book, then, takes as its very foundation the revelation of the Three Hypostases in the Deity; it requires that revelation to justify it. The whole Catholic Church of Christ requires that revelation in order to acquit the acts of the Church, and the acts which she makes every individual member of the Church do. Unless the doctrine of the Trinity is part of the true Christian Revelation, and unless we have that guarantee that the three Persons whom we address in our Prayer-book, and in all Prayer-books, are real existences, what right has the Church to make us address them? It is evident, then, that the Trinity in the Godhead is assumed by the Church as an original revelation to mankind; and the Church from the first, in putting her children into relation to these mysterious Divine Persons, directing their thoughts and affections towards them, and teaching men to apply to them for the supply of their spiritual needs, has done so upon the ground of the existence of these Divine Persons having been revealed, and of the certainty and strength of this revelation. The invisible presence of the Three in One has thus penetrated every corner of the Christian life, and the religious feeling has flowed forth in hymns, supplications, and praises. "The essence of natural Religion," says Bishop Butler, "may be said to consist in religious regards to *God the Father Almighty:* and the essence of revealed Religion, as distinguished from natural, to consist in religious regards to *the Son* and to *the Holy Ghost.* And the obligation we are under of paying these religious regards to each of these Divine Persons respectively arises from the respective relations which they stand in to us. . . . The Son and Spirit have each his proper office in that great dispensation of Providence, the Redemption of the world; the one our Mediator, the other our Sanctifier." . . . And "religious regards . . . are thus obviously due to the Son and Holy Spirit, as arising, not merely from command in Scripture, but from the very nature of the revealed relations which they stand in to us, . . . the relations they stand in to us being matter of pure revelation."[1]

The doctrine of the Trinity, then, constituting, as it does, not only one of the Articles of our Church, but the very foundation of the Prayer-book, and of the devotional life of her children; and the doctrine being thus plainly and absolutely treated by her as a genuine and true part of the Christian revelation;—if condemnatory sanctions are to apply to any Christian doctrine or truth at all, they must apply to *this* doctrine. And how can she withdraw them, therefore, with due regard to her own consistency and the unity of her own teaching? She has a certain constitution and fabric of belief, with which this act of censure is plainly incompatible; and Scripture being answerable for the condemnation of wilful rejection of revealed truth, and the Church confessing that this *is* revealed truth, it is difficult to see how she could harmonise the withdrawal of these clauses with her own constitution and fabric of faith.

It is, indeed, an acknowledged principle in the interpretation of the damnatory language of *Scripture* regarding unbelief, that it is to be understood *with conditions;* and the same rule of interpretation applies to the damnatory clauses of the Athanasian Creed. The omission of conditions is one of those expedients of which language has frequently availed itself for the sake of convenience,—making absolute statements when that which qualifies them is left to be understood. But this is so common, so coeval with language, and so much a part of it, that when it is said that to take language with this understanding is a *non-natural* interpretation of language, we cannot but consider that such an assertion is made in forgetfulness of the whole growth, and of the plainest facts, of language. We justly call it a non-natural explanation when the plain and known meaning of a word is contradicted, and it is explained to mean something else; but simply to supply a condition to a statement, which is understood in it, cannot be called a non-natural interpretation of that statement; rather the contrary would be the non-natural interpretation; rigidly to insist upon

[1] Butler's *Analogy*, Part II. chap. i.

interpreting a statement according to its pure grammar, when the usage of language admits an understanding in the interpretation of it. It is *this* which is to interpret the statement non-naturally. It is non-natural because it is not a carrying out of the *intention* of language, but a thwarting of that intention. Take, for instance, one of those pieces of instruction which we meet with in Scripture—" Give to him that asketh thee." Here is an instance in which the grammar covers any case whatever, and of what kind soever, and whensoever, and wheresoever, of asking: the naked construction logically contains and includes the universal area of begging. Do we then interpret this precept non-naturally when we take it as understanding conditions, and not as applying indiscriminately to all cases whatever of asking? It appears to me that we should interpret it very non-naturally if we did *not* take it as understanding conditions. *That* would be the artificial, the strained, the violent interpretation—the interpretation that went against the natural meaning of the language, considered in connection with the known and familiar practice of language. So of the precept, " Resist not evil." It is obvious that the precept only means to inculcate in a forcible way, generally, the duty of resignation; that the universal form in which it is put is made necessary by the exigencies of the case, because a short and pithy precept was essential to the purpose of instruction; and that the hearer was intended to carry away from the universal precept—" Resist not evil," the main lesson, and to supply of his own common sense the necessary exceptions. It is the Quaker's interpretation of " Resist not evil" that is the non-natural interpretation : upon principles of common sense nobody *could* so understand the command; it is the strained exposition of a sect. Language cannot be held in such a vice. And just as *moral instruction* requires its liberty of speech, and has modes of statement which must not be tied to the letter, so has *judicial and condemnatory* language. The Athanasian Creed uses a universal formula of condemnation. But to take this formula as excluding all conditions in the application of it is to commit exactly the same mistake in the interpretation of it that we should commit in insisting on the literal interpretation of "Swear not at all," or "Pray without ceasing," or any other summary dictum of instruction. The formula is not intended for this strain upon it, and such strain would be in real truth a most non-natural interpretation of it. It is meant to express the truth that eternal punishment is the sentence upon all who reject the true faith, being really *responsible* for this rejection, and having nothing to excuse them in the circumstances of their education and situation, and the influences to which they have been exposed. But to suppose that because the statement is made in a universal form, therefore it is intended to apply to all heretics without discrimination,—to those who have been educated in heresy, and who only hold the creed in which they have been brought up; to those even who have never heard of any other faith;—this is so monstrous an assertion, that we ought not to suppose that the whole Church could have made it, unless there were overwhelming evidence that she accepted this statement in that sense. But the only evidence offered is the universal form of the statement itself. This is no evidence at all, because it is certain that universal statements, intended to be modified and understood with conditions, are incorporated in language, are a part of language, and are coeval with the very structure of language. Were there indeed no controversy stirring, ninety-nine out of a hundred *would* interpret it so as a matter of course; and they would think it an *un*natural interpretation of it to insist upon tying the statement to the rigid letter. They would be right in thinking so. There is no greater non-natural interpretation than the forced and rigid avoidance of qualified interpretation. On the other hand, we cannot call that a forced and strained explanation which we are giving constantly to language, and giving with general consent. This qualification of sense is a treatment of language which we are applying to it almost every hour of our lives. Why, then, should it be non-natural when it is applied to the Athanasian Creed?

The damnatory language of the *New Testament* is put into this universal form; but the universal damnatory assertions of the New Testament have always been understood with tacit conditions; nor has this ever been regarded as a non-natural interpretation of them, but, on the contrary, this interpretation has always been given to them as a matter of course. Our Lord says: "He that rejecteth me, and receiveth not my words, hath one that judgeth him: the word that I have spoken, the same shall judge him in the last day."[1] This is a damnatory assertion applying in terms to all who reject our Lord; but has this assertion been ever taken in a sense of literal universality? It never has been. It has never been supposed, even, that all the Jews in Jerusalem who lived in our Lord's own day and actually heard, or knew of, His preaching, but did not in fact accept it, will be eternally punished. This and other like assertions have been always understood with a condition that such rejection of Christ as is spoken of, is from causes for which the individual himself is morally responsible, and not from any irresistible influence of education and circumstances. Thus our Lord says again: "If ye believe not that I am He, ye shall die in your sins."[2] This also is a universal damnatory assertion, reprobating *all* who did not believe in Him. But this has also been always understood in the same qualified sense. And so to Nicodemus our Lord's announcement is: "He that believeth not is condemned already, because he hath not believed in the name of the only begotten Son of God." This too is a universal damnatory assertion, which has been always understood with conditions. And so when our Lord says in the last chapter of St. Mark, "He that believeth not [or disbelieveth] shall be damned," that too is a damnatory assertion which has never been taken in the absoluteness of the letter, but always as tacitly coupled with a condition.

When, then, we see that universal statements which admit of being understood in a qualified sense have a recognised place in language; and when we see that Scripture itself has adopted that form of statement; and when we see that it uses that form of statement in the very department, with which we are now concerned, of damnatory language; and when we

[1] John xii. 48.    [2] John viii. 24.

ourselves understand these assertions of Scripture in this sense, and so far from thinking it a non-natural sense, would without any hesitation regard the contrary or rigidly literal interpretion as non-natural—as artificial, forced, strained, and unnatural; how can we with this introduction, and having adopted this course in language and in Scripture, twist the whole principle of interpretation right round as soon as we come to the Athanasian Creed? How are we justified in saying that the letter of the grammar is an artificial and false sense in *Scripture*, and the true and natural sense in the *Creed?* How are we justified in fastening the epithet non-natural upon the very same interpretation in the Creed for which in the New Testament we have claimed the attribute of natural? Does Scripture, when it says that everybody is condemned who does not believe aright, *mean* that he is condemned conditionally—*if* it is his perverseness, *if* it is his individual sin, *if* it is his wilfulness, *if* it is his pride: and does the Athanasian Creed, when it says the same thing, *mean* that he is condemned whether it is his sin or not that he does not believe, whether he is wilful or not, whether he is proud or not, and whether he is perverse or not? Such interpretative judgment would involve a conspicuous contradiction and absurdity.

The New Testament lays down one general law upon this subject, and states one fundamental condition upon which all the damnatory language, applied to those who do not hold a right faith, is used; and that is, that the error in faith proceeds from something wrong morally. "This is the condemnation that light is come into the world, and men loved darkness rather than light because their deeds were evil."[1] The rule of eternal condemnation is here expressly declared to be a moral one; and as this rule of Scripture lies at the bottom of all the damnatory language of Scripture, so it underlies also all the damnatory language of the Church. The Church assumes the rule of Scripture, and makes every universal assertion of this kind with this fundamental condition attaching to it, by the necessity of her very root which is in Scripture.

It is sometimes said those who drew up this Creed

[1] John iii. 19.

obviously did not intend the damnatory clauses to be understood in any qualified sense. But we have nothing to do with the sense in which the compiler of this Creed understood these clauses; even if we could ascertain who the compiler was. This is the Church's Creed, and these clauses are imposed upon us to be understood according to the Church's rule of interpretation, and not according to any private interpretation, or any individual's sense : and the Church's rule of interpretation is the rule by which we interpret the like statements in Scripture, which, as we know, is the conditional rule of moral responsibility.

## XIV.—*THE HOLY EUCHARIST.*[1]

THE great result of our Church's review of the doctrine of the Eucharist at the Reformation was to recall the doctrine from the technical and artificial precision and completeness which mediæval philosophy had imparted to it, to a more vague and indefinite, but at the same time more genuine form, and one more like the original. Mediæval thought found the doctrine with a certain obscurity, shadowiness, and incompleteness attaching to it, and left it exact, systematic, and vigorous, every chasm filled up, and the whole rounded and compacted. To our Church, on the other hand, the *undefined* form of the doctrine appeared to be the *designed* form. This incompleteness was intended. It had been officiousness to meddle with it, to improve upon it. Our Church then restored the doctrine to its original and more undefined state, and rejected the new supplementary matter.

1. TRANSUBSTANTIATION.—In the first place, it rejected Transubstantiation. The primitive doctrine of the Eucharist was undoubtedly that of a change in the elements, whereby from being mere bread and wine they became the body and blood of Christ, to the strengthening and refreshing of our souls. The early Church, then, was content with the simple and indefinite idea of a change, a material and natural food,—the food of the body,—being converted into another kind of nourishment, the nourishment of the soul. But when a later age came to the consideration of this subject, it discovered that the idea of change—the change of bread and wine into the body and blood—was incomplete, and stopped short unless it was distinctly stated as a change of substance; that the substance of the former bodies was converted into the substance of the latter. Unless this took place, it was said, there was no

[1] Delivered in the Latin Chapel.

change of one body into another; but a change was granted; therefore this must take place; the substance of the bread and wine must cease, and in its place must be the substance of the Body and Blood—which is Transubstantiation. The doctrine of Transubstantiation was thus in its aim a logical filling-up of the indefinite idea of a change; it resulted from a process of reasoning—that, if there was a change of the material food into the spiritual at all, there must be a change of its substance, and that if one substance was changed into another, the first substance could no longer exist.

But though the idea of change was sharpened, and an apparent void filled up by this logical step, it appeared, as soon as ever a revision took place, that it was a precision gained where it was not wanted. It was not wanted, for what could be more irrelevant to the truth of the spiritual substance, in the sacrament, than the question about the *material* substance of the *bodily* food? The spiritual substance was clearly the one important element in the Sacrament, for which the Sacrament was instituted, and whether or not the material substance had been abstracted in the act of change, or remained after it, would not make any difference to the inward part of the Sacrament or the *res sacramenti*. The distinction was entirely a metaphysical one, and had no spiritual relevance; it did not affect, one way or another, the effect and virtue of the Sacrament. The Body and Blood of Christ has just the same nourishing effect whatever becomes of the substance of the bread; and the notion of substance in distinction to accidents was purely a notion of philosophy introduced into a spiritual subject, where it was altogether an incongruous consideration. The whole was simply a subtle and barren philosophical speculation, ending in mere words, without sense or meaning, and entirely foreign to a spiritual ordinance, and to a channel of divine grace. Our Church therefore, at the Reformation, rejected Transubstantiation, and fell back upon the earlier and more indefinite idea of a change in the elements—as a change, namely, which was *true and real for all the purposes of the Sacrament*, by which the elements became, from being mere physical food, spiritual food. "If these things be true," says Thorndike, "it will be requisite that we acknowledge a change to be wrought in the elements by the consecration of them in the Sacrament. For how should they come to be that which they were not before, to wit, the Body and Blood of Christ, without any change? And in regard of this change, the elements are no more called by the name of their nature or kind after the consecration, but by the name of that *which they are become*. Not as if the substance thereof were abolished, but because it remains *no more considerable to Christians*, who do not, nor are to, look upon this sacrament with any account of what it may be to the nourishment of their bodies, but what it may be to the nourishment of their souls."[1]

Again, with respect to another important point relating to the Sacrament, the primitive doctrine had less speculative consistency, while by that very twofold direction which it took, it comprehended more truth, and reflected more faithfully the nature of the Sacrament itself. I refer to the point of the objectiveness of the *res sacramenti*. Certainly the ground taken by the early Church with respect to the spiritual part of the sacrament of the Lord's Supper—the Body and Blood of our Lord—was *not* that that spiritual part was only an internal matter, a moral effect of the act of participation upon the mind. The Lord's Body and Blood was regarded as a reality external to the mind, even as the bread and wine was; it was considered as joined to the bread and wine, and co-existing with it in one Sacrament. "The eating and drinking of it in the Sacrament," Thorndike says, "presupposed the being of it in the Sacrament; . . . unless a man can spiritually eat the Flesh and Blood of Christ in and by the Sacrament, which is not *in* the sacrament *when* he eats and drinks it, but *by his* eating and drinking of it comes to be there."[2] The language of the early Church on this subject is so well known, and so large a body of it meets us in the writings of the early ages, that we need not dwell long upon this characteristic of early teaching on the subject of the Eucharist. But while the early ages held, as we call it now, the objectiveness of the inward part or thing signified in the sacrament, or that the Body and Blood was the concomitant of and adhered to an external and material thing to which it was united in the

---

[1] Thorndike, *Laws of the Church*, c. iii. § 1.   [2] *Ibid.* c. ii. § 12.

Sacrament, we see at the same time, upon examination of their language, that this objectiveness was held with a very important modification, which gives a double aspect to the doctrine of the Fathers. The modification was this, that the Body and Blood of Christ could not be eaten except by faith, which was the *medium* by which this spiritual food had any operation or function as food. Although, then, the Body and Blood *itself* followed an *external* test of presence, as being the concomitants of the material elements, the *eating* of this Body and Blood followed an *internal* test, and was the concomitant entirely of the state of mind of the recipient of the Sacrament. Thus as food abstractedly the Lord's Body was objective, as eaten food it was subjective, and the result of the faith of the partaker. As eaten food it parted company with the material elements, as the guarantee, and was transferred to a totally different test to be applied to it, the moral and spiritual test, namely, of the disposition of the receiver. And yet the capacity for being eaten is so identical with the very nature of food, that where this capacity is made to follow a moral and internal test, and not an external or objective one, it must be granted that a large qualification has taken place of the objective character of the spiritual food in the Sacrament. Let us not indeed put aside *that aspect* of the Sacrament, that is, the spiritual food, as it is an external reality, but neither let us dispense with the other aspect of it, namely, that the eating of that food is subjected to a moral test.

The language of the Fathers is not indeed free from some real and much more apparent disagreement on this subject. On a subject where language has so many nice distinctions to keep, it will not always keep them; nor avoid indiscriminateness, saying one thing when it means something else close and contiguous to it, but still quite different from it. Thus the rule or custom by which the bread itself was called the Body, as being the figure of the Body; and by which the whole Sacrament, not distinguishing its material part from its spiritual, was called the Body, as *containing* the Body, necessarily led to occasional confusion of language; writers saying that the Body was always, and in any case, eaten together with the reception of the Sacrament, without any condition, when they really meant that the bread, which was the Sacrament of the Body, was eaten. Where, however, this distinction was in the writer's mind, a large mass of language shows that the true Body of Christ in the Sacrament could not be eaten except by the medium of faith. St. Augustine, who is quoted in our Article[1] on this point, has frequent similar statements. St. Hilary says —"The bread which cometh down from heaven is not received except by him who is a member of Christ."[2] St. Jerome says— "Those who are lovers of pleasure more than lovers of God, neither eat His body, nor drink His blood;"[3] though he also speaks of the polluted and unworthy approaching the altar and drinking His blood. But the connection which this latter assertion has with the visible altar and the open reception of the sacrament gives the body and blood here rather the open and sacramental sense just mentioned, than the true sense. "He who obeys not Christ," says Prosper, "neither eats His flesh nor drinks His blood."[4] "He receives who approveth himself," says Ambrose. "The wicked cannot eat the word made flesh," says Origen.[5]

This modification indeed of the objective character of the spiritual food in the Sacrament, involved in the eating of it not being tied to the Sacrament, but depending on the faith of the individual, is an essential consequence of the very nature of the heavenly food itself. The Body and Blood of Christ is not a natural, but a spiritual substance. It can only therefore be eaten spiritually. To suppose that a man's natural mouth and teeth can eat a spiritual thing, would be a simple confusion of ideas. The eating of it must be wholly in the sense of, and correspond to the nature of, the food. It is in a spiritual sense alone that a spiritual substance can be eaten. Although, then, the natural mouth and teeth can eat the bread and wine, which is the sign of the Body and Blood, and the sign to which it is by the divine ordinance joined, the natural organs cannot eat the Body and Blood of Christ, which is wholly spiritual. Only the soul or spirit of man can take in and feed upon a

---

[1] Article XXIX. S. Aug. *in Joann. Tract.* xxvi. § 18.
[2] S. Hilary *de Trinitate*, lib. viii.   [3] S. Jerome *in Isai.* lxvi. 17.
[4] *Sent.* 139.   [5] Origen *in Matt.* xv.

spiritual nutriment. Faith, therefore, as being the spiritual faculty in man, must in its own nature be the medium by which the Body of Christ is eaten; and that Body, though present in the Sacrament, must remain *un*eaten by the partaker of the sacrament unless he has faith. Without faith it can only be eaten *sacramentally*, by eating the bread which is the sign or sacrament of it.

None indeed have ever maintained that the body and blood of Christ are eaten *profitably* except through the medium of faith, or spiritually. It is admitted (even where it is maintained that the Body and Blood are really, and in fact, eaten by carnal and wicked men in the Sacrament), that they are still eaten unprofitably, and to the condemnation of the persons. But nowhere in Scripture do we hear of an eating and drinking of the true Body and Blood of our Lord which is not profitable. The Body and Blood are of that nature, that they are in the reason of the case, by the simple fact of being eaten and drunk, beneficial; and no such thing is contemplated as a *real* eating of them, which is not a *beneficial* eating of them also. "Whoso eateth my flesh and drinketh my blood," saith the Lord, "hath eternal life. . . . He that eateth my flesh and drinketh my blood, dwelleth in me, and I in him. . . . He that eateth me, even he shall live by me."[1] The spiritual food of our Lord's Body and Blood cannot, as has been said, be eaten except spiritually; it cannot be eaten carnally by the mere natural mouth and teeth; such an idea is a discord and a contradiction in reason. But if it cannot be eaten except spiritually, how does the carnal man supply the spiritual medium and instrumentality of eating? The carnal man has only the natural mouth and teeth to apply; this is all he has; but this is totally irrelevant to spiritual food. Undoubtedly the carnal man has a spiritual principle in him, in common with the spiritual man *in this sense*, that he has an immaterial soul; even his wickedness is in this sense spiritual, that it is the wickedness of a spirit, because none but a spirit can be wicked; a man can only be wicked by means of his will, and the will is a property of spirit and not of matter. Thus the devils are

[1] John vi. 54, 57.

spiritual beings in the sense of being immaterial, and St. Paul says: "We wrestle not against flesh and blood, but against spiritual wickedness in high places."[1] But it is not spirituality in this sense, which is all that is meant, when it is said that the Body and Blood of our Lord can only be eaten spiritually; the spirituality requisite for the eater is more than the mere immateriality of a natural soul; and a wicked man could not, by means of his wicked spirit, though it is spirit, spiritually eat our Lord's flesh. To partake of our Lord's Body and Blood implies union with our Lord; it implies the fruition of Him, it implies a cognateness of the eater to the food. The Body and Blood of our Lord are not spiritual food in the immaterial sense only, but they are spiritual food in the *moral* sense, as being moral aliment and nutrition, the goodness and holiness of our Lord infusing itself into the human soul. But to eat what is in this sense spiritual requires a state of mind which is spiritual in this sense. "The Body and Blood," says Thorndike, "is not spiritually eaten and drunk till *living faith make them spiritually present to the soul*, which the consecration maketh *sacramentally present to the body*."[2] The wicked then cannot eat them spiritually, but the spiritual is the only way in which they can be eaten; the wicked therefore cannot eat them at all.

Hence our divines, who maintain with the Catechism that the inward part of the Sacrament is the Body and Blood of Christ, still hold with the Article, that without faith that Body and Blood of Christ is not eaten or partaken of. "Evil men," says Ridley, "do eat the very true and natural body of Christ *sacramentally and no further*, as St. Augustine saith; but good men do eat the very true Body both sacramentally and spiritually by grace."[3] "Those who eat unprofitably," he says again, "eat the Sacrament;" the very flesh of Christ to be eaten must be eaten *spiritually*. "I say," says Cranmer, "that the same visible and palpable flesh that was for us crucified, is eaten of Christian people at His Holy Supper; ... the diversity is not in the body, but in the eating thereof; no man eating it carnally, but the good eating it both sacramentally and spiritually, and

---

[1] Eph. vi. 12.
[2] *Laws of the Church*, c. iii. § 5.
[3] *Works*, Parker Society, p. 246.

*the evil only sacramentally.*"[1] "All that are partakers of this sacrament," says Jackson, "eat Christ's body and drink His blood *sacramentally*, that is, they eat that bread which sacramentally is His body, and drink that cup which is sacramentally His blood, whether they eat and drink faithfully or unfaithfully."[2] He limits the eating and drinking of those who are without faith, to eating and drinking the sacramental sign. Those, says Thorndike, that receive in a dead faith, "*cannot be said to eat the body and blood of Christ*, which is only the act of a living faith, without that abatement which the premises have established, to wit, *in the Sacrament*."[3] "Since I proved," says the author of the *Unbloody Sacrifice*, "that what is eaten and drunk in the Communion is the Body and Blood of Christ *before* it is administered and received, . . . it may with appearance of truth be from hence inferred that I believe the Body and Blood to be received by the wicked hypocritical communicants, as well as by those who receive it with true faith and devotion; and therefore to silence this objection, I shall show from the writings of the ancients (1.) that the wicked communicant does *externally* eat and drink the Body and Blood, but (2.) that he does not do it internally. . . . Although there are very few indeed that cannot externally eat the sacramental Body as to its gross substance, which is bread, yet there are very great numbers of men that cannot receive it internally, as it is the mysterious body of Christ, . . . for it is a spiritual Body, not so much intended for the repast of our palates and stomachs as of our minds."[4] Between such a doctrine as this of faith, as the necessary means by which the Body of Christ is eaten, and Hooker's doctrine, there is some but no very wide interval—the position I mean of Hooker, "that the real Presence of Christ's Body and Blood is not to be sought for in the Sacrament, but in the worthy receiver of the Sacrament,"[5] at the same time that he held a true mystery in the Sacrament itself—that it did not "import a figure only," but had an instrumental virtue and

---

[1] Cranmer, *On the Lord's Supper*, Parker Society, p. 224.
[2] Jackson, *On the Creed: Works*, vol. x. p. 51, ed. 1844.
[3] Thorndike, *Laws of the Church*, c. iii. § 6.
[4] J. Johnson's *Unbloody Sacrifice*, ch. iv. § 5.
[5] Hooker's *Ecclesiastical Polity*, v. lxvii. 6.

power attaching to it. "These holy mysteries," he says, "received in due manner *do instrumentally make us partakers of the grace of that Body and Blood* which were given for the life of the world."[1]

It is not, however, to be inferred, because the wicked do not eat the very Body and Blood of Christ in the Sacrament, that therefore they only eat common bread and wine. They eat consecrated material elements, to which the mysterious property has been imparted that the faithful receive and eat in them the Body and Blood of Christ. Common bread has not this property imparted to it, but the bread in the Sacrament has. When the wicked eat the sacramental bread, then, though they do not eat the Lord's Body, they eat bread which is in a certain intimate and mystical relation to our Lord's Body. But for the wicked to eat bread which is in such a relation to that sacred and mystical Body is a *profanation*. It is a pollution of a hallowed sign and symbol, and an effective sign and symbol, by their unholy touch; and such desecration and profanation of the consecrated elements endowed with so divine a property justly turns to their condemnation. Thus when St. Paul says to the Corinthians, that "whosoever shall eat this bread and drink this cup of the Lord unworthily shall be guilty of the body and blood of the Lord; . . . and eateth and drinketh damnation to himself, not discerning the Lord's body,"[2] it does not by any means necessarily imply that this profanation arises, and this condemnation arises, from the actual eating of our Lord's true Body, but it does undoubtedly imply that there is some sacred and close relation in which the bread and the cup of the Lord do stand to His Body and Blood, which gives to the former a true sanctity, and so renders them capable of pollution and desecration. The wicked eat that to which a divine virtue is joined, even the property of becoming to the faithful the Body of our Lord. This virtue is joined to the consecrated bread, independently of our faith, and the wicked who eat it eat it with this virtue attaching to it, which cannot leave it, namely, that the very same bread, if eaten by the faithful, would be spiritual nourishment to them, which common

---

[1] Hooker's *Ecclesiastical Polity*, v. lxvii. 8.   [2] 1 Cor. xi. 27.

bread could not be. And it appears to me that this is substantially what is meant by the strong statements of Bishop Poynet, with respect to wicked men's mode of partaking of the sacrament,—statements which claim for the material elements a junction with the thing signified by them even while the wicked eat them. "As to the denial," he says, "that the wicked can eat the body of Christ, we must make a distinction. For if we regard the nature of the Sacrament, divine virtue cannot be absent from the sign in so far as it is a Sacrament;" and he quotes Cyprian, who says, "Sacraments cannot exist without their own virtue, nor can the Divine Majesty be ever absent from the mysteries." "The Sacraments," he continues, "so long as they are Sacraments, retain their own virtue, nor can they be separated therefrom. For they always consist of their own parts, an earthly and a heavenly, and an inward and an outward, whether the good take them or the bad, whether the worthy or the unworthy. Howbeit that commutation of the signs and transition of the elements into the inward substance, which everywhere occurs in the ancient writers, cannot exist, if we separate the virtue from the sign, and attempt to take the one apart from the other. But this is to be understood, so long as the sign serves its use and is adapted to the end for which it was destined by the Word of God. . . . Should there be any who think that there is too much here ascribed to the elements, it is not so, but its due reverence is given to the external symbols on account of their sacred use, and the inward virtue which is added by the power of the divine words."[1] What this language appears to mean is, that the material symbols are ever accompanied by a divine virtue and property, which adheres to them, by the very nature of the sacraments, and that therefore even when the *wicked* eat and drink them, that virtue still belongs to and accompanies them; the invisible part is still joined to the visible, but it does not imply that the wicked eat the thing signified itself,—that they eat the Body and Blood which is the inward part of the Sacrament.

[1] Bishop Poynet, *Diallacticon de veritate natura atque substantia corporis et sanguinis Christi in Eucharistia* (first published, 1557), pp. 76-78, 81, ed. London, 1688.

The primitive doctrine, then, of the Eucharist, thus introducing faith as the medium by which the body of Christ is eaten in the sacrament, that is, applying a modification to the external or objective character of the *res sacramenti*, this was departed from in the later and mediæval doctrine. It appeared to be a more whole, complete, and consistent view of the Sacrament, to regard the eating of the Body of Christ as essentially and invariably attending upon the Sacrament itself. And the doctrine of Transubstantiation which inserted the Body of Christ in the place of the very substance of the Bread, thus making it succeed to the position of the very material substratum of the bread, necessarily carried with it this result. But when the doctrine of the Eucharist came under revision at the Reformation, our Church reverted to the original and more modified condition and form of the doctrine, by which, on the one hand, the Body and Blood of our Lord was by the act of consecration, independently of the faith of the individual, the inward part of the Sacrament, and on the other hand, that Body and Blood were not eaten in the Sacrament except by the medium of faith. This was a qualification of the rigorous and compact whole which later speculation had made,—a departure from that unity which one-sided theorising creates; but it was a reversion to the original and genuine doctrine, which, as being less definite and precise, and more twofold in its statements, was also the truer and more authentic. Spiritual truth does not consult the intellectual and philosophical standard, and aim at a systematic unity, but is truth of a vaguer and more natural and more inclusive sort.

2. ADORATION.—Again, upon another subject connected with Eucharistic doctrine, our Church reverted to an earlier application and interpretation of the principle maintained upon this subject. I refer to the question of the adoration paid to Christ's Body in the Sacrament. When we examine ancient language on this subject, we find large differences in its composition; that it contains a great quantity of irrelevant statement which does not really apply to the point at issue, mixed—in a way which makes it very difficult to extricate it—with the really relevant and pertinent kind of statement. Thus there is a large mass of statement to the

effect that Christ should be specially and peculiarly worshipped in the whole act of partaking of the Sacrament of His Body and Blood. But this language has nothing whatever to do with the worship of Christ under material sacramental elements. There are thus two wholly different kinds of statements mixed together in the general language relating to adoration of our Lord in the Eucharist. One of these kinds of statement expresses only an adoration accompanying the act of receiving, the other expresses an adoration of Him as contained in some sense in that which is received: one denotes only the worship of Christ as generally present in and at the Eucharistic rite; the other signifies a worship of Him as specially present under the species of bread and wine. Of these two kinds of statement one, as I have just said, has no real bearing upon the particular question of adoration in the Eucharist, as that phrase is understood in controversy. All Christians, of whatever Church or party, would admit the adoration of our Lord in this general sense in the Eucharist: namely, that when a man partakes of the Eucharist, he does worship Christ. But this is not worshipping Him as present or in any way contained in the bread and wine. "We worship Christ," says Ridley, "wheresoever we perceive His benefits, but we understand His benefits to be greatest in the Sacrament."[1] And in the following extract Thorndike does not express more than what any Christian would admit:—"I suppose," he says, "it is the duty of every Christian to honour our Lord Jesus Christ as God subsisting in human flesh, whether by professing Him such, or by praying to Him as such, or by using any bodily gesture, which may serve to signify that worship of the heart which inwardly commands it. This honour, then, being a duty, . . . . what remains but a just occasion to make it requisite ? . . . . And is not the presence of Christ's flesh in the sacrament of the Eucharist a just occasion to express, by the bodily act of adoration, that inward honour which we always carry towards our Lord Christ as God ?"[2] In this passage then the worship paid to Christ in the Sacrament is not a worship paid to Him as present under the form of the sacramental elements; but it

[1] *Works*, Parker Society, p. 236.  [2] *Laws of the Church*, c. xxxi. § 3, 4.

is only the worship which is *always* paid to Him, as existing invisibly always in the form of man and human nature, only paid to Him upon the particular opportunity of the Sacrament. The Body and Blood in the Sacrament is not the *object* of the worship, but only the *occasion* of it. "The celebration of the Eucharist," he says, "is a competent occasion for executing that worship which is always due to our Lord Christ Incarnate."[1] "Place thyself upon thy knees," says Bishop Jeremy Taylor, "in the humblest and devoutest posture of worshippers, and think not much in the lowest manner to worship the King of men and angels, the Lord of heaven and earth, the great Lover of souls, and the Saviour of the body. . . . For if Christ be not there after a peculiar manner, whom or whose body do we receive? But if He be present to us not in mystery only but in blessing also, why do we not worship?"[2] The worship described in this passage is the worship of Christ present in a special way in the great act of Christian communion, but it is not the worship of Christ under the outward form of the material elements. There is a great difference of course between a general presence of Christ in the act of communion, and a particular presence united to the bread and wine.

Separating this general language then from that particular body of language which asserts an adoration in special connection with the material elements, we find in the first place that in all earlier language, and in the language of our own divines which represents the earlier ages, *adoration* is addressed to the *Body and Blood of our Lord*, and that that, and that only, is the object to which it *is* addressed. Our divines, indeed, when speaking of the *partaking in Communion*, speak of *Christ simply* being received, not making any distinction between the Body and Blood and the divinity of Christ; nor is such an extension of the *res sacramenti* other than natural, nor can any injurious consequence follow it, in connection with the sacrament as spiritual food; the boundaries and limitations of mystical language are not to be very accurately restricted where no practical danger can ensue. But as regards the *adoration* in the Eucharist, the act of *adoration* has been

[1] *Laws of the Church*, c. xxxi. § 6.   [2] Taylor's *Worthy Communicant*.

assigned specially to the Body and Blood of Christ as its object; that being the strict and proper *res sacramenti*; and not to the divinity of Christ, which is not properly or strictly the *res sacramenti*, or united with the material elements. The whole language of antiquity establishes the Body and Blood as that which is in sacramental connection with the bread and wine. The divinity is not represented as placed in this sacramental union with the material elements. It is quite true indeed that wherever the Body and Blood of Christ are, there by strict reasoning must be the human soul and the Divinity of Christ; it is impossible to separate what are in their own nature united. But it must be remembered that this is a mystical subject, and that in mystical doctrine we cannot proceed in this way by logical steps. In mystical doctrine we must take the form of statement which is given to us, and not exceed it; because if the truth is given in a certain form and measure, and with certain limits and confines, we must assume that it is intentionally so given, and for a divine purpose. Earlier writers and our own divines then adhere cautiously and faithfully to Scripture, in speaking of the Body and Blood of Christ as the *res sacramenti* in the Eucharist, and in assigning the act of adoration in the Eucharist to the Body and Blood. It was therefore a qualified and conditioned kind of adoration which patristic theology connected specially with the Eucharist. For the Body and Blood of Christ are not in themselves objects of *divine* adoration and worship; they only admit of a worship which is paid to them indirectly by reason of their intimate connection with that which *is* an object of direct adoration, namely, the Divinity of Christ: they can only receive that reflected Divinity which comes from the Person of Christ, and consequently only a secondary worship. "The Body and Blood of Christ," says Thorndike, "is not adored nor to be adored by Christians for any endowment residing in it . . . but in consideration of the Godhead, to which it remains inseparably united . . . in which Godhead therefore that honour resteth and to which it tendeth. —So the Godhead of Christ is the thing that is honoured, and the reason why it is honoured both."[1] Thus the very constitution

---

[1] *Laws of the Church*, c. xxx. § 2.

of the Sacrament contained in itself a check upon any idolatrous use of it; because by the very law of the Sacrament that which was the inner part or thing signified was confined and restricted to the Body and Blood; which material part of our Lord did not admit of direct adoration being paid to it. The sacramental connection with the material elements only covered an object of indirect worship; the object of direct worship or the Godhead was not contained under the material elements. The Body and Blood admitted indeed only of a higher degree of that worship and reverence which is paid to all objects intimately joined by service or dedication to the Divine Majesty. "The saying, 'worship His footstool,'" says Bishop Poynet, "many understand of the ark of the covenant ... which was to be worshipped on account of the presence of the Divine Majesty. And in the same manner," he says, "we may worship the Eucharist on account of the ineffable and invisible grace of Christ joined to it. 'He,' says Augustine, 'who venerates a useful sign instituted by God, does not venerate the transient thing which he sees, but rather that to which all such things are to be referred.'"[1] "There is a deceit," says Ridley, "in this word '*adoramus.*' We *worship* the symbols, when reverently we handle them. ... If you mean the external sacrament, I say that also is to be worshipped as a sacrament."[2] The reverence then that is paid to sacred signs and symbols, and to all objects which are associated with the Divine Majesty, is a worship or adoration in a secondary sense; and *a fortiori* may our Lord's Body and Blood, as being joined not by association, but by the truth of nature, with His Divinity, receive that worship. But the worship given specially in the Eucharist was such subordinate worship—worship paid to that which was intimately connected with Divinity, not to the Divinity itself. The mind of the worshipper was necessarily carried indeed to the direct worship of the Divinity of Christ, but in so doing it went out of the area and limits of the sacrament, and worshipped the God of God, Light of Light, Very God of Very God, by whom all things were made.

But when later theology took up the subject of the adora-

---

[1] Bp. Poynet, *Diallacticon*, p. 75, *ut supra*.
[2] Ridley's *Works*, Parker Society, p. 236.

tion in the Eucharist, it instituted a very different kind of adoration. In later theology, in the first place, the *res sacramenti* was not only the Body and Blood of Christ, but was the *whole Christ*, Body, Soul, and Godhead. "Totus et integer Christus," says the Council of Trent, "sub panis specie, et sub quavis ipsius speciei parte; totus item, sub vini specie et sub ejus partibus existit." The Council includes expressly "sub specie panis et vini" not only the Body and Blood, but the Soul of Christ, and the Godhead of Christ—"propter admirabilem illam eius cum corpore et anima hypostaticam unionem."[1] But, the inward part of the sacrament being thus defined, when it came to the adoration of the *res sacramenti*, that adoration necessarily became, not the indirect worship of what was in natural conjunction with the Divinity, but the direct adoration of the Godhead itself, existing under the species of Bread and Wine. But without entering into the question of the criterion by which we define idolatry, or at all asserting that the worship of the true God, though under an unauthorised material form, is idolatry, we must still see that this express adoration of the Godhead, as subsisting under the visible material form of bread, holds a place very distinct from, and is divided by a great interval from, the primitive adoration of the Body and Blood. The Roman definition of the *res sacramenti* clears away all modification, frees the worship in the sacrament of all check, and establishes a distinct localised object of divine adoration which the genuine constitution of the sacrament had implicitly provided against.

A different character, again, was given to the act of adoration by insulating it, by making it independent of the act of communion, and separating it from all its natural place in the Sacrament. In early writers it is subordinated to the main object and scope of the Sacrament, namely, a partaking of the spiritual food of Christ's body and blood. Thus St. Augustine's expression, "No one eats that flesh without first adoring," while it inculcates *an* adoration, at the same time, by its very form, implies that it is an adoration given in the course of the act of communion, and in connection with that reception of the

[1] Concil. Trident. Canones et Decreta, Sessio xiii., cap. iii. *ad finem* (p. 67, ed. Lovanii, 1567).

food which is the main design of the Sacrament. But later and mediæval practice divided the adoration from the Sacrament. The Bread was kept for adoration; was elevated, carried in processions, and offered to the worship of the people, apart from, and wholly disconnected with, its office and use in the Sacrament as spiritual food. Our Church recalled the worship not only to its proper kind and nature, as indirect; but also to its proper place, as an act connected with, but subordinate to, the main purpose of the sacrament; and in the 28th Article declared that the "sacrament of the Lord's Supper was not by Christ's ordinance reserved, carried about, lifted up and worshipped."

III. SACRIFICE.—We come to another point. On the subject of the Eucharistic Sacrifice the language of our divines has been very consentient and uniform; they have almost with one voice maintained a commemorative and representative Sacrifice, in agreement with the belief of antiquity. The popular belief of later times exaggerated the Eucharistic Sacrifice till it became, to all intents and purpose, a real one, and "the priest offered up Christ on the altar for quick and dead, to have remission of pain and guilt;" that is to say, offered Him up as a Victim, in a sense which could not be distinguished from that in which He was offered up by Himself on the Cross. It is true that the decree of the Council of Trent just saves itself by cautious, not to say dissembling, language, from the extreme and monstrous conclusion that the Sacrifice of the Mass is the very same with that upon the Cross. It distinguishes between a bloody and an unbloody oblation; and it states that the fruits or consequences of the Bloody Oblation or the Sacrifice on the Cross are "received through the unbloody one"—Oblationis cruentae fructus per hanc incruentam percipiuntur: but at the same time it asserts that the sacrifice of the mass is a really *propitiatory sacrifice—vere propitiatorium*. Now undoubtedly there are two distinct senses in which an act may be said to be propitiatory. The act of Christ's Sacrifice on the Cross had an original propitiatory power; that is to say, it was the cause of any other act, or any act of man, or any rite being propitiatory, that is, appeasing God's anger, and reconciling Him to the agent. We may allow that in common language a man may do something which will reconcile God to him, and restore him to God's favour; but then all the power that any action of man can have for this end is a derived power, derived from Christ's sacrifice, from which any other sacrifice, the Eucharistic one included, borrows its virtue, and without which it would be wholly null and void. There is, then, an original propitiation and a borrowed propitiation, a first propitiation and a secondary one. Why then did the Fathers of Trent, when they had all human language at their command, deliberately choose to call the Sacrifice of the Mass *vere propitiatorium*? They may have said that it was *vere propitiatorium* in the secondary sense; but no one can fail to see the misleading effect of such language, and that nothing could have been easier to the divines of Trent, had they chosen, than to draw a far more clear distinction than they did between the Sacrifice of the Mass and the Sacrifice on the Cross. It is evident that, as ecclesiastical statesmen, they were afraid of interfering with the broad popular established view of the Mass, while as theologians they just contrived to secure themselves from the responsibility of a monstrous dogmatic statement.

It was thus that our Church at the Reformation recalled the doctrine of the Eucharist to its proper proportions, and corrected the errors and extravagances into which later theology had been led. She relieved the change in the elements from the interpolation of Transubstantiation, and from that false, rigid completeness and system which the schools of the Middle Ages had given it. She restored Faith as the medium by which the Body of Christ is eaten. She restored the true limits of the adoration in the Eucharist, and of the sacrifice of the Eucharist.

I will conclude with the reflection, that amid the various explanations of the manner in which the mystery of this Sacrament is to be expressed, the mode of change, the kind of change, the relation of the material element or sign, to the inner part or thing signified; the relation of the whole Sacrament to the mind and faith of the partaker; one central truth remains, retaining which we retain the true substance of the doctrine of the Eucharist, namely, that it is a true participation of the Body and Blood of Christ, which are verily and indeed taken and received by the faithful in that Sacrament. Various degrees of importance may attach to circumstantial points—to Transubstantiation in the Romanist's view, to Consubstantiation in the Lutheran; and different ideas may be entertained among ourselves as to the sense in which the Body and Blood are contained in the Sacrament, or the Sacrament transmuted into them, antecedently to the participation of the receiver. I do not by any means intend to say that upon this latter question there is not a grave truth and a grave error; but I must say with Hooker that the question does not relate to necessary belief in regard to the doctrine of the Sacrament; and that a true participation of the Body and Blood of Christ is the fundamental truth of the Eucharist. In Hooker's language—" Whereas therefore there are but three expositions made of 'this is my body;' the first, 'this is in itself, before participation, really and truly the natural substance of my Body by reason of the co-existence which my omnipresent Body hath with the sanctified element of bread,' which is the Lutheran's interpretation: the second, 'this is itself, and before participation, the very true and natural substance of my Body, by force of that Deity which with the words of consecration abolisheth the substance of bread, and substituteth in the place thereof my Body,' which is the Popish construction: the last, 'this hallowed food, through concurrence of Divine Power, is in verity and truth, unto faithful receivers, instrumentally a cause of that mystical participation, whereby, as I make myself wholly theirs, so I give them in hand an actual possession of all such saving grace as my sacrificed Body can yield, and as their souls do presently need, this is to them and in them my Body.' Of these three rehearsed interpretations the last hath in it nothing but what the rest do all approve and acknowledge to be most true, nothing but that which the words of Christ are on all sides confessed to enforce, nothing but that which the Church of God hath always thought necessary, nothing but that which alone is sufficient for every Christian man to believe concerning the use and force of this Sacrament."[1]

[1] *Ecclesiastical Polity*, v. lxvii. 12.

## XV.—LETTER TO THE REV. PROFESSOR STANLEY ON THE ARTICLES.

### (1863.)

MY DEAR PROFESSOR STANLEY,—You will not, I am sure, be surprised if the appearance of your *Letter to the Bishop of London on the State of Subscription in the Church of England* excites great attention. The proposal to do away with the whole of our existing subscriptions, coming from one of such position—academical and ecclesiastical—such wide and justly-acquired influence, and a personal character which has won the attachment of so many of all parties in the Church, must raise serious thought. You also quote the important observation of the Bishop of London, made in his Lordship's recent Charge, that "the whole subject of what our subscriptions ought to be requires, and must receive, immediate attention"—an observation which, coming from so high a quarter, indicates a critical state of things—that this question is now removed from the settled basis upon which it has so long rested, and is, to a certain extent, re-opened.

I will, therefore, with your kind permission, address a few remarks to you on this subject; and first, I will state the limits which I propose to myself. It is not my intention to go into the whole of the contents of this momentous question, which would be too large a field for a pamphlet. There are particular statements in our Articles connected with the Roman controversy; and there is also the subscription to the Prayer-book, as imposed by the Act of Uniformity. Both of these calls for assent are supposed to constitute a grievance in two different quarters. But I shall take a set of Articles, the characteristic difficulty of which is their apparent collision, not only with tenets of divines, but with common sense and natural feeling—

a ground of objection felt by a larger class than the theological one. I refer to the Articles from IX. to XVII., relating to the process of man's salvation, and containing statements apparently opposed to free will and to the existence of the slightest goodness in man in a state of nature. This is my field of material, then, and with respect to this material I shall limit myself to one point of view which I will explain, and for the explanation of which I will ask a little preliminary space.

It appears to me a point which has not been sufficiently attended to in our controversies on the subject of Subscription, that where the language of a doctrinal formulary and the language of the Bible are the same, whatever explanation we give, in case there is a difficulty, of the language of the Bible is applicable to the language of the formulary as well; and that, therefore, in such a case, the statement in the formulary is no fresh difficulty, but only one which we have already surmounted in accepting the same statement in the Bible. In such a case the formulary is not, in truth, responsible for the apparently obnoxious nature of the assertion it makes; nor does a person who has already assented to the same declaration in Scripture incur any new responsibility when he assents to the formulary. This appears to be a very simple and natural rule, and yet it is one which a great many serious and most intelligent persons never think of applying when they encounter difficulties in our formularies. Their minds are in a different state and attitude when they read the Bible from that in which they read a doctrinal formulary. I do not mean simply that they know the Bible to be inspired, and the other document not; but that, as readers, they are freer, more natural, more liberal in interpreting the meaning of Scripture, than they are in interpreting the meaning of a formulary, even when it is exactly the same language which is used in both. They come with the expectation of finding ugly and repulsive matter in the human document; and when, therefore, they do find what at first sight is such, they fasten upon it that *primâ facie* meaning as the true and real meaning of the formulary, and will not let it go. No; that is its meaning, and that shall be its meaning, and nobody shall persuade them that it is not. Whereas, when they came across the very same statement in the Bible, they accepted it with a natural and obvious qualification.

To take the commonly-quoted instance of the damnatory clauses, as they are called, in the Athanasian Creed, which assert of the "Catholic faith," that "except a man believe it faithfully he cannot be saved." The difficulty which is felt about this assertion in the Athanasian Creed does not at all relate to the nature of the *credendum*, or subject-matter of belief—the doctrine of the Trinity—but to condemnation on account of simple belief. Yet this point of condemnation on account of belief is stated in Scripture as strongly as in this Creed. It is asserted in terms, absolutely and positively, "He that believeth and is baptized shall be saved; but he that believeth not shall be damned." How is it, then, that when those who object to the statement of condemnation on account of belief, when they meet it in the Athanasian Creed, did not object to the same statement when they encountered it in Scripture? The reason is obvious—that when they met this statement in Scripture they gave it the benefit of a liberal interpretation. They did not suppose for an instant that this text *could* mean that God, who is just and merciful, would condemn a man simply on account of his not believing certain truths, apart from all consideration of disadvantages of education, early prejudices, and want of opportunities and means of enlightenment. They therefore regarded it immediately, I might say unconsciously, as containing the unexpressed condition of *moral* responsibility, and understood the condemnation only to apply to such as did not believe in consequence of faults of their own. But if they gave the assertion this liberal interpretation when they met it in the Bible, why cannot they give it the same interpretation when they meet it in the Athanasian Creed? And if they do, this assertion in the Creed can be no burden to them: it only asserts what Scripture asserts, and need only mean what Scripture means.

It often depends entirely on the simple *eye* with which we look upon a statement, whether we see in it a reasonable or a monstrous assertion. In reading Scripture, these interpreters saw the statement I am referring to in a natural light; it never occurred to them to suppose that it could mean, *really*, what it did mean rigidly and literally; they used a free rational discretion in the way in which they understood it. But when they came to the same statement in a Creed, they forgot *natural* interpretation, and adopted *artificial*. I say artificial, because there is nothing in fact so contrary to natural interpretation, in many cases, as naked literal interpretation. This latter is often the most artificial, far-fetched, and distorted kind of interpretation we can give. Human language is an imperfect instrument; it is obliged to adopt many short and summary forms of speech and modes of statement, leaving the reader to supply of his own understanding the proper and intended qualifications. I say, it is *obliged* to do this, because indeed it is necessary for our practical convenience that it should. It must limit itself in expression. Were language really to express the whole amount of unexpressed conditions which are contained ordinarily in it, it would become too cumbrous an instrument for use. All communication between man and man would be clogged. It would take half an hour to make a remark. To ask a question, we should have to start we do not know whence, and end we do not know where. Nor should we gain in perspicuity what we lost in despatch. Language would then be unintelligible from its very fulness and cram. No head could take in such a crowd of detail. How difficult of comprehension, for instance, is a legal document, not from its defect, but its enormous supply of expression, resulting from the cautious determination to state everything which in ordinary language is left to be understood. Human language, therefore, shortens and abridges itself; and it would surprise us if we were to examine, and see how much we leave out in ordinary speech and writing, which the hearer or reader is intended to supply. When then language, by its normal construction, constantly leaves these unexpressed qualifications for us to supply, if we insist on that particular kind of interpretation which does *not* supply them, we do not fulfil our part of the arrangement. The bare literal interpretation in such cases is not a tribute, but a positive injustice, to the statement to which it is applied, misrepresenting its purpose, and distorting its meaning. The literal meaning is just the very opposite to that which it especially pretends to be—the *natural* meaning. It is an *un*natural meaning. It is artificial, when we know—know by familiar and practical experience—that language is a system of *understandings*, as well as of *expressions*, to insist, in all cases, upon the bare expression or the naked letter as its adequate exponent. Yet we see on all sides persons rejecting the warnings, the rules, and the checks of common sense, to exult in this unreasonable law of interpretation.

I do not undertake here to define all the conditions under which the principle of qualification should be applied, and the guarantees for its legitimate operation: I only, as a matter of common sense, assert the existence of such a principle. If a man accepts the Gospel history with the qualification that it is only mythical or symbolical narrative, that appears to me an illegitimate qualification, whether applied to the Gospels or to Lord Clarendon's History. But if either Lord Clarendon or an inspired writer uses some particular expression which seems obviously intended to be taken with a qualification, I would let either have the benefit of it.

I might illustrate this rule of appeal to Scripture by another case, that of the Bishop's address to the Priest in the Ordination Service—" Whose sins thou dost forgive, they are forgiven; and whose sins thou dost retain, they are retained." The hesitation to accept this statement arises, I apprehend, from the impossibility that a mere man can, under any circumstances, possess what is naturally meant by the power to forgive sins—a power which is an attribute of the Deity alone. But that men—some men, who were mere men,—did forgive sins, is the express statement of Scripture. "Whosoever sins ye remit, they are remitted unto them; and whosesoever sins ye retain, they are retained." It is true that the authority which communicates this power is different in Scripture and in the Prayer-book, being in the one case our Lord, in the other the Church; and it is true that the men to whom it is communicated are also different, being in the one case Apostles, in the other priests: but the difficulty that its possessors were men is the same in both cases. When we come then to the attribution of this power to men in the Prayer-book, there is, on this head, no fresh difficulty to which we are subjected, but only one which we have already surmounted in accepting the same attribution in Scripture. In Scripture, we of course assented to it, with the reservation,—"Who can forgive sins but God only?" That is to say, we took it in some sense consistent with that truth; and we have only to give the same explanation to it in the Prayer-book.

Having explained then what I mean by this rule of interpretation, I will proceed soon to apply it to the Articles in question. But, first of all, I must speak of these Articles themselves, and show that they come under that head of formulistic language to which this rule is applicable, namely, that they speak the language of Scripture.

These Articles, then, have been sometimes represented as simply scholastic and controversial; the productions of the laboratories of professional divines: distantly connected, indeed, with some real and essential truth at the fountain-head; but so far removed from it by the successive stages of human speculation through which they have passed, and the human media which have coloured and modelled them, that they have practically ceased to belong to the sphere of revelation, and become a simply human and polemical fabric. Whatever element of divine truth there may be in them has been so completely metamorphosed in the passage, and so buried in the incrustations of foreign matter from the department of speculative thought, that it has virtually lost its identity. But though this is the theological description which is sometimes given of this section of our Articles, I must frankly confess that they appear to me to be, every one of them, the actual statements of St. Paul. For identity of statement literal tautology is not necessary; it is enough if the evident sense and meaning are the same. These Articles appear to me, then, to say exactly the same thing that he does.

I will take the three which contain the substance of the whole—Arts. IX., XI., and XVII. The first of the cardinal statements of the IXth Article is, that "man is very far gone from original righteousness, and is of his own nature inclined to evil." Now what does St. Paul say? I will quote one passage, which only represents more vividly the general purport of his language. In that passage the Apostle is evidently not speaking of any particular corrupt state of society, or corrupt age, or vicious circle; he is speaking obviously of man altogether, of man as such in his natural state, and impersonating such universal man, and therefore, speaking in the first person, he says—"I am carnal, sold under sin ... For I know that in me, that is, in my flesh, dwelleth no good thing ... For the good that I would I do not, but the evil that I would not that I do ... I see another law in my members warring against the law of my mind, and bringing me into capitivity to the law of sin. O wretched man that I am, who shall deliver me from the body of this death?" If man in the flesh, or natural state, is under actual captivity to sin; if he is sold under sin, and if no good thing dwelleth in him, so that he never does the good thing, and always does the evil thing; then man—the natural man—is certainly "very far gone from original righteousness." He is even, if we are to press the term, "as far as possible [*quam longissime*] gone from original righteousness:" for we cannot imagine a condition more remote from righteousness than this. No acts proceeding out of such a condition as this can, of course, be "pleasant to God," as a subsequent Article says.

The other cardinal statement of the IXth Article is, that this sinfulness of the natural man is not the mere fault of the individual, but the "fault of his nature, as engendered of the offspring of Adam." But St. Paul says exactly the same thing. The *universal* sinfulness of the natural man is indeed, *ipso facto*, a fault of nature; for a universal result must proceed from some law, and cannot be simply an "extraordinary coincidence" —so many separate individuals *happening* to fall into the same sinful character. But he also states this truth expressly, sending us to Adam as the origin of the sin of all mankind,— "We are by nature the children of wrath ... The old man is corrupt ... By one man sin entered into the world, and death by sin ... By one man's offence death reigned by one ... Through the offence of one many be dead ... By the offence of one judgment came upon all men to condemnation ... By one man's disobedience many were made sinners ... For since by man [by the analogy, an individual] came death, by man came also the resurrection of the dead. For as in Adam all die, even so in Christ shall all be made alive."

The XIth Article asserts the doctrine of justification by faith only; but this is so constantly asserted *totidem verbis* by St. Paul, that I think anybody will admit that the language of this Article is the language of St. Paul.

The XVIIth Article has been a great bone of contention. Understood grammatically, this Article represents both the ultimate salvation and also the preparatory life and actions of all who are saved, as the certain results of an eternal decree of Predestination. "They which be endued with so excellent a benefit of God are called, *obey the calling*, are justified," etc. This statement, then, encounters the very natural objection that it is opposed to the self-determination, or, as it is called, freedom of the will, and to the Divine justice and impartiality: it is, nevertheless, almost word for word, the statement of St. Paul,—" whom He did foreknow, He also did predestinate to be conformed to the image of His Son "—where that to which the elect are predestinated is evidently not merely the happy end on *supposition* of the qualification for it, but to the means or qualification itself—being conformed to the image of Christ. And so he continues,—" Whom He did predestinate them He also called, and whom He called them He also justified: and whom He justified them He also glorified."

I have just touched upon these Articles enough to show the matter they contain; and now I must repeat, that they cannot be regarded as dry formulæ, structures of logic, and the products of scholastic brains. They shoot up straight from the very fount of Pauline teaching, are fresh from the vital source, and are living and working doctrine, connected with the spiritual sense of Christians. I need not say, in writing to one who has gone so ably into the temper and genius of St. Paul, and described so vividly the characteristics of that Apostle's thought, that it is impossible to read his Epistles without seeing that the mind of this inspired writer was put in possession of a most remarkable body of doctrine respecting the nature and salvation of man—a doctrine substantially the same with that of the rest of Scripture, but certainly assuming in his teaching a developed form. Human nature is first seen in his revelation utterly prostrate and helpless; unable to do anything but sin; but still "alive," in this miserable sense, that it is unconscious of its own degradation, and does not even wish to rise. But then the Law comes and gives the finishing stroke to man,—*slays* him, transfixing him with the sharp consciousness of his guilt, and then leaving him to himself. This completes the work of death. In this state of things, then, the mighty Deliverer appeared, wiped off man's guilt by the unspeakable Sacrifice, and offered to recreate him:—but only on one condition, namely, that the change should be acknowledged as entirely His doing, and not man's. This is the act of justifying faith, which disowns works; upon which act of self-rejection the soul is new-created, and is endowed with a Spirit not its own, which impels, sustains, and elevates it with irresistible might, so that it rises above earth and mounts heavenwards. But why are not all saved thus? It is the "purpose of God according to election . . . having mercy on whom He will have mercy." St. Paul thus begins and ends alike with a profound mystery: he begins with the mystery of the Fall, and he ends with the mystery of Predestination. And in this sphere of inspiration he shoots from depth to height, descends to the lower parts of the earth, and ascends far above all things; sits in the dust with fallen nature, and soars beyond the clouds with renewed nature; not in regular alternations, but with the zigzag of lightning in a storm, giving full vent to that quick and lively principle of openness which expresses every parenthetical emotion as it rises; and makes his style so free and flexible an instrument of his mind, almost like thinking aloud. And both his depth and his height, both his picture of vile and helpless man, and his picture of man upraised and carried on by a divine impulse, have a response in the human heart. They are the doctrines of human nature as well as of revelation. For, in truth, the sense of sin in man is infinite, and the sense of dependence in him and of invisible support is infinite too.

A man cannot measure his sin and say that it is so much and no more; and a man cannot limit that sense of being elevated by a Power outside of him which he has when he emerges from sin; that feeling of dependence which is helplessness and strength combined; which is not sadness, but exultation, because everything seems to be done for him, and he is carried along by an unfailing impulse from without:—a feeling which even great men of the world have often had in their own sphere of action, and which has invariably been, when they had it, their great source of strength. For it is a known fact of human character, that a man is never so vigorous, so decided, so unchangeably resolute and determined, so inaccessible to every attempt to divert him, and so elevated above every obstacle and barrier in his way—if it happens to be a wrong cause—so deaf to all reason, and so irrevocably and incorrigibly pertinacious and obstinate, as when he declares that he himself does nothing and wills nothing, but is only following and receiving an unseen motion from without. I say, then, that the sense of sin in man and the sense of dependence are both infinite. It is this latter principle of self-rejection which constitutes the essence of that act of faith which is said by St. Paul to be justifying. It is a matter of simple feeling and common sense that mere works do not satisfy us, as marks of goodness. Nature herself desiderates a certain running accompaniment of self-rejection, emptying every good work, as fast as it is done, of its merits in the doer's eyes: and this ulterior, more remote, and deeper principle is the secret of that type of character which is an object of love. Do we not sometimes meet persons who suggest the remark, how much more we should justify them, or account them righteous, if they would do fewer good works, and do them better; if their left hand did not know so accurately what their right hand did? It was this deep, ulterior principle, to which good works are but the antechamber, which Luther pursued with eager penetration, grasped with extravagant force, and expressed with blind and headstrong audacity, in some of his well-known dicta in disparagement of works. Such is the witness of nature to St. Paul's doctrine of justification, which embodies a great truth of morals as well as of faith.

This set of Articles, then, appears to me to give a plain, unpretending summary of this language of St. Paul. They adopt the range of St. Paul, beginning with the mystery of the Fall, and ending with the mystery of Predestination, and they follow him throughout. Human nature is prostrate in the IXth Article; it throws itself upon a Redeemer in the XIth, and performs the act of self-abandonment; it is raised to the heavenly life here in the XIIIth; and it ascends to glory in the XVIIth. It is quite true that we miss in them the peculiarly poetical effect which we have in the Epistles of St. Paul. But the defect is one of form rather than of substance. The Book of Job, for example, is a book which contains the most striking, beautiful, and majestic truths respecting Providence, human destiny, and design of our present existence; but these truths owe a good deal of the impression they make upon our imagination to the form in which they come before us— the wildness, the abruptness, the quick exclamation, the impassioned complaint, the angry self-vindication; the indignation turning suddenly into the cry of the supplicant, obstinately unyielding, but conscious of utter helplessness; knowing that it is useless to contend against Infinite Power; and so tenderly deprecating, while he all but defies, the Hand that crushes him. If all this was transformed into twelve propositions with headings, the effect on the imagination would be a good deal impaired. And yet every truth that is contained in the book might be stated correctly in this shape, and might demand our assent as the evident doctrine of the Book of Job.

Although, therefore, one school in the Church is charged with too exclusive a devotion to St. Paul, we must still all acknowledge his teaching to be part and parcel of Christianity. And, therefore, had the Articles stopped with the historical or Gospel account of our Lord, and not gone on to St. Paul's doctrine, they would have been plainly quite defective as a representation of Christianity; giving a part and not the whole. This great Apostle has indeed moulded and worded the theology of Christendom in its internal, or, as it is called, subjective region. We meet him in every Confession of Faith, Romanist and Puritan, and all agree in understanding him to say what these

Articles understand him to say. They extract the same main doctrines from him.[1] Indeed, the most difficult doctrine—that of Predestination—has been interpreted as Calvinistically by the greatest Roman doctors as by Calvin himself.

These Articles, then, being solid portions of Scripture, I will now apply that rule of interpretation to them to which I have called attention,—viz., that in whatever sense, and with whatever explanation, we accept these statements in Scripture, we may understand them in that sense, and apply that explanation to them, when we meet them in the Articles. We cannot suppose that this language has one meaning in the Articles and another in Scripture. It is quite true, that *if* we interpret Scripture wrong, then, by the application of this rule, we shall interpret the Articles wrong: but this is no fault of the rule itself, but of the particular interpretation of which it is made the channel: no fault of the rule of transferring the sense of Scripture to the Articles, but only of the particular supposed sense which is transferred.

Let us take the IXth Article. Here is the statement that man, in his natural state, is very far gone—*quam longissime*—from original righteousness. Was Socrates, then, was Plato, was Phocion, was Titus, was Trajan, was Marcus Antoninus,

---

[1] "Si quis non confitetur primum hominem Adam, quum mandatum Dei in paradiso fuisset transgressus . . . mortem incurrisse, et cum morte *captivitatem sub ejus potestate qui mortis deinde habuit imperium, hoc est diaboli* . . . anathema sit.

"Si quis inquinatum illum mortem tantum in omne genus humanum transtulisse, non autem et peccatum quod mors est animæ; anathema sit."—*Council of Trent*, Sess. v.

"Gratis autem justificari ideo dicamur, quia nihil eorum quæ justificationem præcedunt, sive fides sive opera, ipsam justificationis gratiam promeretur. Si enim gratia est jam non ex operibus, alioquin, ut Apostolus inquit, gratia jam non est gratia."—*Council of Trent*, Sess. vi. c. 8. In Chapter v. the Council denies that any works done before the bestowal of grace *merit* that grace. "Declarat justificationis exordium in adultis a præveniente gratia sumendum, hoc est, ab ejus vocatione, qua nullis eorum existentibus meritis, vocantur." The modification of merit *de congruo*, entertained by one party in the Roman Church, was denounced by another. "Sunt alii non contenti gratia gratis data, sed volunt quod vendatur a Deo, et ematur ab eis aliquo pretio licet vili, congruo tamen ut asserunt, non condigno. Dicunt enim homines ex solis propriis viribus gratiam Dei mereri de congruo, non autem de condigno. Et quia iste error est famosior cæteris his diebus, etc."—*Bradwardine*, lib. i. c. 39.

Bradwardine, called the Profound Doctor, was Archbishop of Canterbury in the reign of Edward III.

as far as possible gone from original righteousness? Were they each and all of them as wicked as they could possibly be? I answer this question by asking another. Were they sold under sin, were they under captivity to the law of sin, and did no good thing dwell in them? These statements of St. Paul apply to all mankind in their natural state; and therefore they include, in their literal scope, Socrates, Phocion, Marcus Antoninus, and every virtuous heathen that ever lived. But when we accepted these statements of St. Paul, we accepted them with the interpretation that they were not intended by the inspired writer to conflict with the plain fact of experience, that men, even in a state of nature, have a certain power of doing right actions and avoiding wrong ones; that some are better than others; and that some have been very good men— a fact which St. Paul himself recognises elsewhere, in the allusion "to the Gentiles, which do by nature the things contained in the law." We have only to apply, then, the same explanation to the same statements in the Articles. It is a right, and a duty as well, to do so; otherwise we make the language of Scripture mean differently in Scripture and out of Scripture; that is, when, simply for convenience' sake, it is extracted from the page of the Bible and put in a separate passage before us. We cannot do this. The language of Scripture is, in truth, always *in* Scripture: if it be separated from it to the eye, it is incorporated with it to the mind. It must always have that meaning which we give to it when we read the Bible and come across it there. We give St. Paul's language, when we meet it in his Epistles, the benefit of what is, in the particular case, a *natural* interpretation: natural, *because* not rigidly literal. We may give the same to the Article.

We come to another statement in the same Article, that this sinfulness of the natural man is the fault of his nature, that is, to the doctrine of Original Sin, or of the Fall of the whole human race in Adam. How is this consistent with the Divine justice? I answer this question also by asking another. How is the same language in St. Paul consistent with Divine justice? When we accepted that whole body of language in St. Paul, which plainly asserts the spiritual death of the whole human race in Adam, we accepted it either in a sense which reconciled it to our own understanding with the Divine justice, or in a mysterious and incomprehensible sense. We can apply the same senses to it when we meet it in the Article.

We come to the XIth Article. Here is the great theme of so many controversies,—the assertion of Justification by Faith only. How is this to be explained in consistency with the express declaration of St. James, that a man is justified by works? I answer this question, too, by asking another. How is St. Paul to be explained in consistency with St. James? When we came across the doctrine of Justification by Faith only in St. Paul, we explained it—as we were bound to do—in some way which made it consistent with St James's *literal* assertion of the contrary; "for we may not so expound one place of Scripture as to be repugnant to another." We have only then to apply the same interpretation to that doctrine when we meet it in the Article. As encountered in St. Paul, it is *ipso facto* consistent with St. James, by reason of the unity of Scripture: and what it means in St. Paul it means in the Article.

We come to the XIIIth Article. Here is the statement that "works done before the grace of Christ and the inspiration of His Spirit are not pleasant to God, but rather have the nature of sin." Was no act, then, of a heathen, however generous and heroic, ever pleasant to God? I answer this question, also, by asking another—the same I asked before, —Was every heathen sold under sin, in captivity to the law of sin? If so, then every act of his must have corresponded to that condition. The literal sense of St. Paul is evidently opposed to the performance of any good action by man in a state of nature. But we have taken the language of St. Paul with a qualification: and we can take the language of the Article with the same.

We come to the XVIIth Article, and the known *crux* it offers. Is everlasting happiness, then, the result of an eternal and sovereign decree on the part of God, predestinating certain persons to it, and to the qualifications for it,—the call, the obeying the call, justification, conformation to Christ's image, and good works? I can reply, what is simply the truth, that

St. Paul says exactly the same thing. His *language* and the Article's *language* are the same. We have only, then, to give the same meaning to it in the Article that we have given to it in St. Paul. One who thinks with Bishop Tomline, that by those who are "predestinated to be conformed to Christ's image," to be called, justified, and glorified, St. Paul only means "that part of mankind to whom God hath decreed to make known the Gospel," will, of course, give that meaning to the same language in the Article. One who adopts the interpretation noticed by Bishop Burnet, that when St. Paul describes holiness of life or conformity to Christ as the effect of predestination, he means that it is the cause of it, will explain the assertion of the Article in the same way. One who adopts the Calvinistic interpretation of St. Paul will give the Calvinistic interpretation to the Article. One who adopts the last-named interpretation of St. Paul, with the reserve that it only expresses one side of a great mysterious truth, will adopt the same interpretation of the Article with the same reserve.

I will venture to hope that my argument up to this point contains a good deal which will more or less meet with your concurrence. And I will hazard the prophecy that you will not stop me if I go a step further, and say that these Articles, interpreted in this way, do not impose any great difficulty upon the subscriber. The difficulty, whatever it may be, has been forestalled; it has been met and dealt with in a prior stage of this business, so that when we come to the Article the encounter is past and over. There is no fresh stumbling-block, but only one which we have already surmounted; nor have we to originate an explanation, but only to repeat one. The whole brunt of the struggle has been borne by Scripture, and under the shelter of that intervening barrier the Articles reclined in peace, and only awaited the issue of the combat outside of them which was to decide their explanation. That is the peculiarity of the position, if we may call it so—the military position of these structures. Their battle is fought upon the ground of Scripture. They are saved the exposure to the open sea of interpretation, the waves of which dash upon the rock of inspiration before they reach them, and having spent their force leave a comparative haven for hard-worked and exhausted exegesis.

And this peculiarity in the position of the Articles should perhaps be remembered when surprise is expressed at the fact that so large a number of propositions should be accepted by so large a number of men. This fact in itself, and independently of its antecedents, would indeed be astonishing, and might well excite an ironical curiosity. But this fact has one very remarkable antecedent, which goes some way in explaining it, and makes it more natural and less extraordinary than it otherwise would be; and that is, that a particular book or collection of writings, namely, the Bible, has been accepted by all Christians as an inspired book, and though we differ among ourselves as to the points to which inspiration extends, all would acknowledge doctrine as coming under the guarantee of it. When a set of articles, then, is constructed, so far as their statements are in the language of Scripture, so far they are *ipso facto* statements universally accepted. The agreement as to accepting them pre-exists in the universal acceptance of Scripture. We start with a common reservoir and depository of language, which at once secures a common reception for all the language taken from it. The meaning will be disputed because the meaning of the Bible is disputed, but the statements are of common acceptance because the statements in the Bible are.

This peculiarity, too, in the position of the Articles, should perhaps be remembered when notice is taken of the great diversity of senses in which the Articles are subscribed. "What discord—what variation," it is said, "what a mockery of agreement is here!—people accepting the same statements, but every one understanding them in his own sense." But does not all this go on long prior to the Articles in the treatment of Scripture? Would not all this go on if the Articles were swept out of existence to-morrow, and expunged from the Church's tablet? There would be still the statements of Scripture accepted by all, but in different senses by different schools. There would be still that formal profession of agreement so far in advance of the reality, which some might call a mockery and pretence, and which, indeed, would be this, as much as, and no more than, our agreement in the Articles.

Should not this peculiarity, too, in the position of the Articles be remembered, when the complicated nature of the structure is noticed? It is true it is a complicated fabric, but is not Scripture as much so—indeed more so—by how much it is, in terms, more comprehensive than the Articles? Upon the subject, for example, of Justification, the *letter* of the Articles is less complicated than the letter of the Bible; the latter consisting of two apparently opposite assertions, the former consisting of only one assertion. But does the attribute of simplicity really belong to the scheme of human salvation, as described in the page of Scripture?—a scheme which, starting with a mysterious depravation of our nature, as mysteriously remedies it, and brings things to their issue by a circuitous process of rectification, instead of by a straight and direct course? I take the actual language of the Bible, as it meets my eye, and I say, it is not simple language. It is complicated language. It is language which expresses a complication of some kind or other in the invisible world of man's relations to God and God's relations to man; something out of order in nature which requires to be met by supernatural means. And St. Paul discloses a human interior corresponding to this intricacy of Divine truth, and illuminates with his torch a cavern awful in its depths and recesses, when he reveals man to himself. And are there not oppositions which can only be harmonised by interpretation in that Volume, which expresses doctrinal truth by statement and counter-statement, but not always by simplicity and unity of statement?[1]

It appears to me, then, that whatever became of the Articles, the self-same difficulties, and the self-same way of meeting them, would go on amongst us; that we should still accept a complicated mass of statement, and that we should accept that

---

[1] The Bishop of Oxford (Bp. Wilberforce), speaking of our Formularies, says: "Such a state of things is rather a combination than a compromise. And this is the special character of Catholic Truth. For all revealed religion rests upon certain great principles; which the human mind can hold together in what it knows to be a true concord, whilst yet it cannot always by its intellectual processes limit, define, and reconcile what its higher gift of intuition can harmonise."—*Charge*, 1860.

mass of statement in a variety of senses according to the particular school to which we belong. The Articles are, many of them, but a reflection of Scripture, and their interpretation but the reflection of the interpretation of Scripture. Were the representative document to go, the original document itself would still remain to be the subject-matter of conflicting explanations, to be language accepted by all alike and understood by different sections differently, and to be the basis of doctrinal variety under the form of one and the same subscription.

There is, indeed, a difference between the language of these Articles and that of Scripture, to which I have alluded. I observe that you characterise the set of Articles which has formed the subject of these remarks as "polemical." I should not myself apply that term to them, but I should admit that they gave a special prominence to one side of Scripture language. I should admit, for example, what is a simple fact, that the XIth Article reflects the language of St. Paul on Justification, and does not reflect that of St. James; and that the XVIIth Article represents the Predestinarian side of Scripture, and not the free-will side of Scripture. But Articles, which are "polemical" only in this sense, that they give prominence to certain statements of Scripture and keep others in the background, offer no difficulty to a subscriber on that account. Because the only question which he has to consider is not whether other statements are *not* in Scripture, but whether these statements *are*. If they are there he has accepted them in their place in Scripture, and he has only to accept them in the same sense in the Articles. He has accepted, for instance, St. Paul's assertion of Justification by faith only. Wherever, then, and whenever, he meets that assertion afterwards, he can accept it. It makes no difference to him that St. James's statement is absent, if the statement which is present is St. Paul's.

I gather, however, from some observations I have met with, that what is called the "act" of subscribing, as distinguished from a general obligation to hold a certain collection of doctrine, is very distasteful to some. I can allow this feeling to be consistent with perfect honesty of subscription. We are accustomed to the private act of understanding language with a certain liberty, and qualifying the letter; and we could not get on without a moderate licence of this kind in our reading or intercourse. I need not repeat the remarks I made some pages back on this point. But when we are—to use a colloquial expression—"pulled up" by a form—a solemn act in the presence of others, we would certainly rather have language which did not require qualification to subscribe to. We are, for example, all agreed upon the qualification we give to the Scripture precept, "Swear not at all;" but had any of us to declare solemnly in an assembly of Quakers that he believed it to be wrong to "swear at all," he would do it with the unpleasant consciousness that everybody present regarded him as taking an unwarrantable liberty in making that declaration in the sense in which he did. Could we call up from their sleep the scholastic doctors of a thousand years, there would be the same feeling in declaring before that venerable assembly our belief in the truth that "he that believeth not shall be damned," because we do not take this text literally, and they did. And so in the case of the Articles—a public act of subscription, even if made only in the presence of a few officials, conjures up in imagination a dissentient row, who would look upon the sense in which we accepted one or other Article as an evasion. But if we are conscious of our own integrity, this feeling, though not unnatural, is easily met.

The formal "act" of subscription, again, in the presence of officials, conjures up the idea of lawyers' documents and lawyers' forms, to which class of compositions qualification does not apply, because it is their very purpose to express all that in ordinary language is left to be understood. But this is not the language in which the Articles of which I am speaking are drawn up. They are drawn up substantially in the language of Scripture; and the language of Scripture is not "lawyers' language," but the natural language of mankind, which sometimes leaves room for qualification. They represent the full and literal sense of St. Paul; but St. Paul writes in natural language, not in "lawyers' language."

Although, therefore, the "act" of subscribing may involve—in an atmosphere of difference of opinion,—a sense of collision with others which is not agreeable, it must be remembered that this collision has really gone on before in the interpretation of Scripture, and that our subscription has virtually been made prior to the formal act, in our own rooms, over our books, in our own thoughts.

It does not appear to me, then, that in the compartment which I have been reviewing, subscription presses hard. I have selected one set of Articles, those relating to the process of man's salvation, because here are statements which come into apparent collision, not only with the tenets of particular schools, but the natural feelings of mankind. And it appears to me that these Articles copy St. Paul's doctrine so faithfully, that we have accepted them in accepting St. Paul, and have only got to understand them in the same sense in which we understand him.—"But if you claim the acceptance of these Articles on the ground that they are the language of the Bible, why not be satisfied with the acceptance of the Bible?" That is a proper question in its place, but I have only to deal here with an alleged difficulty or grievance; and I say that there is no grievance in subscribing to these statements if these statements are in Scripture. "But you are virtually maintaining the German 'quatenus,' that the subscriber's assent to the Articles is only assent to them *so far as* they are in Scripture." No; the rule which I have been applying is the rule, that if the language of an Article and Scripture is the *same*, the sense is the same. The "quatenus," on the other hand, gives the individual the liberty to decide for himself that the language of the two *disagrees*, and to take the one and reject the other.

The conclusion which I arrive at, then, is that, over the ground on which I have been travelling, relief from subscription is not wanted. We may, I think, be quite sure that a very large amount of forbearance will always be secured for the results of individual speculation by the natural operation of reasonable feelings in the members of the Church, without instituting any organic change. Our system is one which raises the greatest possible difficulties in the way of prosecution of individuals—not only formal difficulties, but difficulties of feeling. Ours is a system which encourages inquiry and sets minds to work. When, then, we have sanctioned an active principle of examination at the outset, and when we have lived side by side with the gradual growth of individual thought, in the same institution, under the same roof, the sanction of the process must, to a certain extent, affect us even in dealing with its results, when they are erroneous, and must operate as a great practical check upon the temper in which we condemn them. A limit of course there must be to freedom of opinion within a communion which professes a definite creed. I cordially agree with the remarks of the Bishop of London,[1] made with much vigour and naturalness, upon this combination of duties which devolves upon us. But philosophical feelings, social feelings, and equitable views, will always be a strong self-acting barrier against the impatient treatment of the errors of intellectual men, without recourse to a formal alteration of our ecclesiastical basis.

I am,

Yours very sincerely,

J. B. MOZLEY.

[1] Bishop Tait.

## XVI.—*THE COLONIAL CHURCH QUESTION.*

THE crisis through which the Colonial Church is now passing is the result of a collision between two great principles, one in the faith, the other in the working constitution of our Church; one a religious principle, the other a legal one; one the doctrine of the Inspiration of Scripture, the other "the legal principle of construction," as applied to our Formularies. Were a person asked offhand what the motive working in the present critical movement of the Colonial Church was, he would reply, perhaps, that it was a wish to free itself from the Royal Prerogative. But this would not be a proper description of it. The Colonial Churches do not object to the Royal Prerogative as such; rather they would gladly accept it as a centre around which to gather, uniting them with each other, and with the Church at home, in one ecclesiastical system. What is objected to is a particular legal mode of working the Royal Prerogative; a particular judicial principle with which it is now identified. Nor is it this principle itself, that is, not its ordinary action, which is objected to, but its working in one particular case, and upon one particular question, with which it is in its very nature unfitted to deal.

When we speak of the "legal principle of construction," in its primary sense, we mean a very natural and equitable principle, namely, that when the Church makes a statement, that statement should be interpreted according to its literal meaning. There can be no doubt as to the justice of this principle as applied to all truth which can be put into documentary shape, that is, can be formally stated. "The legal principle of construction" is in these cases only another name for the principle of correct and natural interpretation of language. But when we speak of "the legal principle of construction" in a secondary sense, we mean by it another thing—we mean the *confinement and restriction* of the Church to this naked documentary criterion. The use of the documentary criterion is one thing, the confinement of the Church to it is another thing. "Our ecclesiastical judges," says the Bishop of London,[1] "without absolutely committing themselves to it in the abstract, have practically acted on the principle that they must be guided entirely by the written law of the Church, known and understood and acquiesced in by all who are subject to their authority."[2] In other words, a man is only bound not to contradict the written statements of the Church; if any assertion does not contradict these, he may make it. But in this secondary sense, or as a confining principle, "the legal principle of construction" is defective as an instrument of defence to the Church. For though it deals well enough with truth which can be put into documentary shape or be formally stated, what if there is truth which cannot be put into documentary shape, or cannot be formally stated, but yet for the security of which the Church ought to provide? This becomes then an insufficient instrument, and there is something which has to be guarded, but which is not guarded by this defence. But such a truth is the doctrine of the inspiration of Scripture.

When I say that the doctrine of the inspiration of Scripture is not capable of being formally stated, I mean this :—Did the Church impose upon her members the position that the infallibility of Scripture covers every single statement in it without exception, for example, the minutest genealogical and chronological statement, every physical and astronomical statement? Such a doctrine of the infallibility of Scripture could be *stated*, because it *was* thus universal in application, and covered every particular. But without going into a great and profound controversy, it is enough, in the present instance, to say that the Church does not impose this interpretation of the infallibility of Scripture as *necessary*, and therefore the doctrine of the Inspiration of Scripture, which has to be laid down or assumed in an Article

[1] Bishop Tait.     [2] *Charge*, p. 45, delivered 1867.

of the Church, is a modified and qualified doctrine, or admitting of a modified and qualified interpretation. Such a doctrine is laid down or assumed in our Articles, in which the Bible is said to be "the Word of God." The statement that Scripture is "the Word of God" certainly attaches a general infallibility to Scripture; but it does not in the meaning of the Church *oblige* the extension of the cover of infallibility to every single physical, astronomical, genealogical, chronological statement of Scripture. Again, the Church requires "belief in all the Canonical Scriptures;" but the belief of the person carries the same latitude as the infallibility of the book.

But because the Church thus leaves a margin—if I may be allowed to use such a term upon such a subject—in her doctrine of the infallibility of Scripture, does she acquiesce in the rejection of the historical and other general truth of Scripture to any extent and amount whatever? in a general liberty to attribute error to Scripture judgments on persons and things? in the treatment, in short, of Scripture as an ordinary book generally, only reserving the authority of certain specific statements in it? This is a question of fact, and the answer to it depends on what is, as a matter of fact, the nature of the belief which has been held, and is held now, in the Christian body respecting the inspiration of Scripture. What is the character of this belief? Is it such a belief as does not feel itself at all contradicted or challenged by a wholesale rejection of the truth of Scripture, but feels itself fitting in and uniting with such a rejection? taking it easily, and as a matter of course, as something which came within its own scope, and for which it already allowed? or, on the contrary, is it such a belief as, upon the supposition of Scripture being largely false or fabulous, feels an immediate shock, and revolts from the idea?

This being a question, then, relating to a matter of fact, there can be no reasonable hesitation how it must be decided. I can no more doubt as to the general character of the belief which has been in possession of the Christian body from the first, and is in possession of it now, on the subject of the Inspiration of Scripture, than I can doubt about the plainest facts of history or society. The Christian Church has been always penetrated with an idea of the Inspiration of Scripture which utterly refuses to amalgamate with this critical conception of Scripture, and which demands another attitude towards the Bible. This book stood alone in the world, as bearing the Divine stamp, and being an authoritative account of the dealings of God with man in the great matter of human salvation. This was its great communication; but inasmuch as this extended through a succession of revelations, and involved the career of a whole people, and the varied contributions from national history and personal history to the one leading purpose of God; and inasmuch as all that contributed to the execution of the great plan came under the cover of it, and partook of its spiritual providential character, the seal of inspiration did not attach to one or other part, or to one or other ingredient in the book only, but it attached to the book as a whole. Thus the belief of the Church fits in with one measure of latitude on the subject of inspiration, it does not fit in with another. Differences of degree are not always mere differences of quantity. One measure of personal liberty is consistent with civil government, another is not; one degree constitutes temperance, another intemperance. Distinctions of degree, then, may be distinctions of principle. The Church has treated the difference between one measure of latitude on the subject of inspiration and another as a distinction of principle; and has regarded *one* latitude as inconsistent (and indeed in the actual history of men's minds it appears to be so) with the belief even of a true revelation *in* Scripture.

But though the distinction between one latitude and another in the treatment of Scripture is a real one, and a real practical part of the belief of the Church, it is a distinction which is utterly incapable of being stated in an Article. If a margin on this subject is allowed at all in the belief of the Church, that margin cannot be defined. The merest slip of logical territory, and the breadth which covers the whole domain *but* the merest slip, come exactly under the same formal statement or absence of statement. The infringement of the merest edge of the field of inspiration and the irruption into its very centre come under the same definition or absence of definition. If the most insignificant genealogical fact, or chronological fact, or physical fact, is allowed to escape out of the shield of infallibility, the same opening which lets out these facts lets out logically a thousand more. A chronological fact, a genealogical fact, and even a physical fact, it will be said, is an historical fact; if one kind of historical fact may be wrong, another may be; if one fact may be wrong, a whole history may be.

It is impossible, therefore, to draw a line in an Article between a margin and any invasion the most extensive of the historical infallibility of Scripture. From which it follows that, our Articles leaving a margin, no such invasion contradicts the Articles; and that, "the legal principle of construction" admitting anything which does not contradict the Articles, no such invasion is prohibited by the "legal principle of construction." This legal principle must interpret an *opening*, as literally as it interprets a statement; it binds itself not to meddle with anything; as the opening *is*, so must it *admit;* anything is to go through it which can go through it.

The prohibition, indeed, of one measure of latitude, as distinguished from another, being wanted, people have gone to the Articles for it. "It must be in the Articles; is it in the first, is it in the second, is it in the third?" The truth is, it is not in any Article, it cannot be in any Article; the very nature of the subject excludes it from the defining grasp of an Article. How can a distinction of measure, of degree, of application, admit of formal definition? If there is a difficulty inherent in the subject of Inspiration which throws the doctrine upon the common sense and the fundamental belief of Christians for its treatment, such a circumstance would have a parallel in many parts of the Divine dispensations; but it would plainly take the doctrine out of the sphere of formal propositions. It is sometimes said that the questions connected with the doctrine of Inspiration were not mooted in the days when our Articles were written; and the omission of any statement in them to meet the excesses in the historical criticism of the Sacred Volume has been accounted for on that ground. But the cause of the omission in the Articles lies far deeper; it springs from the very root, and out of the intrinsic complexity of the subject. Were a whole Synod of divines, with the full knowledge of the latest inroads upon the historical region of Scripture, to deliberate together to frame a formula to express the doctrine of the infallibility of Scripture, the formula they would devise, if it did not trench upon the designed latitude of our Articles, would express just as much as, and no more than, the phrase in the Article expresses, namely, that the Bible is the "Word of God." It would be chargeable with just the same defect as a guarantee which accompanies the existing formula. It is no fault of our Articles that they do not state what is incapable of being stated; but that does not alter the matter-of-fact result, namely, that the Articles in their legal construction do not prohibit the extent of criticism now spoken of.

We have got then as far as this—that the Church has a decided belief on the subject of the Inspiration of Scripture; but that, as that belief is incapable of being defined and stated in an Article, the Article in its legal construction does not guard that belief. But, arguing upon principles of equity, does the Church lose her right over truth because she cannot formally state it? That is the next question which comes. Does it debar her in justice from requiring from her ministers a certain mode of treating the inspiration of Scripture, that she cannot formally define that mode? I cannot see, myself, the necessary connection between these two. When the Christian Church started upon her career she found herself in custody of different kinds of sacred deposits. She was, in the first place, the guardian of various doctrines which were capable of being formally stated. These doctrines then *were* stated in Creeds, Confessions, Articles, Formularies; and the doctrines having been stated, those statements are the proper subject of legal construction. No unexpressed intention on the part of the Church has the right to insinuate itself here; she has no right to play fast and loose with the principle of Creeds and Articles; to put forth explicit doctrine and supplement it where she pleases by implicit; when she has made her statements she must take her stand upon them, or, if they are defective, alter them; and the grammatical, the literal, the legal interpretation of these statements is the just one. But there was another sacred deposit which could not be treated in this way. This was not a doctrine or collection of doctrines, but a Book or collection of books. The attitude of the Church toward this Book was what was above described. An infallibility attached to the Book as a whole, but that infallibility at the same time was not, as a matter of necessary belief, strained to include particular minutiæ, where the enforcement of it would indeed, in the opinion of some, have detracted from, rather than added to, its dignity and grandeur. Simply then, and in a word, the doctrine of the Inspiration of Scripture could not be stated. But there *was* a doctrine of it, a strong, a vigorous, a deep doctrine of it in the mind of the Church. A certain attitude was taken toward the Bible, and that attitude was as well understood as anything in religion. A certain mode of treating Scripture would at once have been denounced as in utter discord with the character of the Book. Because then the Church has only stated and documentary rights over truth which she can state and put into a documentary shape, has she no rights which are not stated, and are not documentary, over other truth which is incapable of such expression? Because the general mode of treatment due to the inspiration of Scripture cannot be defined, does she possess no jurisdiction whatever with respect to the general treatment of the Inspiration of Scripture?

I do not see, as I have just said, what is the connection between those two; or that the right to guard certain truth, and require the practical recognition of it, depends upon the circumstance of such truth's capability of being formally stated. This circumstance with regard to the *right* to guard does not appear relevant. If there is a belief respecting Scripture which is deep in the Church's mind, which is a thorough part and an inseparable part of her belief in Revelation, which touches the foundation of her whole faith, which it is all-important and positively necessary to guard for the security of the faith of her members,—to say that this belief cannot be defended because it cannot be put into a formal proposition does seem a kind of pedantry. You have the right to the *thing;* the thing exists all the same, whether or not it can be logically defined. True, if you *can* formally state a truth, you are bound upon the principle of Creeds and Articles to do so, and in lack of such statement you must take the consequences, because the omission is your own fault. But here it is no fault of yours that you do not state the truth, you are not able, the truth is of such a nature ; you are not responsible for the nature of the truth. The only form, therefore, in which the right can exist, being that of a right over an unstated and undefined truth, the right is justified in existing in that form. The impossibility of defining the truth constitutes it legitimate to guard it undefined.

You have a right, I say, to the thing. You have a right to many things which you cannot define in terms ; you have a right to be fairly treated, to be civilly treated. What constitutes honesty, candour, liberality, openness, in any particular case, cannot be defined. A Christian congregation, then, with respect to a certain general treatment of Scripture, says, I have a right to the *thing*, whether I can formally define it or not is nothing to the purpose. Nor is it anything to the purpose, in considering the question of right, whether this idea of the community is logical or illogical ; we have nothing to do with criticising this idea. It is enough that this *is* the idea of the community.

It must be remembered that we assume in this discussion the place which the Bible holds in a Christian community, as being *such* a Book as that the treatment of it like an ordinary book, which carries with it a general exposure to criticism, is irreligious in the eyes of the community. This place, this rank, this character of the Book in the eyes of the community is assumed. Do you mean to say then, that, this being the case, a Christian community has not a right to maintain *as* a community its own fundamental idea of that Book by requiring that that Book shall be treated in a certain general way, answering to this fundamental idea of it existing in the community ? To say this would be to interfere with obvious rights ; for what is the object of persons meeting together in a religious community, unless they can secure a common general ground in the treatment of certain subjects? When they do meet then, the community has a right to make its own terms with its own ministers and officers, to which the latter need not agree unless they please, but by which, if they do agree to them, they are bound. This right applies, then, as to other things, so to the general treatment of Scripture. But if this general treatment cannot be formally stated? The community still does not lose the right, it exists all the same. The fundamental idea which the community entertains of "the Word of God" attaches and adheres to the phrase "Word of God" as the sense and import of that phrase. The sense does not the less go along with the words because it cannot be formally stated. And this being the case, the community has the right to defend, along with the phrase, the sense which attaches to it, and to see that that sense is not violated in the public expressions and ministrations of its own ministers.

The principle of enforcing claims and rights, which are of such a nature that they cannot be formally stated, is well known to law: take, for example, the law of libel. No statute does or can define what a man may say, and what a man may not say about his neighbour. He may certainly say a great many things which his neighbour will not like, and which yet will not bring him under an action of libel. This standard then of illegality in speech and writing affecting our neighbour, which is undefined by statute, exists as a sense and understanding in our courts, and is enforced by the discretion of the jury and judge. The Articles of War do not define what is conduct unbefitting an officer; the criterion exists in an unexpressed shape, and is enforced in the particular case by the discretion of a court.

The standard idea of the Bible as an inspired book thus exists as a fundamental idea or sense attaching to the phrase, in the Christian body; and this sense is defended by a discretionary jurisdiction in the body, which must decide in a particular case whether it has been violated or not. I do not speak of the function of a hierarchy here, but of a public right of a community. The right of requiring a certain mode of treating Scripture, although that mode cannot be defined, is indeed in practical force in every dissenting community in this country. Every Methodist congregation, every Baptist congregation, every Independent congregation exercises it. None of these religious communities have in their written formularies or articles—even if they possess formularies or articles—any definition of the mode of treatment due to Scripture; their ministers therefore subscribe to no such statement: yet it never occurs to any member of these bodies to question the right of the community to claim a certain treatment of Scripture from its ministers. This is assumed as a primary law of the community, which must be known to all who undertake the ministerial office in it.

The same right then exists *radically* in our own Church, and, what is more, it exists in the bosom of the Royal ecclesiastical supremacy as described in our Statutes.

For indeed, so far from the Royal supremacy being in itself chargeable with the legal principle of the reduction of every thing to a documentary criterion, a strong general interposing power was the marked characteristic and a chief function of the Prerogative for a long time in practice, and it is even now so by the letter of our Statutes. By 1 Eliz. c. 1, it is enacted that "such jurisdictions, privileges, superiorities, and pre-eminences, spiritual and ecclesiastical, as by any spiritual or ecclesiastical power or authority *have heretofore been*, or may lawfully be, exercised or used for the visitation of the ecclesiastical state and persons, and for reformation, order, and correction of the same, and of all manner of errors, heresies, schisms, abuses, offences, contempts, enormities, shall for ever be united and annexed *unto the imperial Crown of this realm.*" "There is required," says Hooker, " an universal power which reacheth over all, importing supreme authority of government over all courts, all judges, all causes; the operation of which power is as well to strengthen, maintain, and uphold particular jurisdictions, which haply might else be of small effect, *as also to remedy that which they are not able to help* . . . *when in any part of the Church errors* . . . *are grown which men in their several jurisdictions either do not or cannot help; what-*

soever any spiritual authority or power (such as legates from the See of Rome did sometimes exercise) have done or might heretofore have done for the remedy of those evils ... as much in any degree our laws have fully granted *that the King for ever may do.*"¹ This is the state of the case then. There has always resided in the Universal Church a jurisdiction of a general kind, to supplement her formal statements and written rules, and to act in cases which were incapable of being brought under definite terms. This general jurisdiction is referred to in the statute just quoted as "having been exercised heretofore" in the Church of England by certain "spiritual or ecclesiastical powers" which it does not describe, but which were powers resting ultimately upon the Papacy; and it is asserted that this general jurisdiction has now passed into the hands of the Crown. There can be no doubt that in this general jurisdiction which was exercised in our Church before the Reformation, and to which the Crown succeeded at the Reformation, was included the requirement of a certain mode of treating the inspiration of the sacred volume; and that under that jurisdiction the violation of that treatment would have been disallowed.

It is important, I say, in order to have a true idea of the basis and constitution of our Church—its *Reformation* basis and constitution—to remember that the Articles and Formularies did not stand alone; that there ran parallel with them, by statute and by canons, a recognised and an active general interposing and discretionary power, as a branch of the Royal supremacy, to act in material which could not be provided for in Articles. A power which had always resided in the Church, which resides in every Christian community, by the compact of that day took a particular form, and was transferred to the Crown as its administrator. The secular hands in which it was lodged have disguised it as a Church jurisdiction, and the arbitrary way in which it was often exercised have not recommended it. It was, nevertheless, in however secular a form, in substance a general Church jurisdiction, over and above the

---

¹ Vol. iii. p. 543.

tie of Formularies. And it does now by statute exist, though it is not in force.

For it was indeed inevitable that this general interposing power of the Crown must go. The use of such a power was wholly unfitted to the executive of a popular constitution and a parliamentary majority; and the rights of property, which attached to the tenure of benefices, acted as another obstruction to the use of it. This most important branch of the Crown's ecclesiastical supremacy, which had been so active a branch too, and played so conspicuous a part in our Church history for more than a century after the Reformation, thus fell into absolute desuetude. The letter of our statutes is the only trace we have now of its existence; and with the practical abrogation of a general jurisdiction, the Courts could only fall back upon the written documents of the Church, and their literal or legal construction.

Such is the history of this legal principle, viewed in its technical confining sense. It is an artificial restriction of the Church's area of judgment; the sediment and residuum of jurisdiction which the political circumstances of the country have left in the hands of the Church Courts; the ultimate position which the supremacy has been compelled to take up when driven from its wider range; the gradual formation of legal tradition and caution, when successions of lawyers were obliged step by step to reduce an authority which they were bound to wield with a general regard to the modified constitution of the country. It was thus inevitable that a collision must one day take place between the faith of the Church, on one great subject, and the Church's legal machinery. What the ecclesiastical supremacy of the Crown would grow into under our popular constitution was inevitable; by no fault of courts, or judges, or of any body, but by the inexorable action of events, it has become the "legal principle of construction," simply because its supplement in the Crown's general ecclesiastical interposing power could not be retained. On the other hand, nothing could have prevented the great inspiration question from breaking out some day. The legal loophole was thus inevitable; the question that should slip through it was inevitable. Certain principles working blindly have produced this issue in fact; constitutional liberty, when it attacked the Prerogative, hit something which it did not aim at, but which happened to be *in* the Prerogative, this general Church jurisdiction.

And thus the secret has come out, the disclosure of which was only a matter of time, that the subject of the general treatment of the inspiration of Scripture is not provided for within the legal machinery of our Church. There are all kinds of influences in the Church, the popular faith, the weight of persons in authority, the zeal of the clergy, to compensate for the omission, but the *system* does omit the point. The system allows a margin, and there stops short : it does not interfere with the degree, the extent, the quantity of that margin; it allows a principle of latitude, but says nothing about its application. But upon this subject, degree, extent, quantity, application, are everything; and to abdicate authority on these points is to surrender the treatment of the inspiration of Scripture as a subject of Church jurisdiction. And this, as I have just said, not from any wish or intention on the part of Church or State, but only because, by the inevitable force of events, the discretionary jurisdiction of the Church is gone, the formulary alone is left. Whereas a discretionary power can alone in the nature of the case deal with this subject; a formulary is wholly unequal to it.

The effect of the "legal principle of construction" is, therefore, an abeyance of a branch of Church jurisdiction, of a Christian community's jurisdiction. I cannot deny that this is a serious result, although it is relieved and counterbalanced practically. This legal principle acts with the rigidity of a single angle of fortification, which cuts off one approach, and leaves every other open. There is nothing so mathematically strict and impartial as the action of a *negative* principle, whose prohibitive side being confined to special points, allows a universality on the admitting side, except upon those points; which throws open by the very mode in which it excludes, and liberates by the very conditions by which it ties. One point of view monopolises the ground,—decides legality. Does so and so contradict the Formularies? Certain special, historical, and other statements of Scripture are in the Articles; the legal principle protects *them;* that is the prohibitive side of the principle. But with the general body of Scripture, consisting of history, prophecy, teaching, comment upon men and upon events, it has for all this one general test—belief in the Canonical Scriptures, leaving the whole ground of the application of this test to particulars and to details open.

Now I will, in justice to some who, as learned speculators, apply an expunging criticism to Scripture, say that as parish clergymen they would shrink from using such a criticism as a basis of popular teaching; and that their good taste and common sense would put a veto upon any inculcation and exposition of it in parish discourses. Still I cannot conceal from myself that we should be indebted for that salvo to the good feeling of individuals, and not to the "legal principle of construction." *That* must act with an absolute and geometrical impartiality, let the material of criticism, or its taste and refinement, or its sphere vary ever so much. A university and a parish are the same to it. It could not recognise or take cognisance of any such distinction. The law could not prohibit a clergyman from asserting, as the vicar of a parish, what he had a right to assert as a theological writer. A court could not suspend a clergyman for telling his parishioners what he had a full right to tell the public. When it came to the question of the conditions upon which an incumbent held his benefice, a sermon must be judged exactly by the same criterion as a book, and the only question that could be asked about it would be— Is there anything in it which contradicts the Formularies?

I have before me now two published parish sermons, which will do for an illustration. They are entitled "Apostolical Judgments reversed." In the first the preacher comments severely upon the statement in the Second Epistle of St. Peter, that "Balaam loved the wages of unrighteousness, and was rebuked for his iniquity"—an assertion which he terms "a libel." This "seems to me," he says, "quite a libel upon the honesty of the man, and his straightforward honourable conduct." He passes the same judgment upon the writer of the Book of

Numbers, whom he considers, besides having misrepresented the character, and misinterpreted the acts of Balaam, to have made a positively false statement as regards the commands of God to him; first, not to "go," and then to "go with the men." "It is here," says the preacher, "that we must begin our quarrel with the writer. Whatever may have passed between the soul of Balaam and his God, we cannot possibly believe what the writer here says." He "points out two marks, by which we may clearly perceive how little God had really to do with transactions in which the mistaken writer has so constantly mixed up His Holy Name." And he considers that, though the narrative contains a valuable warning, the warning which it conveys is to avoid the sin of the narrator, not the sin of the subject of the narrative, who is highly commended. "It [this narrative] is of great value as a record of early error on the subject of God's dealings with men; and it would be difficult to find another narrative in the Bible so full of warning against the sin of taking God's Holy Name in vain." The next sermon is on the characters of Esau and Jacob—a subject on which he wholly disagrees with St. Paul, as upon the character of Balaam he differed from St. Peter. "A good deal has been said about Esau selling his birthright; he has been described as 'profane' for doing this, and it has been commented on as a grievous sin. Now, whatever may have been the value of that birthright (and we have no means of discovering now), Esau's answer is a good excuse for his selling it. He says, 'Behold, I am at the point to die, and what profit shall this birthright do me?' . . . Esau was right in his answer—what good could his birthright do him when he was dying of hunger? There is one sense, of course, in which we ought all to face danger, loss, and even death for God's sake, for the sake of our duty. But from this story we cannot possibly discover any particular value in the birthright which should have made Esau care to keep it."

Now this is a specimen of parish teaching which is, I should think, quite unique in our Church. I merely quote it for the illustration of a principle. Most people would say that it ought not to be dependent on the option of the individual clergyman—though it would be very rarely abused—whether such a treatment of Scripture was adopted or not, but that some' jurisdiction in the Church ought to prohibit it. But the statements I have quoted are not, as far as I can see, prohibited by the "legal principle of construction," the rigid nature of which restricts it to one single point of view. The preacher indeed "quarrels" with the writer of the Book of Numbers, and with two apostles; but upon what subject does he "quarrel" with them? Upon any statement of the sacred writer adopted into the Articles? No, upon no doctrine whatever, but only upon a question of fact, relating to the character of two persons. That apostles may not err, and express that error in the canonical Epistles, when the error only relates to a fact of biography, is nowhere stated or implied in any Article or Formulary in its legal sense.

I have been thus particular in describing the working of the "legal principle of construction" in the Inspiration question, because the desire to be relieved from this principle upon this question is at bottom the motive in the present critical movement in the Colonial Church.

When we come to inquire what the question is which has produced this remarkable and critical movement in the Colonial Church, we find it is the question of which we have all along been speaking here—the great question of the Inspiration of Scripture. It so happens that the first great and extensive invasion, in our Church, of the historical truth of Scripture, has been the act of a Colonial Bishop. The Colonial Church, that is, the collection of Churches to which Bishop Colenso belonged, had to deal with that act. That Church considered, then, that the mode of treating the Bible, or the "Word of God," which Bishop Colenso had adopted, was contrary to the whole Christian idea of, and Christian sense attaching to, the "Word of God." The Colonial Church in Africa therefore condemned him, and in condemning him fell back upon its independent basis as a Christian community. There were some complications indeed *at the time* in the legal grounds which the Church took; it partly rested upon Letters Patent; but even then it took the ground of a Church not subject to the Royal supremacy; and it has since fallen back upon a wholly independent ground.

The foregoing pages, then, give us the point of view at which to look at the present critical movement in the Colonial Church. And here I will say, *in limine*, that I am only concerned with the Colonial Church's proceedings against Bishop Colenso upon *one* ground: there were certain doctrinal charges against him, and some have risen up lately; but I only take the inspiration ground of the proceedings, which was of course the main one.

1. It is a great question—the question upon which the Colonial Church moves, and no subordinate or technical one.

2. Upon this question of the treatment of the Inspiration of Scripture the Colonial Church wants to act as a community. Certainly it *could*—it is optional to it—take the line of leaving the whole treatment of Scripture, with respect to its inspiration and infallibility, entirely to the discretion of the individual minister; but it considers this too fundamental a question to treat in this way. It finds itself possessed of a certain idea of what the Bible is, which has come down to it with Christianity, and which indeed is the rooted idea of every orthodox dissenting body as well. This idea of Scripture, therefore, and a corresponding treatment of Scripture, are considered to be essential. And that being the case, the community considers that there is an obligation upon it, as a community, to secure the observation of this treatment of Scripture on the part of its own ministers and spiritual officers. It may be said, few would make a wrong use of the liberty were the subject left free; but whether this is true or not, the community considers that upon a question of such vital importance it is charged with a responsibility as a community; and that it is its duty to treat a compliance on this subject as one of the conditions of the tenure of spiritual office within its pale.

3. But the community could not thus deal with this great question, tied to the legal machinery of the Church at home, which may be very well fitted for securing such Christian truth as can be stated in Articles, but is not equal to the purpose, where the truth is of such a nature that it cannot be

thus stated. The Articles and Formularies, in their legal sense, do not appear to touch Bishop Colenso. The Article says the Bible is the Word of God. Bishop Colenso says the same. He excepts, indeed, from the infallibility of Scripture history a large quantity of historical matter; but the latitude with respect to particulars allowed in the Article is not defined in a way prohibitory of the extent and dimensions to which Bishop Colenso has stretched it, because it is not defined at all. Again, our Formularies impose the "belief in all the Canonical Scriptures." But just the same latitude which attaches to the infallibility of the book attaches to the belief of the individual. "The declaration," says Dr. Lushington, "'I do believe,' must be considered with reference to the subject-matter, and that is the whole Bible, the Old and New Testament. The great number of these books, the extreme antiquity of some; that our Scriptures must necessarily consist of copies and translations; that they embrace almost every possible variety of subject, parts being all-important to the salvation of mankind, and parts being of an historical and less sacred character, certainly not without some element of allegory and figures—all these circumstances, I say, must be borne in mind when the extent of the obligation imposed by the words 'I do believe,' has to be determined. Influenced by these views, I, for the purpose of this cause, must hold that the generality of the expression 'I do believe,' must be modified by the subject-matter; that there must be a *bonâ fide* belief that the Holy Scriptures contain everything necessary to salvation, and that to that extent they have the *direct* sanction of the Almighty."[1] The field of Scripture which is thrown open to criticism by this particular criterion and limitation of the necessity of belief in Scripture is certainly wide enough for all the purposes of an historical critic, who does not concern himself with the doctrines of Scripture, but only with the narrative and description of events. Indeed it is impossible to see how Articles which admitted of *any* latitude or margin on this subject could exclude, by their letter, Bishop Colenso's latitude and margin. The degree of the margin is

[1] Judgment on *Essays and Reviews*.

incapable of being stated in an Article. The opening which admitted others could not be logically constructed so as not to admit him.

4. The Colonial Church, then, in condemning Bishop Colenso, applied a *sense* to the Formularies which was in excess of the legal sense; but which was the sense which attached to the phrase "Word of God" in the mind of the community, and a sense which had been handed down with Christianity. The effect of applying this sense was to restrict and modify a latitude which the letter of the Formularies left undefined; and this restriction condemned Bishop Colenso. But this result could not possibly have been obtained under the legal conditions of the Church at home. The "legal principle of construction" utterly forbids such a proceeding; enforcing the strict alternative—is Bishop Colenso deposed outside of these legal conditions, or not deposed at all? A person may—some do—maintain both that he ought not to be a Bishop, and also that he ought not to be deposed. They object to the result at the cost of the conditions. It is open to them to take either side of the alternative, but is not this the alternative?

5. The Colonial Church only resumes, in this proceeding, its natural jurisdiction as a Christian community. A jurisdiction beyond the letter of Articles, in such matter as cannot be stated in Articles, is inherent in every Christian community. It is acknowledged by every divine of every school who ever wrote about the jurisdiction of the Church: it has always been taken for granted; it has been exercised in the Church Catholic from its very foundation; it is exercised in every dissenting community; and lastly, it resides now, at this moment, in this very Established Church of England, within the bosom of the Royal supremacy, by the authority of Act of Parliament. It is true the Act of Parliament is upon this point a dead letter, but it witnesses to a principle. It is true, there is established by circumstances in the mother Church, and we have become accustomed to, an artificial and conventional *disuse* of this jurisdiction; but an artificial and conventional disuse naturally terminates with the circumstances which produce it; and the use of the natural faculty and

right of the community comes back. The right is gained by taking no new *positive* step at all, but only by *dis*using a disuse, and *dis*continuing a discontinuance.

6. The Colonial Church may well ask—" Why should an old legal instrument, which is made to fit to an old state of things in the mother country, an old forensic formation, an old compact which is part of a past history, be transplanted to the fresh and native soil of the Colonial Church? It may be the duty of you at home to acquiesce in a legal principle which has grown up upon home ground; the more because on the ground on which it has grown up there are many compensations for it; there are old grooves in which things work, long routine, established institutions, venerable customs, ancient seats of learning, the solemnity of old architecture, the Church, the Cathedral, the College, sacred objects and sights, and sources of sacred impressions, on all sides of you, which act as 'aids to faith,' and tend to sustain old ground, when new speculations break out. But *we* should start clear, we want all the strength we can get, and cannot afford to part with any natural right of a Christian community." This is the point of view in which the Royal supremacy is regarded in the Colonial Church. It is no theoretical, it is no canonical, it is no formal ecclesiastical objection to the Royal supremacy which influences her in this mode. It is entirely a practical objection, namely, that the Crown does not, as an existing legal power, possess the means for dealing with this question of Inspiration; that a broader ground is wanted to stand upon than the Crown by legal tradition can use, or allow to itself.

It so happens, then, that just at the time the Colonial Church wants this natural internal jurisdiction for the purpose of dealing with the Inspiration question, this very jurisdiction is apparently, and without any struggle, conceded to it by our courts of law. It is hardly necessary to quote again the statement to which such frequent reference has been made, in the judgment of the Privy Council on Long *v.* Bishop of Capetown, that "the Church of England, in places where there is no Church established by law, is in the same position with any other religious body, in no better but no worse position; and that the members may adopt, as the members of any other communion, rules for enforcing discipline within their body, which will be binding on those who expressly or by implication have assented to them,"—a statement which has been confirmed and carried out by the further position, so well known, laid down in the judgment on the case of Bishop Colenso—" that the Crown, as legal head of the Church, has a right to command the consecration of a bishop, but has no power to assign him any diocese, or give him any sphere of action within the United Kingdom ... or in a Colony or Settlement which is possessed of an independent Legislature." These judgments obviously give the Church in the Colonies the right to adopt the status and enjoy the full rights of a voluntary society, while on the other hand they declare that any legal status which it may appear to have derived from the Crown Letters Patent is wholly illusory, the Crown having no right to create it.

It is true, indeed, that side by side with these important positions laid down by the Privy Council, judgments were given in particular cases which appeared at first sight to be out of keeping with them; but if we examine those particular judgments attentively, we shall find that they are in no real contradiction to these positions. The first case is that of Long *v.* Bishop of Capetown. In the judgment in this case there is no contemplation of the Church in Africa as a voluntary community, having its own rules, obligatory upon Mr. Long as a consentient member. On the contrary, the whole matter between him and the Bishop is looked at from a strictly Church of England point of view. Attendance on diocesan synods is no part of the obedience of a clergyman to a bishop in this country; and therefore it was decided that what was connected with this attendance was no part of the obedience due from Mr. Long to the Bishop of Capetown.

But the peculiar circumstances of the case entirely account for the adoption of an Established Church criterion in this judgment, and omission of a voluntary ground. In fact no voluntary community was before the Court. The Colonial Church in Africa had not formed or organised itself *as a* voluntary community. It did not stand before the Court as a body which had adopted by voluntary agreement terms of union and tribunals of discipline. It was not such a body. It was in fact at that very time committed in part to another and contrary aspect of itself, namely, as possessing jurisdiction from the Crown; for the dioceses, the metropolitanship stood upon the Letters Patent. But under this idea of a Crown jurisdiction, it could not well construct a consensual jurisdiction. The Court, therefore, could not and did not take cognisance of it as a voluntary association; and therefore applied a different mode of treatment to the case, than it would in the instance of a voluntary association have applied. The ground of *contract with a society* is the basis of all judgments with respect to voluntary societies. If an individual enters a society having certain rules and terms of membership, to which he gives explicit or implicit assent, he makes a contract with that society, and that contract is enforced by a Court, by a reference to the rules of the society. But here, there being no organised voluntary society before the Court, the form of the contract underwent a modification and became, from a contract of an individual with a society, the contract of *an individual with an individual*. And this contract between individuals was interpreted by a reference to custom and usage. There were two individuals, two single ecclesiastical persons, before the Court, Mr. Long, a clergyman, and Bishop Gray, a Bishop. Mr. Long enjoyed the endowment of the Church of Mowbray, on the condition of obeying Bishop Gray; what was the particular nature of the obedience due, and did it involve anything connected with Synods? Well, then, if there is any dispute about conditions of apprenticeship, farm service, household service, a Court, in lack of definite terms of engagement, goes to the custom and rule of the district; when a contract involves the employment of certain material, and this is indefinitely expressed, the reference is often the same. In the contract, then, between Mr. Long and Bishop Gray, the condition of obedience was, in the absence of exact specification, construed by a reference to the custom and rule of the district whence the two parties came.

Bishop Gray was consecrated in England by Royal mandate, the Archbishop of Canterbury officiating. The Court, therefore, interpreted the obedience which Mr. Long had bargained to pay to Bishop Gray by an English Church standard; which, as it did not involve the special claim about Synods now made, ruled the case in favour of Mr. Long. No corporate body appeared in this case; there was nobody *over* a diocese; there was nobody *in* a diocese; there was no diocese; there was no Church; there was no community; there were two men; and the engagement between them was interpreted by this criterion.

It must be observed that the peculiar *form* of contract, namely, between two *individuals*, to which the Court was here reduced, was selected because it had to fit on to a peculiar, an intermediate, and a temporary state of things. There are two permanent and regular bases on which religious communions stand; one, that of establishments; the other, that of organised voluntary societies; but here was a communion going on, popularly by the name of the English Church, which did not come under either of these heads,—was not an establishment no the one hand, or an organised voluntary association on the other. It had parted from the former status to which it only hung on by an illusory thread; it had not yet assumed the latter; it was in a neutral intermediate condition. How was it to be treated legally? Had it been an establishment, the question would have been decided by law; had it been a voluntary society, by the terms of the contract with the society; as it was, the fertile imagination of our lawyers hit upon a contract between individuals, which, as a legal contrivance, just caught the Church *in transitu*, and answered the occasion.

The issue then of this judgment was important, as practically interpreting the great *dictum* in it, "The Church (in the Colonies) is in the same position with any other religious body, no better but no worse, the members of which *may adopt*, as the members of any other communion, rules for enforcing discipline, which will be binding on those who have assented to them." The Colonial Church "is" in the same position, etc.: this does not mean that the Church *is* in that position, if it does nothing at all to *put* itself in such a position, if it goes on loosely, in the same state in which it left this country. No: it "may adopt," and if it wants to gain such a position, it *must* "adopt rules for enforcing discipline, which will be binding on those who have assented to them,"—it must formally organise itself as a voluntary communion. There has been, I think, a popular idea that this dictum gives the position of a regular voluntary communion actually to the Church in the Colonies, existing *any how*, but it does not: it only gives the Church the right to *put itself in that position*. The Church cannot put itself into this position in England; it can in the Colonies; that is the difference. We remember the case of Mr. Shore. No section of bishops and clergy could by law establish itself as a voluntary communion upon our diocesan area at home. This prohibition is removed when we get upon Colonial ground. But the Colonial Church is not in this position unless it puts itself into it. Dissenting bodies come into court with their deeds which show their internal government, and justify the act of authority. The Colonial Church must show its rules and tribunals agreed upon by the society. Lord Romilly lays down this right of the Colonial Church just as the Privy Council does. "The members of the Church in South Africa may create an ecclesiastical tribunal to try ecclesiastical matters between themselves, and may agree that the decisions of such tribunals shall be final, whatever be their nature or effect. Upon this being proved, the civil tribunal would enforce the decisions against all the persons who had agreed to be bound by those decisions," and it will do so without inquiring into those decisions. Again,—"If they adopted the Church of England Creed and doctrines, but repudiated a part of its rules and ordinances, they would be bound by those which they had adopted, and not by those which belonged to the Church of England, but which they had rejected. It would, however, be incumbent upon them fully and plainly *to set forth what these rules and ordinances were*, and who accepted them; in order that this might prevent doubt when the Courts of Law were called upon to enforce obedience to these rules and ordinances."

Had the Colonial Church in Africa, then, been an organised

voluntary communion, with certain final episcopal tribunals for the trials of ecclesiastical offences, when Mr. Long entered its ministry; the sentence of one of those tribunals would have been accepted by the Court, and the case would have been decided against Mr. Long. But no such body being before the Court, the case was tested by another criterion, which decided it in his favour.

The other judgment of Privy Council, which took no cognisance of a voluntary communion in Africa, was that given in the matter of the deposition of Bishop Colenso. This judgment only took cognisance of two grounds, that of the Letters Patent, which was the chief and main ground noticed, and that of a contract between two persons, or the alleged engagement of Bishop Colenso to Bishop Gray, by reason of having taken the Suffragan's oath. No voluntary communion ground of the right of deposition was taken cognisance of. But the same reason for the omission of the ground existed in this case that did in the other, namely, that the Church in Africa had not organised itself as, and did not stand before the Court as, a voluntary communion. The African Metropolitan, indeed, while he stated three grounds for the validity of his own jurisdiction, and the act of deposition to rest upon,—his appointment as Metropolitan by Letters Patent,—his mission as Metropolitan from the Church at home, supposed to go along with the Letters Patent,—and the engagement which Bishop Colenso had made in the Suffragan's oath,—did not maintain any ground derived from the agreement of a voluntary community in Africa. Indeed the Church there has suffered all along from what was the result of circumstances—a stand upon two conflicting grounds, either of which incapacitated it for taking advantage of the other. The Letters Patent establishing an Episcopal and a Metropolitan jurisdiction were assumed as legal ground and authority, upon which the Church could act, and it did act upon them till their nullity was exposed. Meanwhile an Episcopacy, with its Metropolitan head, standing as it did upon the legal warrant of the ecclesiastical supremacy of the Crown, did not trouble itself to construct and secure the basis of a voluntary community.

Again, the right of the Colonial Church to do that which no section of the Church at home can do, namely, to put itself into the position of a voluntary community, is not at all affected by the recent judgment of the Master of the Rolls. I have quoted above passages from that judgment, which lay down exactly the same law with respect to this right of the Colonial Church, which the Privy Council has laid down. Upon another question however, which is not in the long-run of so much importance, namely, what the status of the Colonial Church in Africa *is now* at this moment, Lord Romilly appears to be at direct issue with the Privy Council. Contemplated as a formed voluntary association, organised upon a basis of self-government, neither the Privy Council nor Lord Romily have a shadow of a doubt as to the legal status of the Colonial Church, namely, that it is not legally a part of the Church of England, but "in the same position with any other religious body." But the particular question which Lord Romilly had to decide took him mainly upon other ground, and directed his attention to another point of view. He had to consider the Church in Africa not as to what it might be if it chose,—as what it had a right to make itself if it pleased; but he had to consider it as it actually was at that moment. Trust money had been made over to a Bishop of the Church of England; it was due now. Was an African Bishop a Bishop of the Church of England? It was a possible opinion then, even if an off-hand and incorrect one, that the popular sense was enough in the present case, and that he was such in the popular sense. Other grounds, wide of the legal identity of the two Churches, upon which the pecuniary right of the Bishop might be placed, are imaginable. But Lord Romilly decided that the money was due to him, and decided it upon the particular ground of a legal identity—that the Colonial Church in Africa was now, at this moment, *legally* a part of the United Church of England and Ireland.

Perfectly agreed then about a *supposed* Colonial Church,—supposed to be organised as a voluntary self-governing body, Lord Romilly and the Privy Council appear to differ *toto cœlo* about the actual existing Colonial Church. The Privy Council says that "the Crown has no power to assign a Bishop any diocese, or give him any sphere of action in the United Kingdom . . . or a Colony which is possessed of an independent Legislature." The denial of a legal diocese and a legal jurisdiction to the Colonial Church at once cuts asunder the legal identity of that Church now at this moment with the Established Church of England. On the other hand, the Master of the Rolls bases the legal identity of the two upon the affirmation of a legal diocese. "*The law leaves all these* [Episcopal] *functions exactly as by the law of the Church of England they belong to that office. He may as a Bishop visit, he may call before him the ministers within his diocese.*" He is a titular Bishop all the world over, "*he is a territorial Bishop within his see or diocese.*" Certain considerations bearing upon an African diocese cannot, he says, "annihilate the see, or make it cease to be *a legal diocese.*" The legal identity of the Colonial Church with the Church in England follows. "The Church of England may extend and have branches in places where it is not established by law." "The Colony of Natal is a district presided over by a Bishop of the Church of England, which is properly termed a see or diocese," and "the Church in Natal is not a Church in union or full communion with the Church of England, but a part of the Church of England itself . . . in the strict sense of the term."—"So far from no legal identity existing between the Church presided over in the Colonies, and the United Church of England and Ireland, I have arrived at the very opposite conclusion," etc.

Without presuming to criticise legally the judgment of so distinguished a lawyer, I may yet make the observation that such a judgment does run counter to some very natural and ordinary tests.[1] It would ordinarily be thought a condition necessary to being the *same legal body*, that there should be a corporate unity,—one organisation; that it should be under one common head or supreme jurisdiction. The Established Church is under the ecclesiastical supremacy of the Crown. Is the Colonial Church under the same ecclesiastical supremacy? The

---

[1] Mr. Bernard's legal criticism, in his *Remarks on some late Decisions,* etc., brings out with singular acuteness the legal aspects of the case, and the legal principles which militate against this judgment.

test is an exceedingly simple one, and lies in the powers of the Bishop's Court. A Bishop's court, which is *under* the ecclesiastical supremacy of the Crown, must derive powers *from* that supremacy—legal powers from its legal head; it cannot be under it, without being empowered *by* it: it is, as being under the supremacy, the agent and the executive of it. A Bishop's court in this country is thus a court of law, *because* it is under the ecclesiastical supremacy of the Crown. If a Bishop's court, therefore, in the Colonies is under the same ecclesiastical supremacy, it too must be a court of law. But the Master of the Rolls says that it is not, and indeed the fact is very obvious: —" The tribunal of the Bishop [Colonial] is a *forum domesticum*, and not a State tribunal." The Colonial Bishop's tribunal thus derives no powers from the ecclesiastical supremacy of the Crown: the Colonial Bishop's tribunal, therefore, is not *under* that supremacy; the Colonial Church is not under it; and therefore the Colonial Church is not one legal body with the Established Church. The two bodies do not belong to the same organisation. The Colonial Church is outside of that great legal structure which culminates in the Royal supremacy. All that is not under the ecclesiastical supremacy of the Crown is *not* the United Church of England and Ireland or an integral portion of it.

This link between legal powers and legal dependence in the case of the Church is important. There is abundance of language in all quarters to the effect that the Established Church is no part of the constitution of the Colonies, that the Church there has no legal powers; but this language just stops short of the inevitable consequence, namely, that the Church has no legal dependence. There is a half-notion that the supremacy there has rights over the Church, without at the same time giving powers. But the powers and the dependence are but different sides of the same fact, one of which is not had without the other.

But has the Colonial Bishop no kind of jurisdiction because he has not a " coercive " jurisdiction? Undoubtedly he has; but the jurisdiction which flows and is received from the ecclesiastical supremacy of the Crown *is* coercive. If the Bishop's tribunal then has no coercive jurisdiction, it receives no jurisdiction from the ecclesiastical supremacy of the Crown. But the criterion of being *under* the supremacy is receiving jurisdiction *from* it.

"But the Bishop can, for the enforcement of his sentence, resort to the *Civil Court.*" Yes; he can get his sentence enforced, but plainly, by the very terms of the statement, *not* by the ecclesiastical jurisdiction of the Crown. The Master of the Rolls says with perfect truth, "the Bishop is not left powerless, nor can persons with impunity resist his authority. . . . He can exercise all the functions of a Bishop of an English diocese *with this exception*, that his orders are enforced by a civil tribunal." But upon the special point now at issue, is not this "exception" everything? The above statement would leave upon a casual reader the impression that the Royal ecclesiastical supremacy was substantially in the same force in the Colonies that it is in England, only that it acted by a different legal medium, a different instrumental process. But nothing can show more clearly and more directly that the Colonial Church is not under the Royal supremacy than the single circumstance of the interposition of a Civil Court in the matter. The ecclesiastical jurisdiction of the Crown *puts itself* into execution: it flows down in one continuous line from its head and spring in the Crown itself to its terminus in the individual who is the recipient and subject of it. The break of an intervening Civil Court, therefore, is fatal to such a jurisdiction, and nullifies it from the very root; for if it existed it would not want that Court to reinforce it. The same Crown ecclesiastical jurisdiction which tries the case enforces the sentence; but here, one Court tries, another enforces.

It is not then that the Crown's ecclesiastical supremacy is maintained *in a different way* in the Colonies, by a different medium. This language is sometimes used, but such language in truth disguises the real fact, namely, that no supremacy exists at all there but that which is especially *not* ecclesiastical, but only civil; no supremacy but that under which a Baptist congregation comes just as much as the Colonial Church. The Crown has *ecclesiastical* jurisdiction over the Established Church; it decides strictly ecclesiastical questions as the ultimate and supreme tribunal of that Church: the Crown has *not* ecclesiastical jurisdiction over a Baptist community, because it does not decide the religious questions of that body. But the Crown has a *civil* jurisdiction over a Baptist community, to see that it fulfils its engagements to individuals, and does not violate them. That jurisdiction of the Crown, then, which a Baptist congregation is under, the Colonial Church is under, and no other. It would be evidently incorrect to say that the Royal supremacy was maintained in a *different way*, over a Baptist congregation, from that in which it was maintained over the Established Church; because it is *another* supremacy, *another* jurisdiction altogether which is maintained. And the same expression, if applied to the Colonial Church, is incorrect for the same reason.

Lord Romilly bases his assertion of the legal identity of the two Churches upon the affirmation of a "legal diocese." The jurisdiction of the Colonial Bishop is non-legal indeed, and only that of a *forum domesticum*, but his diocese is legal. I am unable to understand how a legal diocese can go along with a non-legal jurisdiction. A diocese is a local area within which a Bishop's jurisdiction is confined. A legal diocese is this area as marked out by law. But a non-legal jurisdiction stands, in the eye of the law, upon a contract between two parties. Can the law then affix a local area and limitation of place to contracts, and say that two parties shall only contract with each other, for their own private convenience, within certain limits? Such a local limitation appears incongruous. It is therefore difficult to understand how a "legal diocese" can be affixed to a non-legal jurisdiction. But supposing one could be, it still would not be a legal diocese in the sense which is here wanted; it would not be a legal diocese in *such* a sense as to constitute a legal identity of the Colonial Church with the Established Church. To constitute that identity, a legal Colonial diocese in the sense of the sphere and area of a legal *jurisdiction* is wanted; in which case a common jurisdiction received from the Supremacy places both Churches alike under the Supremacy, and so satisfies the ordinary test of legal identity. But a "legal diocese," which receives no such jurisdiction from the

Supremacy, does not place *under* the Supremacy, or therefore satisfy the ordinary and natural test of legal identity.

Lord Romilly has made the supposition of a voluntary religious communion in a Colony founded upon the one wish, duly and formally stated, to be in every respect whatever, doctrinal and other, *like* the Church of England. Such a religious association, he says, would be "strictly" part of the Church of England—by strictly meaning, I presume, legally. "If certain persons constitute themselves a voluntary association in any Colony, as members of the Church of England, then, as I apprehend, they are *strictly* brethren and members of that Church. They are bound by the same doctrines, the same rules, ordinances, and discipline. If any recourse should needs be had to the civil tribunals, the question at issue must be tried by the same rules of law which would prevail if the question were tried in England." I will take his Lordship's authority for the latter point, namely, that such an association would have its questions decided by Privy Council sitting as a court of civil appeal, exactly as the same questions would be decided by it, sitting as a court of ecclesiastical appeal, upon cases belonging to the Established Church. But I do not understand how this would make the association legally part of the Established Church of England. The resolution to be altogether *like* the Church of England does not make this body the Church of England. It is still a voluntary association; its very likeness to or resolution to be like the Church of England stands upon a voluntary basis: it may change that basis any day that it likes without the consent of the Crown. It is totally separated from the ecclesiastical jurisdiction of the Crown, which takes no cognisance of its existence.

I am unable to see again what support Lord Romilly can extract for his position from the Long *v.* Capetown Judgment. "This whole judgment," he says, "proceeds on the assumption, and is based on the foundation that the Church [the Colonial Church in Africa] is a portion of the Church of England . . . that the Colony [African] is presided over by Bishops of the Church of England, who have sees and dioceses properly so termed." I am unable to see any diocese in that judgment;

only two individuals. It must be admitted, indeed, that that case was decided by a reference to the Established Church's standard of what was comprised in the Episcopal claim of obedience. But was that because the Church in Africa was regarded as part of the Church of England; or because the terms of a private contract were interpreted by the rule and custom of the Church of England?

The theory of legal identity, then, which the Master of the Rolls has propounded, is one which I am unable to understand. But had his Lordship put a theory of identity into the form of a simple practical assertion, that the Church in our Colonies, until it organises itself as a voluntary association, will be treated in our Courts, *as if* it were part of the Church of England, it does not appear to me that much fault could have been found with his judgment. It is but too likely that this will be the case; the judgment in Long *v.* Capetown speaks to this point in a way that cannot be mistaken. Where no organised voluntary society is before the Court, the principle of a contract between two individuals will be applied, and the conditions of that contract will be interpreted by an Established Church criterion and standard. The practical result then will be the same that is arrived at upon Lord Romilly's theory; and the Privy Council will give, as a civil court of appeal from the Colonies, the same judgments that it would have given had the same questions come before it as the ecclesiastical court of appeal at home. The Colonial Church then must not go relying on that *dictum* of the Privy Council, that the Church of England in the Colonies "is in the same position with any other religious bodies," as if that *dictum* did anything for it without any steps on its own part. It must put itself *under* that *dictum*, by organising itself as a voluntary religious body. The *dictum* supposes this to be done, and does not apply to it existing in a loose unformed state.

The Church in Africa has not hitherto, so far as I am able to recollect, organised itself formally upon a voluntary basis. What it has done has doubtless represented the will, and the intention, and the spirit of the body. Its ecclesiastical structure, as a collection of Churches under a Metropolitan, has doubtless been *implicitly* consented to and adopted by the body. Still this structure hitherto wants a formal *consensual* basis, as well as a formal basis of another kind. It was not erected by Royal Prerogative; it was not erected by any home Church authority, acting along with, and side by side with, the Royal Prerogative, for the Church at home can only act formally *through* the Royal Prerogative; it has not been erected by the voluntary act of the African body; it has only been implicitly acquiesced in by that body after having been erected illusively by Letters Patent. That is the state of things. It is a question, therefore, which deserves the consideration of that body, whether it would not be acting well to rectify the defect, whatever it may be, in its position; and to give this ecclesiastical structure a definite basis, and itself a regular standing of a voluntary communion before our Courts, by organising itself. And, particularly, it is worth considering whether it would not be wise to do this before taking a new important step.

The ground is certainly open, if we are to adopt the plain construction of Privy Council law, for the erection of a new bishopric in substitution for that of Natal; nor can this ground be affected by any doubts that may be raised as to the validity of the deposition of Bishop Colenso. For if, as the Privy Council declares, the Episcopal jurisdiction of the latter never existed, the deposed gains nothing, and the deposer loses nothing, by the defective validity of his deposition from it. His place is, by the original nullity of the creation of it, vacant. Whether we take a legal, or whether we take a consensual ground, the same defect that applies to the position of the Metropolitan who deposed applies to the position of the Suffragan deposed; whose office is on either ground null and void, for the very reason that his deposition is. But though the ground is open, and though a very able person has been chosen to fill it, should not the African Church, before adopting this step, put itself in such a position as not only to *be* a voluntary society, but to be cognisable as such by our Courts; by organising itself upon a voluntary basis, and by putting its rules and regulations, and the constitution of its tribunals, into a documentary shape? The Canadian Church appears already to have put itself in that position.

I am glad to see that the Bishop of Capetown, whose energy and lofty spirit, firmly supported by the Archbishop of Canterbury and Bishop of Oxford, have so sustained his Church under difficult circumstances, announces the design of an assembly, although not an immediate one, of the whole African Church in order "to perfect its organisation." "As to action here," says his Lordship, "I do not think myself the time has yet arrived for our meeting together to consider the state of the Church, or to perfect its organisation. . . . If the time had arrived for action, I should be prepared to invite the clergy and the representatives of the laity to a provincial gathering."[1] A regular organisation would place the African Church upon a totally different ground, with respect to our courts of law, from that upon which it at present stands. No courts take cognisance of it as a voluntary communion now; not the Privy Council, not the Rolls Court. Upon *that* point both Courts agree. But let it only organise itself, and it stands clear of the obstructions which arise in both Courts to its free action. The effect of the judgment of the Master of the Rolls, regarded in a practical light, has perhaps been exaggerated. It only touches, it only professes to touch, the African Church in its state *at the moment*. It does not touch it as an organised voluntary communion which it may become. On the contrary, nobody could state in clearer language than the Master of the Rolls has done, that that Church, as an organised voluntary communion, will be an independent body, and will be treated by a Court of law as such, without reference to any other rules and regulations than its own. His judgment, therefore, only touches the Church *in transitu*, in a passing state, *in the interim* before the Church takes to another basis. If, as must surely sooner or later be the case, the whole Colonial Church does take this other basis, then his judgment in the long-run does not affect it. It only affects it now. It is natural of course that people's minds should be

[1] Letter to the Members of the Church in the Diocese of Capetown by the Bishop of Capetown.

much absorbed in whatever applies to the existing moment; but still whatever admits of being rectified by the work of the future is only a passing concern.

We need not underrate the difficulties of such a future work, or shut our eyes to the important circumstance that there are two parties in the Colonial Church upon this very question of the ground to be adopted by it. We cannot deny the perfect right of any number of members of the Church of England in Africa now to adopt, if they please, and if they can, the Established Church and the Royal supremacy ground, as distinct from the ground of a voluntary communion. If a strict *legal* unity with the Established Church is closed by staying outside of any African organisation, or by forming themselves, according to the supposition of the Master of the Rolls, into a society which would say in terms—I wish to be in everything similar to the Established Church, they might practically pursue this object; and if they did so, they would be only exercising an option and a preference to which they had a perfect right. There would, however, be great difficulties in the way of such object; one especially—notwithstanding the accident of one existing Bishop—the want of Bishops and of Clergy. Such a body would not probably be forthcoming. The cause with which such an attempt would be associated is opposed to the faith of the people. The existing body of Bishops and Clergy has weight and prestige. All these and other considerations point to but one solution of the question before us, namely, the ultimate organisation of the whole Colonial Church upon a voluntary basis. There are difficulties at first starting, but they are only the difficulties of a start; they are complications and intricacies naturally attending the transition from one situation to another. The legal identity of the two Churches is not a favourable ground for trust property to stand upon—as much of it, that is, as would be affected by such a test. I will not, however, anticipate the course of law or legislature. It is only reasonable to hope that things will right themselves; that no unfair advantage will be taken of the complications of an intermediate stage; and that the Colonial Church will ultimately find and fix in her proper position.

## XVII.—DR. NEWMAN'S GRAMMAR OF ASSENT.[1]

THOSE who open this book with the expectation of finding it a controversial treatise in favour of the peculiar doctrines of Rome, will find themselves mistaken. Its purpose is a much larger one; it vindicates the claims of Christianity generally upon human belief. But it deals with the inner foundations of belief, with those processes in the mind which lead to assent, and its great object is to free those processes from the yoke of formal and technical logic. All reasoning, Dr. Newman admits, ought to be prepared to undergo the test of verbal statement, and the external ordeal of syllogism and proposition; and if it is not capable of being drawn out in this form, when the demand is made, he gives it up as unsound reasoning. But he denies that this is the way in which reasoning actually goes on in the mind, even when it is sound and correct. It has short cuts, he says, it puts things quick together, it seizes the conclusion in the premiss, and combines, by a rapid survey, and by an instinctive estimate, the various points of the case in one nucleus, which the individual carries about him, and which constitutes at once his reasons and his belief. He gathers all into a point, instead of drawing it out into divisions and compartments; and the work is done almost intuitively.

"To this conclusion he comes, as is plain, not by any possible verbal enumeration of all the considerations, minute but abundant, delicate but effective, which unite to bring him to it; but by a mental comprehension of the whole case, and a discernment of its upshot, sometimes after much deliberation, but, it may be, by a clear and rapid act of the intellect, always, however, by an unwritten summing-up, something like the summation of the terms of an algebraical series. . . .

"Such a process of reasoning is more or less implicit, and with-

[1] *An Essay in aid of a Grammar of Assent.* By John H. Newman, D.D.

out the direct and full advertence of the mind exercising it. As by the use of our eyesight we recognise two brothers, yet without being able to express what it is by which we distinguish them; as at first sight we perhaps confuse them together, but on better knowledge, we see no likeness between them at all; as it requires an artist's eye to determine what lines and shades make a countenance look young or old, amiable, thoughtful, angry or conceited, the principle of discrimination being in each case real, but implicit;—so is the mind unequal to a complete analysis of the motives which carry it on to a particular conclusion, and is swayed and determined by a body of proof, which it recognises only as a body, and not in its constituent parts."

This is the aim, then, with which this treatise is penetrated—to bring out the reality of reasoning, as it actually goes on within us; its natural and instinctive and intuitive kind of action, which contains all the pith and truth of it, in a more genuine and powerful shape, in consequence of its very condensation, than technical statements and argumentative formulæ do; in which the pungent point of actual nature is drawn out, and weakened by its very extension and its connection with outside casing, and all the leathern apparatus of verbal logic. The mode in which this appeal to Nature assists the Christian argument will appear shortly; but, in the first place, Dr. Newman has to meet and deal with some curious problems which attach to the foundation of human belief, and especially the question,—What right have we to found upon only probable evidence unconditional assent? All assent, says the Pyrrhonist, must be proportioned to the evidence; and therefore, when there is room for greater proof, assent can only be provisional and conditional: unconditional assent is in its very nature an excess—an advance beyond the evidence. A hasty faith is logically forbidden, and a suspense of judgment is imposed. Dr. Newman meets this difficulty with practical answers, but also with a philosophical one of remarkable subtlety and ingenuity. He separates "inference" from "assent," and throws all the burden of obligation to provisional and conditional limits upon "inferences," liberating "assent" from it. While you are reasoning and weighing evidence, while you are deducing from your premisses, you must keep close to your premisses, and what you infer from them must exactly reflect them in degree : but when reasoning is over, the assent which is the consequence of it shakes off the trammels of the subterranean process out of which it has emerged, and the mind having got to the top of the edifice of reasoning, kicks down the ladder by which it ascended. This hardly appears to us a satisfactory explanation of this difficulty—the difficulty that as a matter of fact we do believe with practical certainty upon grounds which theoretically are only grounds of probability. It is quite true that when we obtain our conclusion, we often forget the process of inference and argument by which we reached it; we are lifted up by a happy act of oblivion out of the region of comparison and estimate; still our conclusion is based upon this process, and must be always ready to obey the logical command to recall it when circumstances require. But while we cannot agree with Dr. Newman's solution of this *crux*, perhaps any other definite rationale for it would equally fail. The truth is, Nature takes this matter out of our hands, and upon every plain probability appearing to be on the side of some conclusion in practical life or history, enables us to proceed upon that conclusion as if it were thoroughly ascertained. The pure reason—abstract and unqualified reason—is insatiable and ever hungry for additions to proof; even when gorged with arguments, if it sees but a hollow corner anywhere, it clamours for a supplement; nay, and so ungrateful is its appetite, that it will forget and expunge out of its tablet all past proof, in the eager craving for the further addition, discontented with any amount of actual evidence, so long as it is not all the evidence which is conceivable. The pure reason is thus morbid reason, it weakens while it informs; it paralyses action, and just steps in after all the premises it has gathered to prevent the person from making any use of them. It wants the balance of some other element in our nature, which is not so much an intellectual principle as salutary impulse. The conditions of life and the necessities of action are such, that we must be content with and accept as practical certainty a large amount of probability; and we are enabled in some way, by some machinery in our nature, which is perhaps out of the reach of all analysis, to do this, and to supply by our own confidence the void in the ground of pure reason. It should not be lost sight of that there is, besides the reason, a large, we will not call it irrational so much as non-rational, department in the constitution of the human being which is essential to the success of the rational. We see men who are defective in this supplement to the reason, and who consequently fail in the use of their reason. No evidence gives them strength to act; however massive a body of premisses they have collected, upon the casual glimpse of an unanswered objection, they drop in an instant their conclusion, as if it burnt their fingers, and would expose them to total annihilation at the hand of some master of logic; whose blow would in fact be as light as a feather, did not his antagonist fall down flat on the ground before he gave it.

Supposing, then, a certain amount of probable evidence exists for the truth of revelation, we have not got to prove our right to a positive belief in revelation. That is given us by the constitution of our nature, and the only question we have to decide is, whether there is or not that amount of probable evidence. Upon this question, then, Dr. Newman first observes the plain fact, that what is evidence to one man is not evidence to another. How is this? It is, that judgment upon facts, inference from facts, interpretation of premisses, extraction of conclusions, is after all a personal operation. It depends upon the antecedent assumptions, the knowledge, the disposition of mind, and certain fundamental modes of looking on things, which exist in the mind of the reasoner. Dr. Newman sums up all this in the personal and individual character of what he calls the Illative sense :—

'It is in fact attached to definite subject-matters, so that a given individual may possess it in one department of thought, for instance, history, and not in another, for instance, philosophy. . . .

"Hence it is, that nothing I have been saying about the instrumental character or the range of the Illative Sense interferes with its being, as I have considered it, a personal gift or habit : for, being in fact ever embodied in some definite subject-matter, it is personal, because the discernment of the principles connected with that subject-matter is personal also. Certainly, however we account for it, whether we say that one man is below the level of nature, or another above it, so it is that men, taken at random, differ widely from each other in their perception of the first elements of religion, duty, philosophy, the science of life, and taste, not to speak here of the differences in quality and vigour of the Illative Sense itself, comparing man with man. Every one, in the ultimate resolution of his intellectual faculties, stands by himself, whatever he may have in common with others."

The Illative sense, then, is the same, as regards its own functions, in all cases; but it differs in its conclusions according to the special training and previous experience of the individual and the subjects with which life has made him conversant. It receives its direction from the particular knowledge, taste, and sentiment of the reasoner. It acts well in the individual's special department of art or science, or in his trade and profession, because there he knows the province of his inferences, and starts from correct principles: when it leaves the area of his knowledge it makes mistakes. And when it acts correctly it often acts instinctively and intuitively. The chapter on "Natural Inference" particularly brings out this point. Dr. Newman illustrates this whole subject with all the fertility and vivacity which immense information and a rich imagination impart. He brings his analogies, instances, and parallel cases from all quarters of the philosophical, social, and historical heavens; the reader has a perpetual change, and never knows what fact may turn up next; it may be one at first sight the most utterly removed from the field of discussion. The detection of resemblances amid staring incongruities is one of the most popular and happy gifts of an author; it produces the effect of a constant surprise upon the reader, and something of that gratification which a good puzzle gives.

So far, however, Dr. Newman's vindication of an instinctive and intuitive reason, and of a reasoning faculty which only acts correctly, or obtains sound and true conclusions in the area of the individual's special knowledge, does not come into collision with the position of the religious sceptic. The philosopher will readily admit that reason does act in this instinctive way; and he will also admit that previous experience and special knowledge must make all the difference in the correctness of the conclusions which a person draws from any data which are placed before him. What he objects to is the application of this general position to the religious question. He will not allow to the believer in revelation the right to say that he is in possession of any special knowledge or principles of thought and feeling, any primary judgments which place him at an advantage in the estimate of Christian evidence, and convert that into real evidence which is not evidence to another devoid of these primary ideas and principles. He will not admit any parallel between the knowledge of special departments in the field of life and nature, and the strong hold of certain deep principles and fundamental conceptions which the Christian brings with him to the consideration of the Christian evidences.

That there are then certain primary assumptions or beliefs, which do make an immense difference in the estimate we form of the Christian evidences—which create a presumption in favour of revelation in the minds of those who have embraced them, and which thereby facilitate for those minds the reception of the proof of revelation—is a simple fact which both sides will admit. It signifies little by what name we call these primary beliefs, if we only understand what they are; but Dr. Newman calls them the principles of Natural Religion. These primary beliefs are :—

"A belief and perception of the Divine presence, a recognition of His attributes and an admiration of His person viewed under them, a conviction of the worth of the soul and of the reality and momentousness of the unseen world, an understanding that, in proportion as we partake in our own persons of the attributes which we admire in Him, we are dear to Him, a consciousness on the contrary that we are far from partaking them, a consequent insight into our guilt and misery, an eager hope of reconciliation to Him, a desire to know and to love Him, and a sensitive looking-out in all that happens, whether in the course of nature or of human life, for tokens, if such there be, of His bestowing on us what we so greatly need. These are specimens of the state of mind for which I stipulate in those who would inquire into the truth of Christianity; and my warrant for so definite a stipulation lies in the teaching, as I have described it, of conscience and the moral sense, in the testimony of those religious rites which have ever prevailed in all parts of the world, and in the character and conduct of those who have commonly been selected by the popular instinct as the special favourites of Heaven."

Dr. Newman contrasts this genuine and authentic with a pseudo-natural religion :—

"I do not address myself to those, who in moral evil and physical evil see nothing more than imperfections of a parallel nature; who consider that the difference in gravity between the two is one of degree only, not of kind; that moral evil is merely the offspring of physical, and that as we remove the latter so we inevitably remove the former; that there is a progress of the human race which tends to the annihilation of moral evil; that knowledge is virtue, and vice is ignorance; that sin is a bugbear, not a reality; that the Creator does not punish except in the sense of correcting; that vengeance in Him would of necessity be vindictiveness; that all that we know of Him, be it much or little, is through the laws of nature; that miracles are impossible; that prayer to Him is a superstition; that the fear of Him is unmanly; that sorrow for sin is slavish and abject; that the only intelligible worship of Him is to act well our part in the world, and the only sensible repentance to do better in future; that if we do our duties in this life, we may take our chance for the next; and that it is of no use perplexing our minds about the future state, for it is all a matter of guess. These opinions characterise a civilised age; and if I say that I will not argue about Christianity with men who hold them, I do so, not as claiming any right to be impatient or peremptory with any one, but because it is plainly absurd to attempt to prove a second proposition to those who do not admit the first."

That these elementary convictions of the mind, then, do make a fundamental difference in our estimate of revelation, will hardly be denied. Supposing them, for the sake of argument, to be true principles, so much with respect to their operation as premisses will be conceded. Let us take the single principle of the moral sense, as it is felt in those minds to which we have been alluding, which constitute, in fact, the great mass of mankind; felt, namely, as conscience, sense of sin, an acknowledgment of an external Judge: how at once does this principle act in the way of preparing the mind for a revelation, favouring the need of revelation, justifying the doctrines of revelation; and so facilitating legitimately the acceptance of the evidence of revelation. M. Comte has indeed made us familiar with *a* moral sense, which is a simple materialist force, and a physical phenomenon, coinciding, like heat or electricity, with the vanishing bodily life; presaging no Divine Judge, and aspiring to no upper world. Nobody can deny that something within us, which distinguishes between some actions and others: to say all actions are morally the same, or that there is no such thing as morality, would be denying a palpable fact, like the fact of thought, or will, or sensation. There is, therefore, *a* moral sense. How, then, is it that this moral sense admitted, stops short, in the philosophy of so many, with being a mere physical phenomenon, and an element of sensible life? The answer is, that this is a true fact about the moral sense as far as it goes; and that men have a power of stopping short, and not going on beyond the bare outside of an idea. The ideas in our minds have, if we may borrow a representation from external nature, their coatings; we may go only as far as the coating, or we may go into them, and receive into our minds the full internal substance of them. There runs throughout intellectual nature a use and application of what we may call the shavings of truth, as distinguished from its solid substance. It is this principle or arrangement in nature which enables so many persons of the most different grasp of mind to read the same book, and extract a common meaning and a common criticism from it. The deep man and the shallow man both understand the same character, the same event, the same sentiment, in their respective degrees; and though they come to a point at which one cannot follow the other, they can find a common ground up to that point. It is this provision of nature which enables us to read the same book as children and as grown men, at neither time of life wholly unprofitably, nor without drawing a meaning from it. The child reads Shakespeare and Milton, and skims off a sense from them. Many a one looks back with surprise now at the genuine appetite with which he devoured Scott's novels at twelve or thirteen; and with a feeling of wonder and perplexity as to what it was which he understood in them which arrested him so potently. It is quite impossible that he could have really understood the humour; humour, as distinguished from the mere images which the animal spirits of boys raise, is a discovery of later years, and requires the insight of experience. It is impossible that he could have understood really the characters; and as for the allusions constantly turning up, they must have been a simple enigma to him. Nevertheless, he extracted a meaning out of the scenery and *dramatis personæ* which engaged him and absorbed him. The truth is, what he understood was a meaning which belonged to the book; but it was the coat of the meaning, and not the substance of it. It is the same with an idea.

The moral sense or the moral idea contains in the substance of it conscience, self-condemnation, repentance, the appeal to an external judge; but there is an outer film and superficies of the idea which the human mind peels off from the body of it, when men give a place, *in rerum natura*, to the phenomenon, and at the same time ignore the substance: when just so much of it as agrees with physical utility and the wants of the visible system is allowed, and all the rest is thrown aside as superstition. Take the moral idea as it stands in natural religion. It is a principle of immortality, it indicates a spiritual being, destined to an existence beyond the confines of this material world. Take it as it stands in M. Comte's philosophy, and it is a simple element in a physical system and a vanishing life. The being who has it came up to the surface yesterday, and sinks into the abyssal void to-morrow. The philosopher just sees the idea in that aspect in which it is a necessity of the social fabric; he just cuts off that aspect from it; he peels off the mere simulacrum of the idea, he rolls it up as in the story of "the Shadowless Man" the demon rolled up Peter Schlemihl's shadow; and he presents it to the world as the moral sense. Such a coating of the idea is like the flat surface of the mist, which hid the gorgeous tracery and pillared architecture of the stupendous cavern. As you approach, the unreality of the veil appears, and the real contents of the subterranean vista emerge; yet, at a distance, the surface of mere vapour was the true rock, and the interior was a buried scene. M. Comte, in his moral sentiment, presents to the world a mere superficies, torn from the solid block of the idea, an outer film, which ignores and hides all the depths of the idea, all in it that carries the mind beyond a perishing humanity, all in it that spiritualises and immortalises.

"One man," says Dr. Newman, "deduces from his moral sense the presence of a Moral Governor, and another does not: in each case there may be an exercise, and a sound exercise, of the illative sense; but the one recognises the principle of conscience in his moral sense, and the other does not recognise it,—the illative sense of the one is employed upon and informed by the emotions of hope and fear and the sense of sin, whereas the other discerns the distinction of right and wrong in no other way than he distinguishes light from darkness, or beautifulness from deformity. That is (identifying the apprehension of the subject-matter with the faculty using it), we might say that the one man had the Religious Sense, and the other the Moral."

But although a checked and stunted stage of the moral sense can exist in which it is no introduction at all to revelation —although an abortive form of it can be exhibited in which it is consistent with Atheism and with no future life—although there is a moral sense, which, as Dr. Newman says, "a so-called civilisation recognises, while it ignores the conscience"—still in the way in which the moral sense works in that class of minds which accepts revelation, the moral sense develops and declares itself from the first in the direction of revelation; the moral sense becomes an introduction to the doctrines of revelation. Take the sense of sin. What an enormous difference that makes in our view of the doctrine of the Atonement! It involves the idea of sin as a mystery; we know sin, and yet we do not know it. What is it? The weight of it is a great power within us; it can dispirit; it can crush and prostrate; it can cloud a life; it can produce agony; and lastly, it can fill us beyond recovery with the idea that it is all over with us, and can wind up our mortal existence in despair. But what is sin? If sin is a mystery, then we cannot be surprised that the remedy to it should be a mystery too. An atonement is a natural doctrine of restoration, if we start with the original disease as an enigma. How can we possibly tell, if some incomprehensible entanglement and confusion has taken place, what may be wanted to set it right again? The case is like some difficult piece of business in actual life, when a raw inexperienced mind summarily decides on some one single easy step, which is all that is necessary to rectify the mistake made: but the man of experience says "No; something more is wanted than that—the solution is more complex than you think; a succession of steps will be requisite." So, in the matter of sin, one man says he sees no difficulty—the Divine forgiveness effects the cure in a moment. Another sees in sin "a difficult business," that may not be capable of being set right by one simple step, but may require a complex means for its rectification.

Take another effect of the sense of sin, which is also auxiliary to revelation. It is often said, in arguing against materialism, that the sublime goodness of which man is capable shows that he is a spiritual being. Matter cannot be heroic, cannot be angelic. But may it not also be said that the wickedness of which man is capable establishes the same conclusion? Matter cannot be diabolic. Put before your mind a bad man—armed with all the force and the determination, all the craft and guile, of a corrupt will, devoted inexorably to selfish ends, remorselessly thrusting aside all scruples which threaten to interfere with them, designing and malicious, deep in all the subtle intricacy of vile plots and artful strategics, a miracle of duplicity and dissimulation, a miracle of plausibility and power of self-defence—can this man be a lump of matter? No; he must be a spirit. None but a spirit can be such as he; wickedness is the property of a spiritual nature. Brute matter has, at any rate, the involuntary honesty of invincible stupidity. Its passiveness, its inertness, rescues it from the peril of such guilt. Its torpor is so far its safety. Although a wicked man then undoubtedly presents himself to us in visible form and through a fleshly medium, we are assured that behind the veil of matter there thinks, contrives, and acts a spirit. But such a line of thought as this obviously prepares us for, and inclines us towards, the great disclosures of Scripture as regards the worlds of departed spirits; as well as of good and bad spiritual beings who have not passed through this mortal state; it gives a leaning to the understanding on the side of those agencies not of flesh and blood, against which Christianity in the Apostolic writings struggles,—those " principalities and powers, the rulers of the darkness of this world," the "spiritual wickedness in high places."

The sense of sin, again, must affect fundamentally our estimate of revelation; because this profound affection of the mind must make all the difference in our idea of God: and our judgment on that which professes to be a communication from God must depend upon our idea of Him. There are two ideas of the Divine Being which spring respectively from two sets of first principles—one of which gathers around conscience, the other around a physical centre. There is the idea of Him as a Moral Governor and Judge, expressed in the majestic language of inspiration, which proclaims the "High and lofty One that inhabiteth eternity, whose name is Holy; keeping mercy for thousands, forgiving iniquity and transgression and sin, and that will by no means clear the guilty." And there is another idea of Him as the Supreme Mundane Being, the Impersonation of the causes which are at work in the development and completion of the visible world; who looks —we cannot say from Heaven—with calm satisfaction upon the successful expansion of the original seed which commenced the formation of the vast material organism;—the universal Spectator of the fabric of Nature, the growth of art and the progress of civilisation. These two ideas of the Deity must make all the difference in the aspect in which a revelation presents itself to us: the former will recommend such a revelation as that in the Old and New Testament to us; the latter will create a whole foundation of thought in preliminary conflict with it.

Nor does the recommendation which the ideas and sentiments of natural religion give to revelation stop with the doctrines; it applies also to the external evidences and to the testimony upon which revelation is presented to us. We cannot arbitrarily check the influence of first principles; they have a natural and legitimate bearing upon all the circumstances of the case which they support, and among the rest, upon our estimate of the character of the witnesses in the case. Supposing we are in the first instance deeply impressed with certain views of conscience and sin; if the witnesses to a revelation respond to these views, and if it is the scope of their testimony to acquaint us with a Divine message that meets them; this cannot be other than a favourable mark of, and in a degree a guarantee for, themselves personally. We agree with their tone of mind, their characteristic mould of thought and sentiment, their peculiar moral inspiration, and the profound current of joy and grief, of fear and hope, which runs through the religious composition of their minds. But agreeing with all this, we cannot but repose the greater confidence in them on account of it. The nature of our first principles affects and bears upon the evidence as well as the doctrines of Christianity.

These primary religious assumptions, then, become a basis upon which those who accept the doctrines and evidences of revelation go in the act of accepting them. And to those who have embraced and adopted them this is a philosophical and correct effect of them. They act philosophically, they fulfil philosophical conditions of thought, when they use them in this way, when they give them this recommendatory and preparatory force. We must judge of revelation according to certain antecedent premisses which exist in our minds, according to certain primary notions and impressions existing in us. If these are wrong ones, we are in collision with philosophy in adopting them; but having adopted them, it is quite philosophical in us to argue and judge from them as a starting point—an ἀφορμή, and intellectual base. We cannot do otherwise. But now the further great question arises—What is the character of these first principles, and what is the justice of their pretension to compose a commencement and a base of reasoning? Do they constitute a legitimate and philosophical ground for the mind to go upon, or are they a foundation of mere blind superstition, delusion, and fancy? It will be said the assumptions and first principles which obtain credit in special departments of knowledge, and which direct the illative sense in those departments, are principles which sooner or later approve themselves to the whole of mankind; they are principles which are the result of observation and induction; they stand public investigation, and although they may not at the present gain universal reception, they only wait the sure effect of time, which will establish them satisfactorily and invincibly. Such principles and assumptions as these, it will be said, are a philosophical foundation to go upon, but this cannot be said of the untested and obscure impressions of the religious imagination, pretending to divine what it cannot apprehend, and guessing where it cannot observe,—that collection of dim notions which you call natural religion.

Here, then, the individual and personal character of true reasoning which Dr. Newman has laid down, comes in with remarkable force and point, to sustain those original premisses in the human heart upon which the reception of the proof of revelation is based. He says at once, the truth, the force, the weight, the authority of these premisses is a personal matter. I have these intuitive convictions; others have them. The strength with which these primary ideas are held, the degree in which they penetrate the man, possess him, inspire him; the assurance which they beget, the sense of their reality, the conviction that they cannot be spurious ideas, but represent the truth of things—all this is what makes the very essence of their place as a premiss; and at the same time all this is strictly personal. Formal statements can enumerate and denote, for the purpose of discussion, the ideas of natural religion; they cannot possibly express the depth and intensity with which they are entertained by the individual, or the peculiar significance which they possess in his mind; and their whole weight as a basis depends upon these circumstances. "Every one," says Dr. Newman, "who thinks on these subjects takes a course of his own: every one must use the medium of his own primary mental impressions; I offer my own witness in the matter in question; though, of course, it would not be worth while my offering it, unless what I felt myself agreed with what is felt by hundreds and thousands besides me." "Conscience is a personal guide, and I use it, because I must use myself; I am as little able to think by any mind but my own, as to breathe with another's lungs. Conscience is nearer to me than any other means of knowledge. And as it is given to me, so also it is given to others: and being carried about by every individual in his own breast, and requiring nothing besides itself, it is adapted for the communication to each separately of that knowledge which is most momentous to him individually. . . . I may say all this without entering into the question how far external assistances are in all cases necessary to the action of the mind, because in fact a man does not live in isolation, but is everywhere found as a member of society. I am not concerned with abstract questions."

Dr. Newman's appeal, then, to the individual and personal character of all genuine reasoning is attended by this advantage to the Christian argument, that the fundamental premisses of that argument are seen by means of this appeal in all the cogency and force which they possess as strong individual convictions, as distinguished from their comparatively tame pretensions when they are laid down as propositions and statements. You are carried into a living world of belief. When truths are put forward as statements only, we look on them apart from their vital seat in the individual; they are suspended in the air, and seem to supplicate a proof and a basis; that is therefore a weak aspect of them. But turn to them as they exist in the individual, and the individual is a basis. He can say, " I find these particular original convictions in me, that is, I find a *belief* in me; it is, therefore, too late to ask me to account for my belief; there it is, I have it, I cannot help myself, it is a fact of my own mind, it is part of myself; if I believe I believe. It is true I cannot prove them to others, but that does not prevent their self-witness to me; if I cannot help a certain belief, that is the fullest justification of myself that there can possibly be." When truths are put forward as propositions, they suggest our going further, getting behind them, or underneath them; they challenge inquiry, and in the anticipation of this inquiry they lack the confidence of a strong position. But as felt in the individual, they are a belief to begin with; the step is taken, their position is as strong as it can be made by a decision for them at their very starting. Nobody can say a word against a man for being convinced of his own convictions.

T

The primary ideas and sentiments, then, which constitute natural religion, are a legitimate basis for the mind to proceed upon in its estimate of the proof of revelation; they correspond to the principles in special departments of knowledge, which enable those who are acquainted with those departments to judge of evidence on matters belonging to them; only with this difference, that the principles of science ultimately compel universal reception, the moral set of principles does not. But this distinction does not interfere with the right of assertion, as regards those principles, on the part of those who have them; they have a right to assert as truth what is irresistibly true to themselves and which others cannot disprove. Those who find these original convictions in them have a right to appeal to them as their starting-points and their reasoning base. They cannot of course appeal to their own original belief as binding others, but they can appeal to it as the full justification of themselves, and of that favourable attitude toward revelation which may be drawn from it. Such a primary belief is, therefore, a strictly philosophical premiss, for the purpose for which it is used. Were it used indeed for the purpose of proving revelation to those in whom the belief does not exist, no premiss could be more unphilosophical: but it is not used for this purpose; it is only used for the purpose of recommending revelation to ourselves, and to others who have the same primary belief with ourselves, and for this purpose it is a philosophical premiss.

Take, for example, the instance which we used lately—the sense of sin. This is a knowledge which those who possess it start with as an advantage in the estimate of the Christian revelation, that is, they have the right to say that they do. It is not knowledge in a scientific sense, but it is knowledge in such a sense as that those who have it are instinctively assured that they are in possession of some truth, and are influenced by it in their judgment of revelation and its proof. It is knowledge so far as it is a kind of insight, partial, but real as far as it goes, into the nature of something in which we are fundamentally concerned, and on which God's dealings with us in revelation profess to hinge. It corresponds, in its place and results, to a principle of knowledge in some special department. It is impossible not to see what a strong root of Christian conviction and belief, what an introduction to the Christian dispensation, this sense of sin in the mind of St. Paul was. St. Paul filled two remarkable places; he was at once the first philosophical teacher of Christianity, and the first great convert of promulgated Christianity. What is the most conspicuous premiss, then, which we observe working in his mind, to beget his belief in the Christian dispensation, and assure him of its being a real authentic revelation from God? We see it in the Epistles which succeeded his conversion. It is the sense of sin. The apprehension of the tremendous, mysterious fact of sin pervades all his Epistles, as th great preliminary to the acceptance of the Gospel. It was an assurance in his mind, which was of the nature of a profound knowledge, answering to the accurate acquaintance with some truth in some special department. Could any human being have persuaded St. Paul that he knew no more about sin than Gallio or Herod, and that he and the Sadducee Ananias stood exactly on the same level upon this article of knowledge? He felt he had a knowledge of this subject which other people had not. This formed the basis of the Christianity which he preached and propagated; and if he persuaded himself by the same arguments by which he persuaded others, it was the basis of his own conversion to Christianity.

These moral and religious starting-points present themselves indeed to us in the first instance as belonging rather to the department of the affections than of knowledge; and we are asked—What have the affections to do with deciding a question of reason, such as that of the evidence of revelation? We are not concerned with the affections here, it is said, but with the understanding only. It is the understanding alone which judges about truth; and to introduce the affections into the inquiry is to mislead the judgment, and to carry it away from evidence to enlist it unlawfully on the side of mere wishes, fears, and hopes. But the truth is, that in moral subjects we cannot separate the understanding from the affections. The affections themselves are a kind of understanding;

we cannot understand without them. Affection is a part of insight, it is wanted for a due acquaintance with the facts of the case. The moral affections, for instance, are the very instruments by which we intellectually apprehend good and high human character. All admiration is affection—the admiration of virtue; the admiration of outward nature. Affection itself, then, is a kind of intelligence. Feeling is necessary for comprehension, and we cannot *know* what a particular instance of goodness is, we cannot embrace the true conception of goodness in general, without it. These primary convictions of which we are here speaking, then, are not prevented by being affections from being knowledge—knowledge in the sense of a certain kind of insight,—which those who have it are justified in acting upon as knowledge, in regarding as authoritative and qualified to command their acts.

Dr. Newman's appeal to the personal and individual character of true reasoning thus combines the strength of an enthusiastic ground, on the side of revelation, without its weakness. It is a common remark that the enthusiast is logical *upon* his premisses. Grant him the intensity of his own primary convictions—the truth of his own starting-points—and you cannot confute his conclusions from them; but his position has the great defect, that his primary convictions—his starting-points—are his own and nobody else's; they are singular and eccentric: he cannot appeal to any witness in human nature, to any either whole or partial consensus; he is an isolated man, and there is no body of sentiment and belief in the world which he can claim as concurring with him. His premisses, therefore, are fantastic, and with them his conclusions. But the appeal to the individual in the matter of the primary truths of natural religion gains one of these results, without incurring the other. It gains the strength of the enthusiast's ground, because the enthusiast's strength lies not in his being eccentric, but in his being internal: if he is internal, an ordinary believer is as strong in his belief as an enthusiast. And it avoids its weakness, because the individual is in concurrence and agreement with a whole world of other individuals who think with him. In the fundamental ideas of natural religion there is something approaching to a consensus, and his own personal conviction finds an echo in the voice of human nature. His principles, then, have all the strength of the enthusiast's, while they are the premises, at the same time, of the great body of mankind. The individual's strong sense of them justifies their influence, while such general concurrence in them is a guarantee against their fanaticism.

The logical posture, then, of the Christian and infidel toward each other, is, according to Dr. Newman, this: One of the parties taking certain fundamental perceptions—or what appear to him to be such—which form the substance of natural religion, as his starting-points, and judging from them as a reasoning base, accepts *from* that base of judgment the evidences of Christianity. Can the other refute his inference? He cannot, for he does not know his base. He knows the truths of natural religion in the form of propositions; he cannot possibly know them as they exist in the individual's mind. He cannot know then how much legitimate force they exert in the estimate of the evidences of revelation. Can he then disprove the principles themselves? He cannot, for they are not in opposition to any known truth; while the immense concurrence in them, and the homage of the great mass of mankind to them, protects them from the charge of fanaticism. The inward premises, then, and the conclusion, are alike out of reach of refutation, and safe from the disputant's assault.

In this state of the case the *Grammar of Assent* may be usefully studied by those who direct the sceptical press in this country. They will not be converted to the belief of Christianity by it, but they will perhaps be able to understand that Christianity has something more to say for itself than they suppose. They assume a tone of very comfortable certainty, that the evidences of Christianity have been tried and found wanting. These gentlemen recommend a philosophical suspense of judgment, and declaim against positive conviction; but their own minds are entirely made up. The age of Pyrrhonism is past; men could be Pyrrhonists in the groves of Academia; but in the roar and conflict of the hodiernal arena of opinion they find that the voice of doubt is not heard, and that decision is in request. They bow, and apparently without any great reluctance, to the public need. They assume the falsehood of Christianity, that reason rejects its doctrines, and experience its evidences. The dogmatic infidel suggests suspense of judgment to the Christian believer, but as for himself he is far in advance of the beggarly elements of doubt and inquiry, and with downright assertion as his own weapon, he gags his antagonist with Pyrrhonism. This is the philosophy of the sceptical press. We do not know whether it is intended to be looked upon as literary pleasantry; but the conductors of it must have a very low idea of the intellect of their opponents if they think that it can be contemplated as serious controversy. For how stands the matter?

There is a certain set of fundamental ideas which, when embraced with a depth and reality of conviction, practically leads to the acceptance of Christianity and its evidences. They have done so with an almost unbroken uniformity; they do now; and consequently we have every reason to expect that they always will do. The connection, then, of these ideas with the acceptance of Christianity cannot be set aside as the result of fancy or chance; the foundation supposed, the edifice stands legitimately upon it. But these writers look upon the evidence of Christianity as it presents itself to themselves without this preliminary foundation, and by it judge the evidence as it presents itself to others with it. They apply their estimate of a structure of belief, which has not a basis of introductory truths, to a structure of belief which has one. They forget that they are not in the same position, and do not stand on the same ground, as judges of evidence, with their opponents. But if they ever do remember that there is such a thing as a ground of natural religion, if they ever do bring themselves to recognise the existence of a certain class of primary ideas and instinctive impressions which exist in the human mind, the mode in which they treat the fact when they take cognisance of it, is worse than their blindness when they forgot it. They treat these rooted convictions as if they were only plastered upon the surface of man, and could be taken off. These ideas must be simply erased, effaced, and expunged from the tablet of the human mind. But what process has been invented for erasing and expunging what is *de facto* part of human nature? And what ground is there for the assumption which is constantly made that the progress of science and civilisation will destroy these fundamental sentiments and convictions? Let us take first practical civilisation. By this we mean the multiplication of the resources of society, facilities for doing things, means of communication, comforts, accommodations, conveniences. They assume a hostile logic in these facts to that original creed of the human heart. Yet it is difficult to see why a man's expectation of a future judgment should be altered, because he can get to Australia in two months, whereas some years ago he could only reach it in eight. A belief in heaven and hell cannot at all depend on the success or backwardness of steam navigation. It is as little easy to see why the same belief should be affected by postal communication, the submarine telegraph, the tubular bridge, the discovery of a new propulsive power, the purification of gas, draining, the steam-plough, and sanitary improvements. If there is any argument against that primary creed in these facts, the human mind is so incorrigibly illogical that one man was an atheist under the reign of packhorses, and another man is a believer in the era of goods trains. It is as difficult to see what is the logic in physical science which is in antagonism to natural religion, or to revealed either. The truths of these respective departments are the truths of two different spheres, which cannot come into contact with each other. If men feel a conscience within them, if they acknowledge its presages, and respect its voice as judicial; they must do so all the same under the Ptolemaic and Copernican theories of the Solar System. If they derive from conscience the sense of sin, they must derive it whether light is explained upon the theory of emission, or the theory of undulation. There are difficulties in a Personal Deity, and there are difficulties in a personal immortality: there are difficulties attaching to prayer, and there are difficulties attaching to special providences; but those difficulties are exactly the same, whether the cellular theory is true or false, and whether the sun is fed by the mechanical collision of asteroids, or by the continuous condensation of its own matter. Freewill is not contradicted by the Uniformitarian in geology, and Predestination is not contradicted by the Revolutionist in geology. Scientific analysis cannot possibly discover any fresh objection to the doctrine of the Trinity, the doctrine of the Atonement, the doctrine of Grace, or the doctrine of the Sacraments. If the Zwinglian doctrine of the Sacraments is our conclusion,—it is our conclusion whether there is a space-filling ether, or whether there is a total vacuum in space; if the Anglican theory is our decision, it is our decision whether we accept or not the convertibility of heat into motion, and motion into heat; and if Transubstantiation is true, it is true whatever hypothesis we maintain as to the ultimate indivisibility and weight of atoms.

Sometimes, indeed, science appears to threaten the very foundation of a spiritual existence, and some theory pushes forward into the first ranks which seems to convert our very personality into a development and form of matter. Men tremble at the approach of the giant who comes, with uplifted arm, to aim his blow; but if they only stand their ground the spell is broken, the descending stroke falls harmless upon us, and the spectre vanishes. We shake ourselves, and feel whole and untouched. All that is required for successful resistance in these encounters is distinctly to see that A is not B. The theory of the correlation of vital, physical, and chemical forces, while it reduces some life to the same head with material properties, does not touch the spiritual being or self; consciousness witnesses to that ego as distinct from the mere living bodily organism. The theory, again, that a living organism can develop itself from inorganic matter deals with the origination of one fact, while that which we are conscious of is another fact. Thus material science, even granting its pretensions, only advances as far as some facts which come under the head of life; it then stops upon the outer brink, and can only look from thence upon an unsolved personal being.

No reason, then, can be given why the progress of civilisation or science should expunge from the human mind the ideas of conscience, sin, repentance, judgment, which, as a matter of fact, lead to the Christian belief, and feed the Christian Church. But when reasoning ceases, prophecy begins. There are no more persistent and determined prophesiers in the world than infidels; they make sure of the future. Mankind do not at present think with them, but they will do. The day is coming; the edifice of superstition will fall; principles long rooted in man will disappear; it will be seen that their lurid and misty light is a deception; the human mind will be rescued from the thraldom of them. This will be the issue of civilisation; this will be the history of mankind. Thus when logic fails, they foresee; and when science refuses to contradict religion, they discern the rupture in a vision. We have two great prophets among us who prophesy resolutely and prophesy perpetually,— the Infidels and Millennarians.

We could wish, however, that Dr. Newman had treated the exceptional case of those who, while they would profess a code of natural religion approaching to his own, still do not proceed thence to the acceptance of the Christian evidences. There are those who believe in morals and in religious morals, but shrink from miracles or doctrines. There are those even who accept Roman morals, who admire the ascetic type, who embrace counsels of perfection, who still decline to believe either in the Gospels or the Epistles. The Gospels deter them by their outward miracles, and the Epistles by their inward— by forgiveness, justification, and salvation, through the blood of an Atoning Sacrifice. The acceptance, indeed, of an ascetic standard of morals by persons is quite compatible with cowardice and weakness in the acceptance also of the yoke of physical impression;—is compatible with a dogmatic imagination binding their sense of possibility to the routine of material laws, and disabling them from believing miracles in Nature or mysteries in truth. The more we know of practical human nature, the more we become alive to its piecemeal composition, and to the mistake of taking men as consistent wholes. They are often collections of fragments, reflecting a past succession of different and discordant influences, like geological compounds, which represent the action of past disturbing forces.

We could wish, again, that Dr. Newman had treated the case of some who even admire the distinctive mysteries of Christianity, but who have not come to an understanding with themselves whether those mysteries are sublime truths or sublime fictions. They are captivated by devotion, and by devotion founded on certain ideas and upon the existence of a certain supernatural world; but whether the truths exist or the world exists anywhere else than in the worshipper's own mind they are not prepared to say. They will follow, with even the enthusiasm of partisans, the devotional assertions of a high religious rite, while they do not, at the same time, think it particularly signifies whether these assertions are true or not: their intellect inclines to the latter alternative. The doctrine of the Atonement is true to them in a ritual, and false as a statement in Scripture or in a Creed. The appeal to the "Lamb of God that taketh away the sin of the world" is quite correct in a litany; but when they meet with the same truth in a theological book, they turn away from an assertion with which their intellect is not in harmony. Our own Eucharistic service and the Roman Mass alike are founded upon the doctrine of an Atoning Sacrifice: that doctrine is the very fibre of them, and they are utterly hollow and mere unmeaning structures of words without it; yet one of these minds will respond to the service and reject the doctrine. Why so? The dignity of language is its truth; and if an idea is false it ought not to be in a ritual—if it is true, it ought to be accepted as a statement. Why should ritual enjoy the very unenviable privilege of false assertion? And why should the language of prayer and supplication be esteemed noble and sublime if it issues out of the worshipper's mouth directed to a personage who does not exist, on account of an office which does not exist? The fact is, however, that ritual is regarded by this class of minds only as the expression of subjective religious truth. It relieves the worshipper's mind by the vocal and symbolic utterance of certain religious conceptions, profoundly poetical, and stimulative of deep emotion; and the whole adoration of the congregation goes out toward a mysterious personage, who has done a mysterious work for them; but whether there are in the invisible world any realities which correspond to these ideas, whether there is any such personage or any such work, whether there is any objective truth which answers to this subjective is another question, which they prefer not having to deal with. A statement in Scripture, a Creed, or an Article, puts this question before them, and therefore they dislike a statement in Scripture, a Creed, or an Article. A Creed asserts an objective truth, a ritual to them asserts a subjective one; and subjective truth is interesting to them as revealing the fertility and wealth of the human mind, its poetry and its fancy; objective truth is a dull dry formula. Even a Resurrection and Eternity are dull and insipid to these minds as Articles in a Creed: if they are ideas enriching a ritual, they welcome them; if they are really to be believed, they give them but a freezing reception. Yet it was in this very character, as the vehicle of objective truth, that the formulary of faith appealed of old to Christian poetry and imagination. It was not treated like a dry skeleton and framework of words, but the statement was glorious and elevating because a positive statement; it asserted the objective reality of the thing stated; it gave an opening into another world, and an absolutely real world. Contemplate the grave, precise, and formal statements of a Christian Church in this aspect, and they lighten up with beams from the very fountain of light. They represent the faith of generations of Christians in the ineffable condescension of God and the highest destiny of man. They announce by their very rigidity the external seat of truth; that truth is a fact which exists independently of us, our own belief, or our own imagination.

We do not profess to have given our readers more than a slice of Dr. Newman's elaborate and acute investigation into the processes of the reasoning faculty; and the part we have taken has been that which combines the writer's application of the general principles he has laid down in the body of the treatise to the particular case of the evidence of revelation. For Dr. Newman's treatment of the whole department of reasoning we must refer our readers to the treatise itself, which brings to the subject the subtlest discrimination and most penetrating force, and an eye for the nicest distinctions, aided by the richest imagination and the most inexhaustible fertility of illustration. We cannot part from Dr. Newman without assuring him how glad we are to meet him on common ground. We do not, of course, agree either with all his philosophical positions, or with various particular observations which we come across in the treatise. He sometimes speaks from the basis of his own communion, and of course all his defence of the Christian revelation he himself considers to belong to the Roman interpretation of that revelation. We have preferred, however, to call attention to agreement rather than to differences; and we have treated his Essay as what it really and in substance is, a defence, and powerful defence, of a common Christianity; which has filled up a vacant place in Christian apologetics, and has given a substantial position to a part of the Christian argument which had only received an informal and allusive notice before, namely, the antecedent and introductory principles which lead to the acceptance of the Christian evidences.

# EGYPTIAN DOCTRINE OF A FUTURE STATE.

### (NOTE TO PAGE 56.)

THE doctrine of Metempsychosis was less in conflict indeed with the truth of human personality, when it employed the brutes as its instruments, and represented the souls of men as passing upon death into the bodies of animals; for the man prevailed over the lower personality or impersonality of the brute, and was safer from a rival self. But the doctrine of animal metempsychosis could not at the same time exist without degrading the human soul in its own eyes, and polluting the sense of immortality. Something is due to the human soul even in a state of sin and degeneracy; to unite it to the nature of brutes and send it through an almost endless cycle of brute life, migrating into one animal after another, was to degrade not only the guilty soul but the soul. M. Bunsen indeed says,—" the groundwork of this doctrine is a consciousness of moral responsibility, and a belief in the personal indestructibility of the human soul. A judgment is passed upon it at the point of death, the punishment in its being condemned to be lowered from human to animal life."[1] But even punishment, and especially purifying punishment, should be something that is suitable to man, nor should the nature be degraded in chastising the sin. M. Bunsen sees indeed in the doctrine of animal metempsychosis the foundation of the whole Egyptian animal worship. "This community between the human and animal soul once admitted, one can understand how the Egyptians at last arrived at the idea of worshipping in animals a living manifestation of the Divinity."[2] But he could hardly have given a greater proof of the degrading character of the doctrine, than that it involved the principle of "a community between the human and animal soul," and laid the basis for the revolting animal worship of ancient Egypt.

M. Bunsen is disposed to excuse the animal metempsychosis of the Egyptians in consideration of their idea of a personal immortality. He regards the truth in the system as atoning for the corruption, the corruption as merged in the truth; and so he arrives at a very high estimate of the Egyptian doctrine of a Future State. But upon this plan we may raise the rank of any religious teaching whatever, that is, if we sink the bad parts, and only judge by the good. We must not

---

[1] Bunsen's *Egypt*, vol. iv p. 641.      [2] *Ibid.*

do this, but we must take the system as a whole. All Pagan teaching on this subject had its good side; it contained the idea of a personal eternity; but this high idea was debased by the mode in which it was dealt with. So with the Egyptian doctrine in particular—it had this idea in it; but this idea was joined to the vilest corruptions. Could any community, that had the slightest pretence to advancement in religion, hold the Egyptian doctrine of a future state *as a whole*—with its animal metempsychosis attaching to it? If this is impossible, then the Egyptian doctrine was a low one as a whole. In these combinations the good parts raise the bad a great deal less than the bad parts drag down the good. If there is a strong vile idea in a religion, we may be quite sure that that in some way impregnates the whole. A spurious form of a truth is at great distance from that truth. The Pagan mythology *contained* the idea of the unity of God. Mohammedanism recognises Christianity. Fragmentary truth,—a high idea existing in the distance, while all the near ground is occupied with the grossest matter,— is a very weak thing. Animal metempsychosis filled the whole foreground of the Egyptian doctrine,—it was the strong coarse material which came in contact with the popular mind, and made the impression; the eternal world was in the remote horizon of the system.

M. Bunsen indeed appeals to the recently discovered piece of Egyptian Ritual, called the "Book of the Dead," in which a soul is represented as urging its claim before the supreme tribunal of the invisible world to eternal communion with "its father Osiris," in heaven. It recounts all its own merits, and asseverates its own purity with the solemn repetition, "I am pure, I am pure, I am pure, I am pure;" the Judges assent; "it is stripped of its body and makes its way to its father, the self-created soul of the Universe;" when it sings in ecstasy, "I am the ruling spirit of Osiris who loves me."[1] It is not indeed easy to repose a perfect faith in hieroglyphics, or to understand what all this means, even if we do; but if this piece of ritual means that some souls enter, immediately on death, upon an eternal and heavenly life, we must take this doctrine as interpreted by antiquity; and the statement of antiquity is that the eternal life beyond the stars to which select souls ascended immediately upon death was a *divine*, rather than a strictly human state. "There was another state," says Warburton, who here reflects antiquity, "in the ancient pagan mythology, which had the same relation to Elysium that Tartarus had to purgatory, the extreme of reward, as Tartarus of punishment. But then this state was not in the infernal regions, but in Heaven. Neither was it the lot of common men, but reserved for heroes and demons."[2] And again,—"We are to know that the Ancients distinguished the souls of men into three

[1] Bunsen's *Egypt*, vol. iv. pp. 644, 646, 665.
[2] *Divine Legation*, vol. ii. p. 125.

species, the human, the heroic, and the demonic. The two last, when they left the body, were indeed believed to enjoy eternal happiness for their public services on earth; not in Elysium, but in heaven, where they became a kind of demigods."[1] The heavenly eternity, then, to which some souls were admitted at death, was a Divine rather than a human state in the Egyptian system, if we are to interpret that system by antiquity at large. The semi-divine life soared instantly to its native empyrean, but the human future life opened upon the gross earthly cycle of the animal metempsychosis. We see in such an arrangement a latent indulgence to human disbelief. It provides a future human life indeed, but at the same time it encloses this life within the bounds of this material world; it lodges departed souls in tabernacles of brute flesh, till the end of an enormous cycle, when what becomes of them is too distant a thing to be taken in by the imagination. Its real future is thus in this world; while its eternal world is an abstraction, an ideal sphere of gods and godlike beings, and not a human eternal residence. What is at the bottom of such an arrangement? Obviously, the difficulty of entertaining the idea of a real world of departed men. They live indeed, but it is under different forms in *this* world, or as ideal beings in another. Egypt could make them gods, or make them brutes, but could not make them eternal men.

[1] *Divine Legation*, vol. iii. p. 136. He quotes Cicero:—" Omnibus qui patriam conservarint, adiuvarint, auxerint, certum esse *in cœlo* ad definitum locum, ubi beati ævo sempiterno fruantur."—*Somn. Scip.* c. iii.

www.ingramcontent.com/pod-product-compliance
Lightning Source LLC
Chambersburg PA
CBHW071958220426
**43662CB00009B/1177**